Weird Tales of Modernit

Weird Tales of Modernity

The Ephemerality of the Ordinary in the Stories of Robert E. Howard, Clark Ashton Smith and H.P. Lovecraft

Jason Ray Carney

McFarland & Company, Inc., Publishers
Jefferson, North Carolina

ISBN (print) 978-1-4766-6803-1
ISBN (ebook) 978-1-4766-3614-6

LIBRARY OF CONGRESS AND BRITISH LIBRARY
CATALOGUING DATA ARE AVAILABLE

Library of Congress Control Number 2019943529

© 2019 Jason Ray Carney. All rights reserved

No part of this book may be reproduced or transmitted in any form or by any means, electronic or mechanical, including photocopying or recording, or by any information storage and retrieval system, without permission in writing from the publisher.

Front cover illustration by Ezume Images (Shutterstock)

Manufactured in the United States of America

McFarland & Company, Inc., Publishers
Box 611, Jefferson, North Carolina 28640
www.mcfarlandpub.com

For my mom and dad

Acknowledgments

I want to thank Jeffrey Shanks, Rusty Burke, and Mark Finn for their kindness and intellectual hospitality. My thanks go to Bill Cavalier, Frank Coffman, Dierk Guenther, Nicky Wheeler-Nicholson, Patrick Scott Belk, Justin Everett, Chris Gruber, Todd Vick, Karen Kohoutek, Bobby Derie, Scott Connors, Daniel M. Look, Patrice Louinet, Mark Hall, and Nathan Madison for contributing to the scholarly milieu to which this book responds. Kurt Koenigsberger, Mary Grimm, and Michael Clune provided me with academic mentorship for which I will always be grateful. I also want to thank my colleagues in the English Department at Christopher Newport University, particularly Jean Filetti, Mary Wright, and Trevor Hoag. I want to thank my students there for their enthusiasm. Finally, I want to thank Nicole, my wonderful wife, for her encouragement.

Table of Contents

Acknowledgments — vi
Preface — 1

1. Introduction — 7
2. Pulp Ekphrasis, History, and Deformation — 21
3. A Real Weird Magazine — 42
4. Clark Ashton Smith and Artistic Form — 65
5. The Failure of Clark Ashton Smith — 81
6. The Cultural Alienation of Robert E. Howard — 100
7. Robert E. Howard and Rendering the Real and the Unreal — 114
8. Cthulhu Is Beautiful — 136
9. Lovecraft and the Threat of Modernism — 152
10. Conclusion: Form and Formlessness — 166

Works Cited — 187
Index — 193

Preface

The world is changing. It has always been changing. It will continue to change. For many, particularly those invested in a concrete configuration, order, or ordinary, change is frightful.

Fear is a powerful aesthetic resource.

"The oldest and strongest emotion of mankind is fear, and the oldest and strongest kind of fear is fear of the unknown," states H.P. Lovecraft in the introduction to his literary history of horror, *Supernatural Horror in Literature* (1041). How time will inevitably deform our present is a terrible unknown. Writing to Robert E. Howard on January 30th, 1931, Lovecraft expresses such a fear: "What the country will look like in 2031 is more than I would care to picture" (*Freedom* 135).

Reflecting on the interbellum economic turmoil that symptomatized the changes wrought by modernity, Clark Ashton Smith wrote to Lovecraft in November of 1930: "The general condition of things, from what one hears, is a terror" (CAS Selected Letters 138). He continues, "Undoubtedly, modern science, with its labor-saving machinery, is much to blame for the situation of unemployment" (138). Smith wasn't alone in his fear of the effects of mechanization. Robert E. Howard, in January of 1931, also writing to H.P. Lovecraft, provided this speculation about the future: "Doubtless in a few more generations all the United States will present one uniform pattern, modeled on the mechanized fabric of New York" (*Freedom* 128).

The economic and technological symptoms of modernity were not these writers' only objects of fear, for they also condemned modernity's cultural manifestations, particularly modernism. The same year Howard anticipated sociocultural homogeneity wrought by mechanization, Smith shared his opinion of modernist art with Lovecraft: "My frank opinion regarding the new stuff is that nine-tenths of it is plain, colossal humbug, which the critics and public have been hypnotized or bulldozed into thinking, or pretending, that they like" (CAS Selected Letters 165). Lovecraft replied later that month to affirm Smith's contempt of modernism: "I hardly know how much of this modern art is sincere & authentic, & how much is error & pretense" (*Dawnward* 334). And in the following month, Howard characterizes modernist literature to Lovecraft in this way: "sophisticated trash, novels dealing with perverts and half-baked pseudo-artists" (*Freedom* 151).

The three writers who are treated in this book were unified in their fear and hatred of modernity and the modernist art that seemed to them one as of its primary symptoms.

For Lovecraft, Howard, and Smith, the ordinary is ephemeral, and its fearful ephemerality, seen most vividly through the prism of modern art, represents a fecund aesthetic resource. Thus, much of their work is an ekphrastic account of a new art that, like a microscope, telescope, or spectroscope, reveals the secret truth of history as a terrible process of deformation articulated most famously by Marx and Engels in *The Communist Manifesto*:

> All fixed, fast-frozen relations, with their train of ancient and venerable prejudices and opinions, are swept away, all new-formed ones become antiquated before they can ossify. All that is solid melts into air, all that is holy is profaned, and man is at last compelled to face with sober senses his real conditions of life and his relations with his kind [12].

Attempting to face the real "with sober senses," i.e., the process of historical progress exemplified by an oil booming Texas town, Howard has the protagonist of his autobiographical novel, the pulp writer Steve Costigan, express his hatred thus:

> Here was drama, swift-moving action, and great material for story, but Steve moved among it untouched, despising oil and everything connected with it, hating the roughnecks who swaggered and jostled their way through life, and detesting loud-mouthed, steely-eyed promoters, the keenest of whom never opened any book in their lives [...]. Steve spoke the truth when he said he hated them all too much to write about them [*Post* 65].

Smith and Lovecraft shared Howard's sentiments as regards modernity and the change it represented, and thus viewed it as a cruel process of deformation, a monstrous challenge to which art must respond. For example, in his essay, "Heritage or Modernism: Common Sense in Art Forms," Lovecraft repudiates modernity and the modernism that sought to express it artistically in this way: "Our longing for familiar symbols—our homesickness, as it were, for the things we have known—is in reality the most authentic possible expression of the race's persistent life-force" (193). This celebration of the familiar is surprising for a writer like Lovecraft, whose oeuvre of fiction relies on violating the literary effect of reality. Indeed, Lovecraft affirms Smith's celebration of the unfamiliar elsewhere: "There is absolutely no justification for literature unless it serves to release the imagination from the bounds of every-day life" (CAS Selected Letters 123).

In November of 1936, perhaps still coping with the death of his mother, the suicide of Robert E. Howard, and the illness of his elderly father—who would succumb in just over a year—Smith expresses his devotion to art in this way: "I feel in myself an urge and ability to fare even further afield into the cosmic dreamlands I have yet gone" (CAS Selected Letters 275). Lovecraft would die of cancer four months later.

From a certain perspective, they (and we) are correct to fear time above all.

Among the Clark Ashton Smith papers at the John Hay Memorial Library at Brown University is an account of a 1912 dream that has been anthologized in *Strange Shadows: The Uncollected Fiction and Essays of Clark Ashton Smith*. The account narrates the rising of an alien sun that "flared suddenly to a vast circumference of incandescent flame" (245). This explosion is quickly succeeded by an entropic reversal: "Then all its fires shrank instantaneously back upon their center; and the sun went out" (245). The account ends with this reflection: "My heart seemed to suspend its beating with the heart of the sun" (245).

Why did Smith record this dream? We can speculate that it impacted him deeply, or at least distinctively enough to merit preservation. One course would be to examine the contents of the dream and psychologize Smith. What was on his mind? What anxieties might have caused this nightmare?

Of particular interest, however, is the dream's status as a quasi-literary artifact. Could Smith have recorded this dream because he thought it was suitable for treatment in poetry? If so, then the account of the dream becomes less a matter of psychology and more a matter of literary thematics. The account is artifice, the deliberate aesthetic focalization of a theme. What is that theme? In the image of a star exploding and then collapsing we have the inverse of a famous sonnet written by a poet to which Smith was often compared. I refer to "Bright Star," by John Keats:

> Bright star, would I were stedfast as thou art—
>   Not in lone splendour hung aloft the night
> And watching, with eternal lids apart,
>   Like nature's patient, sleepless Eremite,
> The moving waters at their priestlike task
>   Of pure ablution round earth's human shores,
> Or gazing on the new soft-fallen mask
>   Of snow upon the mountains and the moors—
> No—yet still stedfast, still unchangeable,
>   Pillow'd upon my fair love's ripening breast,
> To feel for ever its soft fall and swell,
>   Awake for ever in a sweet unrest,
> Still, still to hear her tender-taken breath,
> And so live ever—or else swoon to death

In Keats's poem the speaker ekphrastically thematizes endurance over time. The star "hung aloft the night" is "steadfast," "unchangeable," and "eternal." Moreover, the star's eternal nature throws into stark focus the contrasted finitude and ephemerality of the speaker and his love lying winded in post-coital embrace.

The sun functions in the exact opposite way in Smith's dream. In the sun's swift expiration, it evokes ephemerality, the undeniable passage of cosmic time and thus heralds horror. In Smith's poetic universe, not even a star is inoculated against the deforming power of time.

Comparing Keats's poem to Smith's dream limns the distinctive way the *Weird Tales* Three—Lovecraft, Howard, and Smith—respond to the deforming threat posed by time. The temporary forms exuded by the fecund but finite play of matter, stained by the inevitable triumph of formlessness, cannot bear the symbolic weight of hope. To recognize time, for the *Weird Tales* Three, is to recognize hopelessness; thus, modern art becomes the token of hopelessness.

This book examines select works of the *Weird Tales* Three, Robert E. Howard, Clark Ashton Smith, and H.P. Lovecraft. It argues that a central thematic preoccupation of their work is what I call "the ephemerality of the ordinary," an insight into the accelerating pace of historical change in the era of modernity. Many desire to view these pulp fiction writers as merely storytellers, entertainers who wrote sensational fiction for adolescent readers of science fiction, fantasy, and supernatural horror. Others see these writers' work as possessing great philosophical depth. To an extent, the *Weird Tales* Three are both of these. They are fundamentally pulp writers who eschewed the intellectualist literary trends of their day to concentrate on stirring their readers with wonder, horror, and excitement; accordingly, they were ambitious literary artists who took their pulp fiction craft seriously and encoded thoughtful philosophical speculations in their fiction. Put another way, they were literary artists who had no faith in literary immortality, who viewed their work soberly, as ephemera, as pulp, as decaying plant matter.

The present work makes its case through close analysis of specific works of the *Weird Tales* Three, but it makes no claim to be anything other than a speculative enterprise, the articulation of one complex thematic pattern among many possible ones. Literary interpretation is an art and consists not simply in uncovering hidden meanings, as if by x-ray, but also in artfully composing compelling readings of works that can bear multiple readings by virtue of their vital complexity. In this context, the question is not of the truth or falsity of claims but of their plausibility and viability. Too often do literary critics demure from acknowledging the obvious fact that we project ourselves onto the works we read, as if the painter is ashamed of his or her brush strokes.

The work begins with a theoretical orientation (Chapters 1 and 2) and proceeds with a brief historical account of pulp fiction magazines that ends with the story of *Weird Tales*, the magazine that brought the *Weird Tales* Three together (Chapter 3). It then proceeds to treat each writer individually: Clark Ashton Smith (Chapter 4 and 5), Robert E. Howard (Chapter 6 and 7), and H.P. Lovecraft (8 and 9). The book's conclusion (Chapter 10) proposes the literary antecedents of the *Weird Tales* Three and situates them in a wider literary historical context.

The chapters are deeply intertwined and therefore the book should be read from beginning to end, rather than piecemeal.

1. Introduction

The Non-Literariness of Pulp

To understand the literary historical significance of the literature we sometimes refer to as "pulp fiction" and its intimate relationship to violating what Roland Barthes calls the *effet de réel*, its imbrication with a literary technique that can be termed "de-reification," the artfully rendered staging of deformation, we must first come to terms with the flaws that invalidated pulp fiction in the past for some literary elites. These unforgivable flaws made pulp unworthy of deep appreciation and analysis for many reasons, among them pulp's non-literariness, its dependence on a socially and commercially conventionalized rhetoric of fiction, i.e., its unenlightened use of referential language and literary techniques to create imaginary, virtual worlds of the ordinary and the extraordinary. In contrast to the diverse characters and plot elements of pulp fiction—the hardboiled detective, the fast-draw sheriff, the alien invader—its narrative technique is often dismissed as unoriginal and homogeneous, as innumerable passé repetitions of a conventionalized literary realist technique first pioneered in the eighteenth-century novel. Contrasted against "artistic literary fiction," a diverse field of distinctive narrative rhetorics where, through aesthetic efforts, signification is made thick and attention worthy, where the technique of narration is equal to and often ambitiously commensurate with the theme, pulp fiction seems oblivious to the synchronic/linguistic structure of narrative. Pulp seems to concentrate on the imaginary "intra-textual" signified or the virtual world it evokes through the rhetoric of narration. Pulp fiction relates in a "non-literary" fashion to the "ready-to-hand" aspects of language, i.e., the functional and rhetorical nature of story and poetry rather than the "present-at-hand" aspects, i.e., its ontological status as textuality and aesthetic form. Pulp fiction myopically focuses on the rendering and fictionalization of a virtual and unreal story world, while artistic literary fiction strikes a resolution between a bloated signifier and the diminishing and deferred signified. Artistic fiction, in contrast to pulp fiction, becomes worthy of deep appreciation and technical analysis by virtue of its authors' formal awareness, originality, and complexity, qualities often lacking in what we might call pulp fiction, the fiction of base matter.

Pulp Fiction and Conventionalized Realism

To refer to the formal rhetorics of pulp fiction as conventionalized realism is not, at base, to dismiss that technique as an uninteresting subject of literary analysis or aesthetic judgment. Achieving a literary effect of reality is a complex rhetorical and technical activity, and the extent to which pulp fiction works succeed in creating literary effects of reality for their readers and even conditionally reifying the virtual worlds, characters, and artifacts they fictionalize has occasioned compelling scholarship, such as Michael Saler's *As If: Modern Enchantment and the Literary Prehistory of Virtual Reality* (2012). Instead, the idea of the conventional nature of the narrative technique of pulp fiction is emphasized to come to a clearer understanding of its commonplace unattractiveness and apparent superficiality to literary criticism and certain literary elites. Though perhaps most pronounced in the era after the disciplinary consolidation of modernism in the Anglophone literary academy, 1923–1938, this negative interpretation of and distracted attention to pulp fiction lingers today; indeed, it is this widely unanalyzed inartistic appearance of pulp fiction from a literary elitist perspective that structures current pulp fiction reading practices: distracted "extensive" readings are widely preferred over attentive "intensive" or more properly critical and formalist modes of reading, analysis, and appreciation.

Viewed from a wide angle, it seems two major arguments support literary elitism's oscillating indifference and hostility toward pulp fiction. These two arguments endorse extensive reading practices over intensive reading practices, and they are linked to distinctive formalist and ideological perspectives within the discourse of literary criticism (1). The formalist perspective, perhaps strongly associated with, for example, modernist fiction writers such as Joseph Conrad, Ernest Hemingway, James Joyce, and Virginia Woolf, justifies indifference to pulp fiction on the grounds that such narratives are not literary. Literary art, according to this perspective, is distinct by virtue of its awareness of the formal elements of literary technique, and wide-angled surveys of the massive archive of pulp fiction have often confirmed the idea of its formal naiveté, its unoriginal and unskilled storytelling conventionalism (2). The ideological perspective, perhaps associated with early twentieth-century literary gatekeepers like H.L. Mencken, Edmund Wilson, Theodor Adorno, and Max Horkheimer, and several others, manifests hostility toward pulp fiction on political partisan grounds: pulp fiction works appear as outgrowths of the literary marketplace as opposed to its foil, the non-commercial realm of aesthetic ideals, a realm often marked by dissent regarding the commodification of literary art. The idea of the contaminating influence of implicating the artistic activity of writing fiction with capitalist and corporate networks of editors, publishers, and the degraded tastes of a distracted and ideologically brainwashed reading public predicates this perspective.

Pulp Fiction and the Profane

Both formalist and ideologist, however, come to pulp fiction with specific questions of concrete reading practice: does pulp fiction merit intensive reading? Is pulp fiction worthy of sustained yet finite intellectual labor, deeper appreciation by virtue of sincere hermeneutic scrutiny? Neither perspective offers a basis for criticizing wide-angled, inattentive extensive readings of popular writing, such as, for example, Ezra Pound's twenty-part study of popular journalism, published throughout 1917 in *The New Age*, titled "Studies in Contemporary Mentality." Broadly considering the massive archive of pulp fiction for sociological knowledge or an evening's distraction, rather than aesthetic, philosophical, and/or spiritual nourishment, is perhaps understandable. From these sometimes commensurate, sometimes incommensurate perspectives, a non-aesthetic, non-formal skimming of pulp fiction is all such work deserves, leaving unquestioned basic assumptions about the discursive value of the concept and the corpus to which the designation "pulp fiction" might refer. Read a pulp fiction, toss it aside. Read another, toss it aside. Like the trash heap overshadowing Walter Benjamin's Angel of History, let the pile of putrescent, acid-rich paper grow ever higher.

This study proposes a useful way of understanding literary elitism's legacy of hostility and indifference toward pulp fiction by situating these within the ancient allegorical framework of flesh and soul, matter and spirit. The formalist glories in the abstract and pure aesthetic form of literary language, praises its disembodied synchronic structure, the way it seems to augment, like a powerful prosthesis, our degraded perceptual processes, and thus disclaims the fleshy, the contingent, the finite, the rhetorical, and the ephemeral. The ideological critic views the real as degraded, as contaminating slime, and the apparent alliance between pulp fiction and the profane signals its unconscious political unity with modern history understood as an unfolding catastrophe, a fall, a steady process of accelerating alienation and dehumanization. Viewed in this way, both literary elitisms are haunted by a legacy of noble failure, a Sisyphean search for a nonexistent entity: a pure and enduring form that transcends formlessness, that's fetishistic value coheres in its ability to exist without a body, liberated from history, contingency, finitude, and fluidity. It appears as a property without an object, a musical note yet to be acoustically imprisoned in sound, a color without a substance to modify.

Understood in this way, literary elitism projects onto pulp fiction the appearance of being partisan to the profane, the formless, the fluid, the ephemeral, in other words, the trashy. Is such a perspective valid? Is pulp fiction trash? If the answer is yes, then perhaps we should follow popular fiction scholar, Scott McCracken, when, in *Pulp: Reading Popular Fiction* (1998), he writes, "Despite their differences, all theorists of mass culture agree that popular culture cannot be understood in terms of individual texts" (24). If the answer is no, then by what principle can we seek individual works of pulp fiction art to appreciate, to exalt with our finite attention?

1. Introduction

The receding horizon of understanding pulp fiction and its intimate relationship to de-reification and artfully rendering deformation, its ideological function as branding foil to artistic literary art, lies along the path of these questions. And the work of answering must begin with establishing a more specific idea of what we are referring to when we discuss pulp fiction.

Pulp and the Masses

In his history of intellectuals and mass culture, *The Intellectuals and the Masses* (1992), John Carey exposes the fear and contempt held by literary elites toward "the masses," the burgeoning populations documented by sociologists and historians of working class and middle class individuals who had but recently acquired widespread literacy. Here is one of Carey's several insights: "The principle around which modernist literature and culture fashioned themselves was the exclusion of the masses, the defeat of their power, the removal of their literacy, the denial of their humanity. What this intellectual effort failed to acknowledge was that the masses do not exist. The mass, that is to say, is a metaphor for the unknowable and invisible" (21).

Equally so, pulp fiction and its associated narrative technique, conventionalized realism, are formally indefensible metaphors; they are superficial, though perhaps discursively useful, intellectual place markers for holding in the mind an "unknowable and invisible" plenitude of heterogeneous printed material—dime novels, pulp magazines, and paperbacks—as well as numberless narrative techniques employed by so-called pulp fiction writers. As Carey argues, the metaphor of the masses insulated the literary elites of the early twentieth century from the threat of anonymity represented by the mustering swarms of individuals who intruded upon them, whose vulgar tastes, appearing to crystallize as commercially motivated conventionalism, seemed to produce an inauthentic popular culture and pulp fiction of the market, the parlor, the counting room, and the newsstand.

So, too, does the metaphor of pulp fiction and conventionalized realism protect literary critics from the sublime archive of writing produced during the twentieth century. For the literary elite drowning in a heap of printed material, the idea of pulp fiction, like the idea of the masses, justifies and even necessitates (in some contexts) the extensive reading practices of the sociologist and the historian surveying a massive archive. Juxtaposing Carey's study with the idea of pulp fiction suggests that those engaged in producing elite literature and those ascribing to its particular brand of literary elitism share cognitive strategies and intellectual technologies for coping with excess, cognitive strategies comparably applicable to crowds of immigrants, phalanxes of industrial workers, and multitudes of bourgeois families as to piles of paperback books and magazines.

Critical Method

This study approaches pulp fiction from multiple angles: formalism, historicism, periodical culture studies, and biography. But unlike centrifugal studies that ambitiously treat broad concepts like "Science Fiction" and "Modernism," this study proceeds centripetally; whereas some studies are telescopic, scaling individual texts down, integrating them into an ecology or framework, and thereby adopting the perspective of an observer contemplating systems' illuminated connections, this study's approach is micro-scopic. This book considers the canonical pulp fiction works of a canonical pulpwood magazine, *Weird Tales*, during its greatest decade (1929–1939), i.e., cherished literary artifacts that have been painstakingly preserved in print, valued despite their initial inartistic and acutely ephemeral contexts, and extolled in robust, academically-autonomous discourses. In other words, my study does not attempt to describe and interpret pulp fiction by executing a longitudinal study of pulpwood magazines, tracing their historical origins, and abstracting out to argue for their cultural significance. This is a non-literary and historiographical project that is being skillfully executed elsewhere by others at the specialized conventions and in the publications of private pulp magazine collec-

1. Introduction

tors who, perhaps until Sean McCann's *Gumshoe America: Hard-Boiled Crime Fiction and the Rise and Fall of New Deal Liberalism* (2000) and Erin Smith's *Hard-Boiled: Working Class Readers and Pulp Magazines* (2005), were relatively lonely in their stewardship of this important archive of literary culture. General elements of the historical context of the pulpwood magazines archive are briefly surveyed, but a rigorous historical approach to the print media in general would be at variance with this study's literary artistic concern with the pulp fiction aesthetic, its intimate association with de-reification.

While discussing intellectuals' vexed relationships to the masses, Carey refers to the "redemptive genius" of the "Holmes method," i.e., Sherlock Holmes's quasi-magical ability to identify and individuate an anonymous person after scrutinizing him or her briefly: profession, criminality, the depths of the very soul were yielded to Holmes's probing intelligence. Of this unreal intellectual, he writes, "His function [is] to disperse the fears of overwhelming anonymity that the urban mass brought. Holmes redemptive genius as a detective lies in rescuing individuals from the mass" (Carey 8). In approaching pulp fiction and its relationship to de-reification through what are the quintessential and most artistic representatives of it in *Weird Tales* and its three most celebrated literary artists—Robert E. Howard, H. P. Lovecraft, and Clark Ashton Smith—this study aims to highlight these literary artists from the unreal mass while empathically insisting on their identity as pulp fiction writers.

The Weird Tales *Three as Corporate Author*

The literary artists treated in this book, Howard, Smith, and Lovecraft, who will be referred to collectively as "the *Weird Tales* Three" due to their famous association with that pulpwood magazine, were emphatically pulp fiction writers. No apologies. Indeed, one of this book's goals is to firmly situate the *Weird Tales* Three in this profane pulp fiction context rather than, as others have laudably sought to do, strategically recontextualize them and place them in a more exalted literary context. This overdue work of appreciation continues to be an important enterprise that this study is indebted to and that premised the logistical strategies of preservation, curation, academic popularization, and discursive elevation that my study leans on for support. And yet, to argue too strongly that the *Weird Tales* Three connect to canonical traditions of literature by manifesting the canon's literary values risks dulling Howard, Lovecraft, and Smith's radical alterity, their self-aware "otherness" regarding traditional literary canons, and, most importantly, the extent to which their "pulp fiction" context informs and syncs with their thematics, their deep insights about the aesthetic as an exceptional category, the profane, and the ephemeral. The *Weird Tales* Three were pulp fiction writers, yes, but they were also literary artists.

Historical and Thematic Uses of "Pulp Fiction"

Pulp fiction is an unpredictable term marked by combating ideas that needs initial exploration. When we discuss pulp fiction, we can mean several things, but most of us use the phrase in either a historical or a thematic context. This distinction is important. Pulp fiction used in a historical, print culture context refers to a specific print medium, the pulps, woodpulps, also known as the pulpwood magazines, which were a cheap magazine type engineered in the late nineteenth century, ubiquitous on North American newsstands in the early decades of the twentieth century (particularly so in the 1920s and '30s), and marked by decline and disappearance in the 1950s. Pulp fiction used more broadly in a thematic context refers to a kind of profane, sensational, violent, melodramatic type of story that is often badly written and unconcerned with traditional standards of literary value; this is a transhistorical designation of literary value that conceptually privileges entertainment over insight, excitement over thought, action over atmospherics. Pulp fiction, in this context, refers to thematic or generic expectations and does not refer exclusively to the fiction printed in the 1920s and '30s in cheap periodicals adorned with colorful and sen-

1. Introduction

sationalist covers. Dime novels of the 1880s, 1950s romance novels, 1960s science fiction digest magazines, contemporary film novelizations, and much more can be pulp fiction in this transhistorical context to the extent that this or that object manifests certain thematic qualities.

There is a motif uniting these two distinctive senses of the phrase, and that is the idea of artistic value or merit. It seems plausible to assert that both meanings of pulp fiction signal a kind of writing that is unconcerned with traditional ideals of artistic merit or literary value. Viewed from the wide perspective of the printed commodity, the pulp fiction magazines of the 1920s and '30s, which are a concern of this book, appear to us as mere entertainment, as inartistic ephemera, popular culture distractions that suited a modern subject seeking to escape the increasingly impossible demands of life in the rapidly modernizing West. Accordingly, when we judge a work as pulp fiction in the thematic sense—e.g., a contemporary and cheap romance novel that involves a sensational plot featuring melodramatic love affairs, pornographic renderings of sex, and wooden characters—we frame that work as inartistic, non-serious, and imply that it is unconcerned with traditional notions of artistic value; we may also even assert that some of its unique pleasures are associated with a strategic flouting of artistic concerns. "Why do you read such garbage?" a literary elite might ask. "Why not Proust? Woolf? Eliot? Conrad?" "Because," answers the degraded reader, "I don't want to think. I prefer this distraction."

The Weird Tales *Three and Pulp Ekphrasis*

The *Weird Tales* Three were pulp fiction writers, but they problematize this historical and thematic dualism. They published in interwar pulp fiction magazines such as *Weird Tales, Strange Tales of Mystery and Terror, Astounding Stories,* and several others for little pay and were read and enjoyed by a mass audience. And, arguably, their fiction, from their best story to their worst, is clearly pulp fiction in the thematic sense: sensational, often ineloquent or excessively ornate in style, and concerned with inciting raw emotions in readers—such as wonder, joy, excitement, and cosmic dread—rather than providing philosophical insights or didactic guidance. And yet—and yet!—the best work of the *Weird Tales* Three is supremely serious, is centrally concerned with art, the role of art in life, its value, its function, and the stakes involved in the most ambitious of artistic enterprises. This quality of seriousness, this unexpected preoccupation (even obsession) with the ontological status of art, artistic form, and aesthetic experience is compelling and surprising, and particularly so given Howard, Smith, and Lovecraft's context of publication in the inartistic and unpretentious pulpwoods. Furthermore, Howard's and Lovecraft's (though not quite Smith's) contemporary preeminence, ubiquity, and enduring influence in contemporary popular and mass culture, fields imbricated with anti-elitist notions of art-as-commodity, risks blinding us to their sincere artistic and philosophical ambition.

Therefore, the pulp fiction of the *Weird Tales* Three functions as a discursive space for a sophisticated project of aesthetic theorization, a type of "pulp ekphrasis," that probes the very essence of distinctively modern art, the condition of art in modernity, and its surprising goal. Furthermore, though this theoretical project of pulp ekphrasis was never systematized or translated into a philosophical idiom, it nevertheless articulates, even in its unfinished and fragmented form, a unique critique of modernity by framing it as an inhumane process of cruel historical acceleration bolstered by an unperceivable agency. Allegorized in their pulp fiction as an enduring inhuman form of absolute novelty, for these writers the truly modern work of art functions as a revelatory lens. Modern art, from the perspective of the pulp ekphrasis of the *Weird Tales* Three, is a haunted fetish that functions as a cognitive prosthesis not unlike the mad scientist's, Crawford Tillinghast's, bizarre sensory-amplifying machine fictionalized in H.P. Lovecraft's early story, "From Beyond," published in a privately printed, not-for-profit fanzine, *The Fantasy Fan*, just about three years before his death. The waves produced by the machine activate thousands of dormant qualities of the human sensorium thus revealing an infinite, and unfortunately hostile, strangeness just beyond the range of ordinary empirical perception. In the spirit of Tillinghast's machine, the *Weird Tales* Three fictionalize distinctively modern art, transform it into a kind of "shadow modernism," a sensory amplifying art device that functions to expose a fundamental, hidden quality of the cosmos and our relationship to it: the ordinary is ephemeral; the strange, though occasionally domesticated, conversely, is eternal.

From the pulp ekphrastic perspective the *Weird Tales* Three, modern art is no mere delight, a Paterian wellspring of life that invigorates the soul, nor a rare commodity to be simply bought and sold at auction. For these pulp fiction writers, modern art, specifically shadow modernist art, is an inhuman, alien technology, more specifically, a dangerous prosthesis, for bringing the ephemeral, contingent, and ordinary projected by the human mind in contact with the enduring, eternal, and extraordinary figured as alien in the deepest sense of the word. Put another way, the pulp fiction of Howard, Smith, and Lovecraft, via ekphrastic rendering, stages and dramatizes, through the shared trope of the enduring inhuman form of absolute novelty, the dissolution of reality, the decreation of the anthropocentric world, the ephemerality of the ordinary.

Some Notes on Discourse

The dominant scholarly approach to the pulp fiction of the *Weird Tales* Three seems to be influenced by two major, often overlapping sources: (1) the fecund tradition of a sophisticated fan discourse and criticism emerging in the letters to the editor section of *Weird Tales* at the outset, evolving in "fanzines," such as Charles D. Hornig's *The Fantasy Fan* (1933–1935), and achieving academic status in several academically-supported anthologies and journals, e.g., *Lovecraft Studies* (1979–2001), *The Dark Barbarian: The Writings of Robert E. Howard, a Critical Anthology* (1984), and *The Freedom of Fantastic Things: Selected Criticism on Clark Ashton Smith* (2006), and several others, such as *The Unique Legacy of Weird Tales: The Evolution of Modern Fantasy and Horror* (2015); and (2) "academic popular culture studies," a field historically linked to folklore and literary studies.

It would be reductive to use broad strokes to make anything other than weak and local claims about such a diverse field with undefined edges that incorporates academic monographs, mimeographed newsletters, blogs, podcasts, and several other media; diverse critics, scholars, fans, fan-critics, fan-scholars, etc., approach this material in heterogeneous ways for a variety of purposes; however, one strain in this diverse field of scholarship and fan writing against which this work foils is critical treatments that do not attend to the formal distinctiveness of the pulp fiction of the *Weird Tales* Three and the philosophical and historical import of this distinctiveness. This formally indifferent approach to the pulp fiction of the *Weird Tales* Three assumes the conventional nature of Howard, Smith, and Lovecraft's narrative technique and thereby focuses on the virtual worlds these writers render with their skilled construction of literary artifacts. The pulp fiction of the *Weird Tales* Three in this formally indifferent view becomes less literature and more virtual reality, a sinister transformation that brings with it the distracting pitfalls of, say, attempting to codify Lovecraft's fictional mythology or of chronologizing the career of Conan the Cimmerian. We must never forget these worlds are merely literary effects. There is no Arkham, no Aquilonia, no Averoigne. Bearing this in mind will prime us to locate the core aesthetic effect of the *Weird Tales* Three not in mere trick of establishing verisimilitude but in establishing verisimilitude *and* then shattering it, a literary formalistic gesture akin to the creation of the delicate sand painting of a mandala followed by its symbolic destruction.

Despite their interesting particulars, the diverse virtual worlds established by the *Weird Tales* Three are subjects of inquiry literary criticism is not uniquely equipped to understand. This is not to suggest that those trained in academic literary criticism lack the resources to discuss, say, the way racist discourses of eugenics influenced Howard, the way Lovecraft's xenophobia in Brooklyn influenced his renderings of aliens, or the way Smith's association with the writers and artists of the San Francisco Bohemian Club influenced his work. Indeed, many writing about the *Weird Tales* Three are concerned with how sociohistorical echoes into the virtual worlds of Cthulhu, Conan, and Malygris the Sorcerer. And yet, when Nathan Vernon Madison, the author of a comprehensive study of pulp fiction magazines, *Anti-Foreign Imagery in American Pulps and Comic Books* (2013), offers his important conclusion that "a small collection of narratives fairly tolerant and sympathetic" of differences of race are present in pulp magazines—a powerful thesis in direct opposition to traditional understandings of pulp fiction magazines as interwar sites of racist fantasy and cruel nativist sentiment—he convinces by virtue of extensive rather than intensive reading (206). Madison, like several others who treat the *Weird Tales* Three, is concerned less with literary form and more with social reality as seen through the distorting prism of virtual reality rendered in literary form.

For some critics, what distinguishes literary narrative from other forms of art is not its direct relationship to history, society, i.e., the actual, a relationship all art forms, to some extent, can claim; it is instead literary narrative's ability to fictionalize a recognizable human experience while concurrently transforming and strategically distorting that experience for aesthetic effect. For example, in his *Writing Against Time* (2013), Michael Clune frames the non-referential features of literary language as its greatest asset, the source, at least at this moment, of a knowledge unique to it: "At this moment in the history of the disciplines, literary criticism's best opportunity for creating new knowledge lies not in the description of art's embeddedness in contexts recognizable to historians or sociologists, but in the description of the forces by which art attempts to free itself from such contexts and such recognitions" (17). By focusing on how art is transformed and fictionalized in the story worlds of the *Weird Tales* Three rather than, say, how it historically reflects actual art contemporary to it—e.g., movements such as Cubism, Modernism, Futurism, Surrealism, etc.—this work aims for the "new knowledge" Clune speculates literature can render; put another way, after analyzing the renderings of shadow modernism, the outré art objects, bizarre artists, and weird experiences of art fictionalized in the work of the *Weird Tales* Three, the interesting question becomes not what do these strange things refer to *in* history, but how do these renderings permit us to *influence* history and modify our understanding of actual modern art, actual aesthetic experiences, actual artists. After reading Lovecraft, Smith, and Howard, do we look upon the ordinary with suspicion?

The Portal Opens

The narrative technique of the pulp ekphrastic works of the *Weird Tales* Three appears to be a naive conventionalism and thus signals to some the absence of a powerful or interesting literary effect worthy of intellectual labor and intensive reading. This prejudice is a historical legacy of academic and elite writing and reading practices, a literary culture that was canonized at the same time as Anglo-American literary criticism's institutionalization in the interwar period. "Modernism," a corpus of literature resembling in literary contexts sacred texts and often distinguished by its formal novelty and engineered linguistic overdetermination, continues to inform the tastes of literary gatekeepers and to justify their maintenance of an immutable canon or at least to sanction them to perform institutionally credentialed canonizing gestures. Quasi-religious expenditures of attention over solitary worthy texts—intensive scrutiny over extensive reading—continues to be valued. Thus, pulp fiction continues to be misunderstood as a commercially uninteresting assimilation of literary realism, rather than a distinctive aesthetic mastered by the *Weird Tales* Three in their stories of shadow modernism: strange art, artists, and experiences of art created in reaction to modernity.

Conventional realism might be considered metaphorically as an imposing slab of stone covered with undecipherable legends, an obstacle that confronts the serious critic of the quintessential work of pulp fiction, the artistic allegories of the *Weird Tales* Three. Such realism is a door to a sinister vault, not unlike the one featured in H.P. Lovecraft's, "The Tomb":

> The vault to which I refer is of ancient granite, weathered and discoloured by the mists and dampness of generations. Excavated back into the hillside, the structure is visible only at the entrance. The door, a ponderous and forbidding slab of stone, hangs upon rusted iron hinges, and is fastened *ajar* in a queerly sinister way by means of heavy iron chains and padlocks, according to a gruesome fashion of half a century ago [40].

Like the protagonist of Lovecraft's story, Jervas Dudley, the curious reader who wishes to get beyond the misleading narrative conventionalism of pulp fiction will require sustained attention and even perverse scrutiny: "I now formed the habit of *listening* very intently at the slightly open portal, choosing my favourite hours of midnight stillness for the odd vigil" (43).

The tomb's portal opens.

2. Pulp Ekphrasis, History, and Deformation

"Pulp Ekphrasis" and the Secret of History

Though not their exclusive role but nevertheless a key one, the *Weird Tales* Three function as ekphrasists. In several of their enduring works, Lovecraft, Howard, and Smith engage in a form of artistically inflected criticism termed ekphrasis. They do so by fictionalizing modernism, by transforming this real artistic movement into an unreal shadow modernism, a strategic distortion of actual modernism. After many creative iterations honed over several stories—e.g., Pickman's demented art, Malygris's sorcery, the fell mirrors of Tuzun Thune—this shadow modernism becomes an inhuman form of technology that, functioning like a cognitive prosthesis in the virtual world of fiction, thereby reveals the secret truth of history: history is a cruelly accelerating process of deformation. The ordinary is ephemeral. History is the interplay of form and formlessness with formlessness terminally ascendant.

I refer to the ekphrastic discourse of the *Weird Tales* Three as specifically pulp ekphrasis because its unique vitality draws from the artistically alienated perspective that contextualizes and informs it. It is significant that Lovecraft, Howard, and Smith identified themselves as artistic outsiders, as creating pulp literary artifacts at radical odds with the dominant artistic tastes of their cultural moment. Nevertheless, such an ekphrastic engagement with modernist art, the use of modernist art as a cognitive prosthesis for perceiving historical change, is not exclusive to the work of the *Weird Tales* Three and can be seen as part of a broader interwar cultural logic. It can be identified in other contexts, in journalistic accounts of modernism, philosophical speculations about modernism's significance, early twentieth-century parodies, and elsewhere. This more general cultural logic of modernist ekphrasis, locatable in these broader contexts, centers this chapter.

I will clarify this central concept—the pulp ekphrastic enterprise of the *Weird Tales* Three—by treating several examples of similar ekphrastic engagements with actual modernist art. The first example is José Ortega y Gasset's philosophical account of modernism in his essay, "The Dehumanization of Art" (1925). The second example is Malcolm Cowley's reflection on modernist art and culture in general in his literary memoir, *Exile's Return* (1934). The third is Berenice Abbott's attempt to render as static, with photography, the active process of New York City deforming from 1929 to 1939. The fourth is Walter Benjamin's reflection on a Paul Klee painting in "Theses on the Philosophy of History." The fifth example is a story from *Weird Tales* titled "A Square of Canvas."

Why Ekphrasis?

One might wonder why use the specific term "ekphrasis" instead of more encompassing phrases like "critical interpretation" or "aesthetic reflection." When a scholar like Ortega y Gasset analyzes a work of art, this is criticism. When a literary artist, like Smith, artistically describes or fictionalizes a work of art by transforming it into an unreal echo or shadow of the actual, that is ekphrasis.

What is at stake by incorporating an understanding of critical engagement into a broader concept of ekphrasis?

This collapsing of methodological and reading practice distinctions is strategic. The archetypical modernist work of art (if such a thing can be said to exist) can be defined by the extent to which it appears to violate an organic continuity with previous traditions of European art. It unsettles, disorients, and shocks; therefore, historically situational intellectual engagement in writing with modernist art often takes the form of first principle orientation. By way of analogy, the critic becomes a detective coming upon a mystery constituted by a failure of recognition, a suspension of the ordinary followed by aporia. One can imagine the detective, and by analogy the critic or artist, first speechless and then stammering as they struggle to describe, with starts and stops, the scene, i.e., the shocking and confusing modernist work of art.

This unique manner of relating to art is significantly distinctive to merit a qualifying terminological modification that avoids the neutrality and attitude of mental tranquility perhaps implied by terms such as "critical reflection." Homer's description of Achilles's shield, Keats's description of the Grecian urn, Oscar Wilde's haunted picture of Dorian, Lovecraft's fictionalization of Henry Anthony Wilcox's bas relief, Walter Benjamin's description of Paul Klee's *Angelus Novus*: these literary artistic/critical gestures invite a distinctive categorization as ekphrasis by virtue of their intensity and the way the artifact that conditions them seems to enthrall the artist rendering them in various forms of discourse such as criticism, fiction, poetry, and so forth.

The Dehumanization of Art

Madrid-born philosopher José Ortega y Gasset is perhaps best remembered for his contributions to metaphysics and epistemology, but he was also a theorist of distinctively modernist art. Viewing modernism from a quasi-sociological perspective, he argues, quite sensationally, that the modernist artist of the early twentieth century was driven to create their novel artifacts by a hatred of European traditions of art, which were, in essence, linked to a particular nineteenth-century bourgeois reality that young artists sought to escape through, among other things, rhetorical acts of aesthetic violence. He articulates this thesis in an enduring essay, published in 1925 and translated from Spanish as "The Dehumanization of Art." This essay provides a good starting point for a discussion of the ekphrastic treatment of modernism, of which the *Weird Tales* Three's unique pulp ekphrasis is an important example.

Ortega y Gasset embarks in his essay to come to terms with "the unpopularity of new music," of which the Impressionist Claude Debussy is his prime example (4). He concludes that modernist art, inflected by the modernist artist's unique sense of oppression, can be defined by inhumanity, lack of pathos, and a strident refusal of didactic utility. Why so? Why would the artist degrade art in this way, relegate it to a marginal, antisocial status? Ortega y Gasset poses the question and answers it in this way: "Why this disgust at living forms? Like all historical phenomena this too will have grown from a multitude of entangled roots which only a fine flair is capable of detecting. An investigation of this kind would be too serious a task to be attacked here" (39). And so, he attempts to unravel these roots, concluding that dehumanized modernist art serves but one unflattering function, i.e., it "helps the elite to recognize themselves and another in the drab mass of society and to learn their mission, which consists in being few and holding their own against the many" (7). This elitist function of modernist art, Ortega y Gasset speculates, is an outgrowth of the cultural logic of his contemporary historical milieu, interwar modernity, a period when "art has changed its position in the hierarchy of human activities" (48). Art has degraded from an important discourse to a marginal, comparatively subordinate one: stripped of its earlier functions, art has become a mere social symbol, an index of quasi-tribalistic belonging, a degraded emblem of clique solidarity, like a badge, medal, or corporate logo.

An Empire of Decaying Bodies

There are several avenues for critiquing this famously hostile view of modernist art, to defend modernism, but such is not my task at hand. Here what is most important about Ortega y Gasset's polemic essay is its curious function as an ekphrastic treatment of modernism, the distinctive way it uses modernist art as a cartographic technology for coming to understand the secret of history generally and the hidden nature of moder-

2. Pulp Ekphrasis, History, and Deformation

nity specifically: modern history is an accelerating process of change and deformation, a nature he succinctly refers to in his conclusion as "there is no turning back" (50). Like a telescope or microscope, Ortega y Gasset looks through the aperture that is modernist art to see the terrible secret of modern history, its violent tendencies toward a shocked human subject driven fiercely into the disorienting future where recognizable forms dissolve into formlessness. Although art in modernity has, by becoming equivalent with anti-popular taste, been degraded to the status of mere social branding, its secondary and perhaps more useful function is as exposé of a buried conspiracy against the people, a check on their orienting powers of recognition. For Ortega y Gasset, like an arcane cryptolect translated, modernist art reveals a terrible social logic, the inevitable rise of a ruling elite:

> A time must come in which society, from politics to art, reorganizes itself into two orders of ranks: the illustrious and the vulgar. The chaotic, shapeless, and undifferentiated state without discipline and social structure in which Europe has lived these hundred and fifty years cannot go on. Behind all contemporary life lurks the provoking and profound injustice of the assumption that men are actually equal [7].

Here Ortega y Gasset paints a terrible tableau, an inhuman world where most of vulgar humanity finds itself at the mercy of a terrible power, a situation not unlike the "baleful despotism" described in Clark Ashton Smith's, "Empire of the Necromancers," a fantasy story published in *Weird Tales* in September of 1932. After drawing a "threefold circle," two necromancers ploy their death magic:

> Thus did the outcast necromancers find for themselves an empire and a subject people in the desolate, barren land where the men of Tinarath had driven them forth to perish. Reigning supreme over all the dead of Cincor, by virtue of their malign magic, they exercised a baleful despotism. Tribute was borne to them by fleshless porters from outlying realms; and plague-eaten corpses, and tall mummies scented with mortuary balsams, went to and fro upon their errands in Yethlyreom, or heaped before their greedy eyes, from inexhaustible vaults, the cobweb-blackened gold and dusty gems of antique time [196].

Ortega y Gasset's dehumanized modernist art is transformed here into a fictional shadow modernist art object in the form of the necromancers' three-fold circle. In the place of humanity, decaying corpses; in place of government, a despotism of initiated thaumaturges.

Actual Modernism versus Shadow Modernism

This is not to suggest that Smith's pulp fiction is a direct allegorization of Ortega y Gasset's critical account, his sensational critique of modernist art in "The Dehumanization of Art." Similarities are, nevertheless, undeniably notable: the three-fold circle of the necromancers stands in for the dehumanized work of modernist art, and the division of humanity into an occult-initiated caste of necromancers and undead thralls and distinguished elite and vulgar masses is suggestive. What is the nature of this relationship? Mere coincidental resemblance?

Ortega y Gasset and Smith are both engaged in a form of ekphrasis, a speculative description of distinctively modern art produced in the unique conditions of modernity, a condition of accelerating deformation acutely thematized by the symbol of a decaying corpse. In the case of Ortega y Gasset, he probes his uneasy feelings linked to actual modernist art to discover its associated historical implications, i.e., that the steady deformation of the traditional cultural and artistic forms of European civilization is co-equivalent with the acute amplification of social, political, and economic inequality. In the case of Smith, he explores his uneasy feelings linked to actual modernist art by fictionalizing and distorting it, as if by a funhouse mirror, thereby rendering an unreal shadow modernism that reveals a similar historical secret: Ortega y Gasset's anticipated actual despotism is comparable to Smith's unreal one. Both Ortega y Gasset and Smith use modernist art to produce something like knowledge, a sinister intimation that the future, as its recognizable forms deform, will grow increasingly strange. Thus, in its strangeness, it will become less recognizable and more fully inhuman.

Certainly, the ekphrastic treatment of modernism and the rendering of shadow modernism cannot be the wellspring of strange prophecy? Surely dehumanized art, like a necromancer's occult charm, cannot prefigure such a "baleful despotism," a strange empire of rapacious necromancers rendered inexhaustible tribute by disintegrating and decaying thralls? Is this knowledge? If not, what is it? By looking through the distorting lens of modernist art, who else might expect such a quasi-occult revelation, a rare but fleeting glimpse of the ephemerality of the ordinary? Who? Let us briefly treat self-identified champion of modernism, Malcolm Cowley, who wrote this in his celebrated book-length reflection and memoir of modernism: "The 'artist proper' must always prophesy, explore, lead the way into new countries of emotion; and they cannot turn back" (144).

Malcolm Cowley and the Formlessness of Hell

Most will remember Malcolm Cowley not as an ekphrasist but as a young associate of Edmund Fitzgerald, Hart Crane, Ernest Hemingway, and other exemplars of specifically literary modernism, as well as, in his more mature years, a tireless champion of a misunderstood and controversial modernist literature in the 1940s and '50s. Indeed, his role as a public champion of modernism is particularly apparent in terms of the mass-appeal literary modernist artifacts he edited, i.e., the Viking Portable Editions of Ernest Hemingway (1944) and William Faulkner (1946). Less acknowledged is his role as literary chronicler and ekphrasist. Like Ortega y Gasset and the *Weird Tales* Three, Cowley engages in the ekphrastic treatment of modernism; he uses modernism as a prosthesis, engages modernist literary history to understand a secret truth of modernity, its sinister nature as inhumanly accelerating change, the deformation of recognizable forms.

Cowley's engagement in ekphrasis is emphatic in his memoir of the 1920s literary culture titled *Exile's Return*. First published in 1934, *Exile's Return* charts the development of literary culture in the early decades of the twentieth century. It incorporates Cowley's personal stories and related anecdotes about his and others' relationships with several artists and writers active during those years although it focuses on the post–World War I period. It is a compelling look into how Cowley, critics like him, and the educated public viewed modernism as a shocking but enthralling tool for assessing the first decades of the twentieth century specifically and modernity generally. Cowley describes *Exile's Return* as a "literary odyssey," i.e., an adventure thematically unified around the intellectuals and artists who produced the experimental literature and art of the '20s. Reflecting on 1929, the final year he chronicles, he states,

> It was a year of suicides, not only among stockbrokers but also among wealthy dilettantes. It was a year when faces looked white and nervous; a year of insomnia and sleeping tablets. [...] Most of all it was a year when a new mood became perceptible, a mood of doubt and even defeat. People began to wonder whether it wasn't possible that not only their ideas but their whole lives had been set in the wrong direction [306].

"In the wrong direction." This directional metaphor recalls Ortega y Gasset's characterization of modernity as an acute awareness that "there is no turning back" (50). Similar in rhetorical technique and tone to Ortega y Gasset's reading of modernism as dehumanized art, here Cowley uses the macro-text of Anglo-American modernism as a conceptual unity to throw into relief the flow of history, the intrusion of accelerating change into the space of the ordinary. Comparing modernism to a succession of alcohol-soaked parties attended by a bohemian friend, Cowley describes participating in that culture this way:

> The room was smoky and sweaty and ill-ventilated; all the lights were tinted green or red, and, as the smoke drifted across them, nothing had its own shape or color; the cellar was like somebody's crazy vision of Hell; it was as if he was caught there and condemned to live in a perpetual nightmare. When he came out on the street, he said, it was bathed in harsh winter light, ugly and clear and somehow reassuring. That was the way a decade came to its end [323].

Inconceivable Chambers Beyond Time

Like Ortega y Gasset, Cowley ekphrastically translates actual modernism into a theme, an abstraction, and proceeds to meditate on this theme and so engages it as a lens for revealing the secret nature of history as a process of deformation. Looking through this thematized practice of modernist art, Cowley, like Ortega y Gasset, perceives accelerating and inhuman change, the blurring together of heaven and hell, excess and dearth, a phantasmagoria not unlike that rendered by Lovecraft in his imagist montage, "Nyarlathotep," a dream-like narrative that treats, among other things, an alien god who personifies modernity as a grotesque mixture of antiquity and technology. Published in the November 1920 issue of the *United Amateur*, a low-circulating non-commercial magazine, the story

2. Pulp Ekphrasis, History, and Deformation

treats a technological showman "twenty-seven centuries" old who, with a camera, projects prophecies onto a "screen in a darkened room," and thereby reveals to a group of spectators the secret of history as allegorically comparable to a Dada-like song and dance (203):

> Through this revolting graveyard of the universe the muddle, maddening beating of drums, and the thin, monotonous whine of blasphemous flutes from inconceivable, unlighted chambers beyond Time; the detestable pounding and piping whereunto dance slowly, awkwardly, and absurdly the gigantic, tenebrous ultimate gods—the blind, voiceless, mindless gargoyles whose soul is Nyarlathotep [205].

For Lovecraft, modernity is allegorized here as a parody of formless modernist music and Dadaistic dance, a bizarre experimental opera supplemented by modern technology and framed by ancient prophecy. It resembles Cowley's interpretation of the modernist enterprise of the 1920s as a series of alcoholic benders ending in a shame-filled, pain-wracked morning of harsh winter light.

Ortega y Gasset and Cowley, like Lovecraft and Smith, use modernism—actual modernism and unreal shadow modernism—to perceive an otherwise hidden secret of history: the process of history leads intractably toward an inhuman world dominated by an elite.

A few years after Cowley published his memoir, Hitler was appointed Chancellor of Germany, the Spanish Civil War began, the Nazis invaded Poland, and, in due course, our next ekphrasist, Walter Benjamin, overdosed on morphine.

Tick tock.

Walter Benjamin and Perceiving History

Like Cowley and Ortega y Gasset, Walter Benjamin is an ekphrasist who treats modernism; although, most will remember him as cultural critic, associate of the Frankfurt School, and author of *The Arcades Project*, a philosophical travelogue. In his "Theses on the Philosophy of History," Benjamin uses modernist art as a cognitive prosthesis to view the otherwise hidden secret of history. Let us examine one of the most famous examples of the ekphrastic treatment of modernist art, i.e., Benjamin's interpretation of Paul Klee's 1920 modernist watercolor painting, *Angelus Novus*, as a depiction of "the Angel of History," a symbol for him of humanity's tenuous historical agency. Viewing the idea of humanity's mastery of historical forces as a universal self-aggrandizing delusion, Benjamin portrays "the Angel of History"—the symbol of our agency, our collective grip on the "steering wheel" of history—as teetering on the brink of a horrible disaster:

> His face is turned toward the past. Where we perceive a chain of events, he sees one single catastrophe which keeps piling wreckage upon wreckage and hurls it in front of his feet. The angel would like to stay, awaken the dead, and make whole what has been smashed. But the storm is blowing from Paradise; it has got caught in his wings with such violence that the angel can no longer close them. The storm irresistibly propels him into the future to which his back is turned, while the pile of debris grows skyward. This storm is what we call progress [258].

Here is a subtle allegory inspired by and thereby intertwined with a preceding two-dimensional one created by Klee. The angel Benjamin describes is not, strictly speaking, Klee's angel, but an unreal facsimile of it, a virtual and calibrated echo and ekphrastic description. The actual paint strokes constituting Klee's angel function as an object of ekphrasis, and via translation from a painting into a literary image, Benjamin projects his interpretation, thereby shaping it for his rhetorical aims. This is more than mere interpretation or allegoresis. It is also not neutral journalistic description. It is explicitly rhetorically-motivated ekphrasis. Benjamin is using Klee's painting like a prosthesis to perceive what is otherwise invisible with the limited scope of his all too human sensorium: the broad-scale historical change characteristic of modernity.

Benjamin's Bad Feeling

Benjamin's image of disastrous loss of agency parallels in important ways another one, a central one to the nineteenth-century critical tradition he inherits in the interwar period: "Modern bourgeois society with its

2. Pulp Ekphrasis, History, and Deformation

relations of production, of exchange and of property that has conjured up such gigantic means of production and of exchange, is like the sorcerer who is no longer able to control the powers of the nether world whom he has called up by his spells" (Marx 14). From the image of a sorcerer losing control of the demon he has conjured, we come to the image of an angel, wings flared, blown wildly out of control by a gust from heaven. In Marx's image, it is the bourgeoisie who have lost control; in Benjamin's image, it is all of humanity. In these two images, separated by one century, we must bear in mind a distinctive transformation of pathos: Marx's ecstasy in the dialectical materialist eschatological unfolding of utopia transforms a century later into Benjamin's genuine horror in the certainty of not mere dystopia but universal apocalypse. But it is important to append to this emotional transformation that has been outlined above as Benjamin's methodological distinctiveness: Marx comes to have faith in his vision of the bourgeoisie's lost agency by virtue of the logic of what is now considered his discredited labor theory of value. As few continue to subscribe to his economic theory, we no longer anticipate his utopia on those grounds, and so his metaphor, although compelling, is less convincing. But Benjamin comes to his horrible flash of insight, his unfaith in historical "progress," not through economic theories but by meditating on and describing a modernist painting.

Unlike Marx, who as a materialist and economist theorist, seeks verifiable knowledge of history, Benjamin seeks a knowledge-like foundation of belief constituted affectively and mystically, something more like a hunch, intuition, or formless "bad feeling." In Benjamin's final utterance, Marx's dialectical materialist philosophy has been discarded in favor of a free associative series of mystical images that render spontaneous nonsyllogistic insight based on emotion and inspiration. The rhetorical effectiveness of Marx's metaphorical sorcerer and demon is predicated on the viability of his theory; the rhetorical effectiveness of Benjamin's image is predicated not on theory but on pathos. His rhetoric does not make the same appeals as Marx's. Moreover, it is less respectable from a philosophical perspective. Benjamin would not be judged by logical consistency but by affective intensity. He grasps the secret of history as an unfolding disaster, a descent into formlessness, not by the logical power of the syllogism but by the mysterious quality of his virtual *Angelus Novus*, his transformation of Klee's painting into a horrible literary allegory. In this way, it is less a form of dialectical materialist philosophy and more like Lovecraft's tale of an insane painter, "Pickman's Model," first published in *Weird Tales* in October of 1927.

Pickman's Modernist Paintings

The story tells of Richard Upton Pickman of Boston and the circumstances of his disappearance. Although Pickman's bizarre paintings had been censured by most art critics as too bizarre and morbid, the sensitive protagonist of Lovecraft's tale, a Benjaminian figure, sticks by him and acknowledges the demented artist's genius. Consider the narrator's description of one of Pickman's paintings, an example of pulp ekphrasis and a rendering of shadow modernism:

> There was something very disturbing about the nauseous sketches and half-finished monstrosities that leered around from every side of the room, and when Pickman suddenly unveiled a huge canvas on the side away from the light I could not for my life keep back a loud scream—the second I had emitted that night. It echoed and reechoed through the dim vaultings of that ancient and nitrous cellar, and I had to choke back a flood of reaction that threatened to burst out as hysterical laughter [68–69].

For Benjamin, who committed suicide to escape the Gestapo, the idea of historical progress rendered in the brushstrokes of Klee's painting were a horror, no less horrible than the fictional work of Lovecraft's fictional Pickman's. Pickman's paintings, like Klee's, reveal the instability of the ordinary, the sinister presence of a subterranean race of flesh-rending ghouls, literally agents of human deformation. Registering historical change as a catastrophe, Benjamin's acute consciousness of history as disastrous deformation appears as an insight of horror, a terrible epiphany precipitated by his encounter with Paul Klee's angel, an encounter not unlike the protagonists of "Pickman's Model." Not only does Benjamin's reading of *Angelus Novus*, in paralleling the protagonist of Lovecraft's story, exemplify his suspicion of modernity during the increasingly unstable interwar period, it also instances a distinctive ekphrastic strategy it shares with Lovecraft. Both Lovecraft and Benjamin use modernist art

2. Pulp Ekphrasis, History, and Deformation

for perceiving the unfolding present of modernity, for perceiving the otherwise hidden secret of history.

Lukács and the Secret of History

The secret of history, i.e., the phenomenon of broad-scale historical change, the dissolution of recognizable forms, is something we have difficulty perceiving while dwelling in the ordinary, a space defined by recognizability and thankfully constrained by the narrow boundaries of a solitary embodied sensorium. We can perceive broad-scale historical change as distinct events in newspapers, newsfeeds, broadcasts, and public political displays, but barring war-zones, in the myopic, limited field of our day-to-day lives, change is vegetable in velocity. Forms endure. For example, even though one might sit calmly, this does not mean that the world is not a swirl of accelerating broad-scale historical change. Migrations, regime-changes, technological and scientific developments, and unfolding ecological disasters are happening, but through the tiny aperture of a single human sensorium, there appears to be comparable stasis. The individual sitter's smallness limits their ability to perceive such large-scale changes in an immediate way. The illusion of historical stability, this veil of the ordinary and the endurance of form, is a function of our limited human mode of perception. The issue is that there is something about this mode of perception that prevents us from perceiving this unrelenting, large scale, and rapid change. But by gazing on and becoming enthralled by a strange work of modernist art, engaging it as a prosthetic technology, Benjamin has managed to expand his sensorium, to lift the veil, and grasp the secret of history as a process of deformation.

On an elemental level, Benjamin's leveraging of Klee's painting for historical perception of change evidences the inflammation of what Georg Lukács theorizes as modern historical consciousness in his 1937 study *The Historical Novel*, which he describes as a manner of perceiving the flow of history in the arena of daily life unique to the experience of modernity. For Lukács, the extent to which we can conceive of ourselves as occupying a point in history, as being historically unique, as being modern, is predicated on our ability to perceive a certain intensity of change. Obliquely engaging in a phenomenology of history, Luckás attempts to answer the bizarre question of how we perceive or intuit significant historical change. But we need to qualify this. The central question for Lukács is not, for example, how do we know change is happening intellectually. The question is, rather, how can we see, hear, taste, smell, and even touch and thereby register historical change in our immediate lives and environments. Can we?

Lukács's answer to this mystical question convinces because of its commonsense character. For him, "the concrete possibilities for men to comprehend their own existence as something historically conditioned" emerged in the Western world approximately around the time of the French Revolution as a result of the intensified intrusions into daily life of the concrete, material consequences associated with political reorganization: e.g., the wiping away of the estate system and associated sartorial laws in France, the public execution of the Louis XVI, the massive conscription of citizen soldiers, the economic scarcity associated with large scale warfare, etc. (24). In other words, Lukács speculates that our ability to perceive history, to perceive large scale change, to grasp it mentally as a force that matters, is equivalent with our ability to register its effects within the range of day-to-day activities.

Though speculative, this is not a radical idea. One will, of course, be comparatively unaware of history while sitting alone in a coffee shop. The coffee will slowly cool. One will sip it. But do these "events" constitute history? Of course not.

But when scarcity results in hunger, when officers forcefully conscript someone I care for, when I smell corpses rotting and witness the beheading of the king, when I am dragged before a magistrate on charge of treason, then, in this disorienting swirl of deforming social forms, I become acutely aware of something called "history."

Benjamin and the Cognitive Prosthesis of Art

Lukács's theory of historical perception begins to but does not completely domesticate the rhetorical distinctiveness of Benjamin's transfor-

2. Pulp Ekphrasis, History, and Deformation

mation of Klee's *Angelus Novus* into a literary image. Seen from the perspective of this theory of the formation of modern historical consciousness, section IX of Benjamin's essay just might signal the philosopher's acute historical consciousness, his modern way of thinking time. But this does not fully domesticate the strangeness of Benjamin's ekphrastic gesture, his transformation of Klee's *Angelus Novus*. It is important to hold in mind the distinction that Benjamin's situation is radically different from Lukács's hypothetical French peasant. The fictional peasant perceives history through the sight of Louis XVI's execution, the movement of armies, the smell of rotting flesh. In the instance of the peasant, to be conscious of history during the revolution it is enough to possess a sensorium. Thus, the strange question must be posed in this way: why is it that Benjamin, over two centuries later, seems to require a modernist painting to perceive his modernity, to perceive rapidly accelerating change? Can he not be conscious of history without the map or prosthesis of a modernist painting? Without ekphrasis? Can he not simply perceive history directly by watching it through military parades? Newsreels? By listening to radio broadcasts? Contemplating photographs? By reading sociological studies?

Benjamin's reading of Klee brings into focus the interpretive limits of Lukács's theory of historical perception. But his theory is invaluable to the extent that it conditions us to understand how Benjamin and Lovecraft are deploying an ekphrastic technique that leverages a sensible element, the phenomena of the "new art"—as represented by Klee's actual *Angelus Novus* ("the New Angel") and Pickman's unreal paintings—in order to gain phenomenological access not simply to the flow of history but its deepest secret: its nature as accelerating change, a process of transforming novelty into ordinariness and ordinariness into novelty. Put simply, for Benjamin and Lovecraft, to be enthralled by a work of modernist art is to look upon modernization during its terrible unfolding and to apprehend thereby its full significance: the pace of change is accelerating. Form decays into formlessness. The ordinary is finite, conditional, and fragile.

It is by translating the "new art" into a virtual literary image that history, that the catastrophe that is modernity, can be apprehended not merely by the corporeal sensory organs but by some other means: an emotional mode of understanding, knowledge via pathos.

Cresting Concrete Waves

Let us briefly turn to another ekphrasist who treats modernism, Berenice Abbott (1898–1991), who illustrated the first edition of Malcolm Cowley's *Exile's Return*. From 1918 until 1921 Abbott shared an apartment in Greenwich Village with Cowley along with many other important American artists and intellectuals, such as Djuna Barnes and Kenneth Burke. She befriended Marcel Duchamp and Man Ray when they visited Greenwich Village. She eventually set up a portrait studio in Paris with Man Ray where she composed iconic photographs of figures associated with the modernist movement: James Joyce, Sylvia Beach, Jean Cocteau, Peggy Guggenheim. But Abbott is not only interesting as a modernist. Abbott's ascendency, her most significant contribution for this study, corresponds not to modernism proper but to the period after modernism. Her significance is not exhausted by her sometimes role as illustrator or by her friendship with Cowley, Burke, Barnes, and other interwar modernists. She becomes most interesting for this study as an ekphrasist who uses modern architecture as a prosthesis for perceiving an otherwise invisible process of historical change.

After forsaking Greenwich Village in 1921 to study sculpture in France and Germany, Abbott returned to New York in 1929. Stirred to her core by dramatic changes that had taken place during her travels, she secured employment taking photographs of the economically depressed city for the Federal Art Project. She collected them into an exhibition titled *Changing New York*. Consisting of over 300 black and white photographs taken from 1929 to 1939, selections of this project were published in a 1939 book that garnered universal acclaim, acclaim that had not ceased by as late as 1973 when Pulitzer Prize–winning art critic, Ada Louis Huxtable, looking back on photography projects that sought to capture the essence of New York, described Abbott's exhibition as "unequaled" (182). Describing Abbott as the photographer "who saw the city most truly," Huxtable describes the appeal of her photographs in this way: "They are primarily and penetratingly real. There is an extraordinary sense of the urban essence, of the entire physical and human conurbation rather than of something skimmed off the top" (182). More contemporary accounts

2. Pulp Ekphrasis, History, and Deformation

of Abbott's important project attests to her power to capture and stabilize in enduring aesthetic form the otherwise visible, yet not self-evident, phenomena of New York in the process of changing. For example, in the preface to the companion to a 1997 re-exhibition of Abbott's 1939 *Changing New York* project, Robert P. Macdonald, then director of the Museum of the City of New York, states, "Abbott understood the novelty of her subject: a city analogous to the mythical phoenix, raising out of its nineteenth-century physical forms and the human ashes of financial collapse into a new, astonishing world that was both promising and harsh" (8). In other words, whereas most look upon the skyline of New York as a stable pattern, an enduring form of stone and steel, Abbott sees the cresting of concrete waters, the secret truth of the ordinary reality of New York from 1929–1939.

A Gigantic Montage of a Thousand Negatives

Abbott proposed her project to the Federal Art Project as a documentarian accounting of New York City in the process of changing. Thus, we should consider her photographs "action shots" of a city changing, forming, and deforming. In a typical photograph, "Brooklyn Bridge, Water and Dock Streets, looking southwest, Brooklyn," for example, Abbott uses the modern architecture that is under construction as equipment to perceive the dissolution of the ordinary, to hold in stasis radical, large-scale change with her camera. Could one be inclined to read the photograph as prophesying the inevitable eclipse of a view of the East River and the sky?

Such a speculation cannot be supported by a mere fragment of larger text, which is what a single photograph extracted from the whole of Abbott's project inevitably becomes. But the conventions of Abbott's photographic enterprise rely on a kind of scopic dismantling, a carving up of the city and holding out for observation its change as a disunity. The rhetorical effectiveness of conveying "changing New York," however, was weakened by this scopic dismantling. What adequately conveying this change requires is a theory of "ruthless unity," a phrase Theodor Adorno and Max Horkheimer applied to the culture industries of film, radio, music, and popular magazines (1112). Abbott's deconstructive gesture of 344 highly-composed photographs hides the secret of history, the fact that interwar New York captured by her photographs was literally dissolving. However, reconstructing them, suturing them together, reveals this secret. The secret of history becomes more apparent through the prism of a fuller archive, a point Abbott was aware of as indicated by the answer she gave to an interviewer of *Popular Photography* in 1940. Asked to select her favorite photograph from the project, Abbott refused. Her answer: "Suppose we took a thousand negatives and made a gigantic montage; a myriad-faced picture combining the elegances, the squalor, the curiosities, the monuments, the sad faces, the triumphant faces, the power, the irony, the strength, the decay, the past, the present, the future of the city—that would be my favorite picture" (qtd. in Yochelson 9).

Abbott's gigantic montage of undeveloped film echoes Benjamin's "pile of debris" growing ever skyward, and it anticipates the plenitude of stories printed on disintegrating pulpwood paper in *Weird Tales* that fictionalize shadow modernism. In this way, Abbott's answer allows us to understand how, in a picture like "Brooklyn Bridge, Water and Dock Streets, looking southwest, Brooklyn," we can perceive the secret of history haunting modernity, albeit in a fragmentary way. Grasping it fully requires reflecting on a wider archive. In *Changing New York*, the modernist photographer, the technology of the camera, and the modern architecture fuse to render unto the sensorium the ephemerality of the ordinary.

In this chapter, several examples of the ekphrastic treatment of modernism have been discussed. Ortega y Gasset uses modernist art to make prophetic claims about the structure of European historical progress. Malcolm Cowley uses modernist art to render modernity as a hellish space hostile to the human subject. Walter Benjamin uses modernist art to interpret modernity as an unyielding and irredeemable catastrophe. And, finally, Berenice Abbott uses modern architecture to render the process of a city dying and yet transforming. In all these instances of ekphrasis, a secret of history is revealed: modernity is the condition whereby the ephemerality of the ordinary becomes undeniable. In other words, in all these examples of ekphrasis, modernist art is used to support speculative claims interpreting history as the acceleration of a process of de-reification and deformation. In these works, history bends from form toward formlessness.

2. Pulp Ekphrasis, History, and Deformation

Weird Tales *and the Pulp Aesthetic*

In the following chapters, I argue that key works of the *Weird Tales* Three constitute a special form of ekphrasis termed pulp ekphrasis. The key works by Howard, Smith, and Lovecraft, like the texts considered above, engage modernist art as a prosthetic technology/tool but do so in a specific way: these works fictionalize modernism, strategically distort and transform it into shadow modernism.

Lovecraft, Smith, and Howard are not the only interesting authors who published in *Weird Tales*, of course, but this study has no pretension as a survey or comprehensive account of all the work published in that magazine. The pulp ekphrasist works of the *Weird Tales* Three, nevertheless, deserve special mention to the extent that, as central works in the emerging canon of pulp fiction, they exemplify something like a transhistorical, or at least contextually transferable, pulp fiction aesthetic. Contra stereotypes about pulp fiction, this tradition and aesthetic enterprise, like modernism, is concerned with art, with creating non-market value, and with examining, self-reflexively, the conditions that allow the possibility of something like artistic authenticity.

The pulp ekphrastic works of the *Weird Tales* Three are a good place to begin this defense of pulp fiction and the unreal and speculative literary traditions that extend from it, such as science fiction, fantasy, and supernatural horror. And yet, these works' obsession with art could be considered a symptom of the larger community they constellated around, namely, the magazine that connected them. To demonstrate this rich connection to the magazine discourse community in general and to conclude, consider a story published in *Weird Tales* before Lovecraft, Smith, or Smith appeared in its pages, Anthony Rudd's, "A Square of Canvas."

Anthony Rudd: Form Toward Formlessness

Rudd's "A Square of Canvas" exemplifies the theme of monstrous experimental art that centers the pulp ekphrastic works of the *Weird Tales*

Three. Rudd's story fictionalizes a modernist artist as a shadow modernist and a modernist art object as a work of shadow modernism. In Rudd's story, the modernist artist becomes a sadist who sacrifices life and provides pain for the recompense of art. Modernist art, accordingly, is rendered in this story as a non-representational, deforming style that begins as naturalism and ends as formlessness. In this way, it executes a similar thesis to Ortega y Gasset, Cowley, Benjamin, and Abbott: seen through the perspective of distinctively modern art, history is a secret process of accelerating deformation.

Published in *Weird Tales* in 1923—the second year of *Weird Tales'* publication—"A Square of Canvas" stages the transformation of modernist art into a demonic and formless painting, an entity that not only challenges interpretive systems but also signals the end of signification by a descent into formlessness. In terms of genre, the story is a demented künstlerroman. The fictional artist, Hal Pemberton, relies on the mutilation of bodies for artistic inspiration. As a student, he struggles to receive praise from his teachers until, in frustration, he kills a beetle and experiences an artistic inspiration: "Before my eyes I saw the picture I wished to portray—the play of protest against death. I drew the death struggle..."(4). As the story proceeds, Pemberton's artistic needs are no longer satisfied by insects, and so he moves on to torturing rabbits:

> I seized by the long ears the white-furred animal which had stared at me. The warm softness of the palpitating body raised my artistic desire to a frenzy. I pulled a table from the wall, and holding down the animal upon it I drew my knife. Overcoming the mad, futile struggles of the rabbit, I slit long incisions in in the white back and belly. The blood welled out [...]. Perfect fury of delight sent me to my canvas. My fingers trembled as I mixed the colors, but there was no decision now [...]. You perhaps, have seen a reproduction of that picture? It was called *The Lusts of the Magi*, and now hangs in one of the Paris galleries [6].

Pemberton proceeds with his mutilations and continues to create art that shocks and thrills the art and critical community. He moves on from torturing rabbits to horses, and finally, after torturing large mammals no longer satisfies him artistically, he kills and mutilates his wife to create his final masterpiece.

> This was the logical, inevitable conclusion! She was my mate; was in duty bound to furnish inspiration for the picture I must paint [...]. To show her that I loved her still, no matter what duty impelled me to do, I kissed her hair, her eyes, her breast. Then I set to work. [...]. In a few minutes I was away and painting as I

never painted before. A red stream dripped from the steel cot, down to the floor, and ran slowly toward where I stood. It elated me. I felt the fire of a fervor of inspiration greater than ever beset me. I painted. I painted. This was my masterpiece [11].

When his masterpiece is revealed at the end of the story it is "a blank square of white canvas" (12). From form, through deformation, into formlessness, the logic of pulp ekphrasis is succinctly executed here.

Rudd's story of a demented modernist artist harmonizes with several of the later pulp ekphrastic works of the *Weird Tales* Three. For example, in Pemperton's artistic ecstasy in torture, we can see glimpses of Clark Ashton Smith's "Isle of the Torturers," a story that features the sinister people of Uccastrog who turn torture into an art form and the groans of the tortured into music. Pemberton's disturbing paintings call to mind the horrible bas-relief of Henry Wilcox in Lovecraft's, "The Call of Cthulhu" and Richard Upton Pickman's "modern studies" in "Pickman's Model." And as Pemberton tortures his wife in response to his high-minded artistic compulsion, he comes to resemble the sorcerous Master of Yimsha in Robert E. Howard's, "The People of the Black Circle," who asks this elitist question of his unfortunate prey: "How can I explain my mystic reasons to your puny intellect? You could not understand" (54). Rudd's story of a shadow modernist creating shadow modernism through torture is an early form of the pulp ekphrasis, a discourse that emerged in *Weird Tales* at its outset. Pulp ekphrasis would become a literary enterprise that the *Weird Tales* Three would master together. Whereas Rudd's Pemberton renders shadow modernism as meaningless, as a mere blank canvas that communicates nothing at all in its absolutely formlessness, the *Weird Tales* Three would come to speculate about what, such a blank canvas, such a descent into formlessness, might signify: history's secret nature as deformation.

3. A Real Weird Magazine

The Pulpwood Magazine Context of Weird Tales

To understand the most enduring literary art of the *Weird Tales* Three, to see their writing as pulp ekphrasis, and to comprehend their fictional art objects as shadow modernist works that artfully stage de-reification into formlessness, one first needs to grasp the specific literary and print context from which their pulp fiction emerged. This specific print context is, of course, the experimental pulp fiction magazine, *Weird Tales*, the legendary magazine that, as a carnival-space to the otherwise regimented pulp fiction marketplace, provided the unique discursive conditions for Lovecraft, Smith, and Howard to master the pulp fiction aesthetic, disseminate their work, and to pass it on for others to study and preserve. But to understand *Weird Tales*'s under-acknowledged experimental nature and how the *Weird Tales* Three artistically capitalized upon it, one first needs some general sketch of the pulp fiction magazine marketplace that allowed *Weird Tales* to exist as a viable, though troubled, business enterprise. And so, let's begin with an August 28th, 1935, anonymously authored article that appears in *The New York Times* that analyzed the pulp context of *Weird Tales*.

Titled "Fiction By Volume," the purpose of the article is somewhat contradictory: it is to reveal to the reading public something they were seeing but not seeing, the "invisible visibility" of a print media that they may have perceived superficially but did not know. Deliberately designed to thrill them, yet failing to attract their attention, it was always there, a "voluntary circulation" among the distractions of interwar New York, unacknowledged every time they purchased a newspaper, a pack of cigarettes, a cup of coffee (16). This was the lurid print media that caused every newsstand in New

York City to swell in the 1930s, the all-fiction magazine printed on pulpwood paper: "the pulps."

This article describes the pulps as "little known and officially unrecognized publishing world," a term which highlights the idea that this is a quasi-literary world the reader is not familiar with but is, in reality—at least in terms of sight—familiar with (16). And this "world" is defined in direct opposition to the "great publishing world," where "manuscripts are being examined on the score of style and originality" (16). This "officially unrecognized world" was the all-fiction publishing business, a business that produced *Weird Tales*, the self-styled "unique magazine."

Why does the writer feel a need to reveal these magazines to readers, considering their ubiquity? Could it be that the readers of *The New York Times* never looked beyond the section of the newsstand shelf that held their periodicals of choice? Reflecting on the vast number of pulp fiction magazines being published and sold at the time, the writer observes, "The result of this production system is inevitably an emphasis on quantity rather than quality" (16). The writer concludes the article on a surprisingly positive note, mirroring the paradoxical nature of the term "officially unrecognized" (16). He frames pulp fiction magazines as both a site of hackwork as a well-spring of literary talent. He ends his article by calling—particularly for publishers—to explore deeply the seen but unseen pulps, those garish magazines that clutter the newsstand.

This article is a rare attempt to maintain the intellectual value of "intensive" readings of pulp fiction while at the same time justifying "extensive" reading practices of the commodity literature published in pulpwood magazines "by volume." The pulp magazine marketplace is framed as a formless compost heap, not unlike the rubbish heap that crowds the ankles of Benjamin's Angel of History. For the most part, the writer argues, the pulpwood publishing world is constituted by trashy ephemera; and yet, such a polluted mass just might obscure an important literary work, a diamond in the rough.

The Degraded Nature of Pulp Fiction

Such a nuanced and nonjudgmental view of pulp fiction magazines seems to have been a rare one; during their ascendency in the interwar period, few seem to have attempted to engage with the pulps in this subtle way. Moreover, even fewer went further and called for more people to buy and read them. Searching the newspapers of the interwar periods reveals a more common pattern of dismissal on moral and class-prejudiced grounds: pulp magazines are more often framed not only as degraded literature, as contaminated entertainment by virtue of their appeal to the masses, the working classes, the immigrants, but they are also framed as an intellectual menace, a sentiment that links the philosophically rigorous invectives of the Frankfurt School concerned about the "culture industry" with the sincere complaints of a frustrated high school teacher: "Ninety percent of high school students read 'pulp' magazines and the material contained in them constitute a menace to the pupil's morals, his English and his mind," decries Anita P. Forbes, a high school teacher quoted in a November of 1936 *New York Times* article with the headline, "Pulp Magazines Called Menace" (27). Forbes goes on to speculate about their appeal: "They afford thrills, they help while away idle minutes and they require no mental effort from the reader" (27). She summarizes the threatening capacity of the fiction published by pulp magazines by saying it's too easy for students to read to cultivate deep reading skills: "How is that habit of active perception and appreciation to be formed in minds accustomed in finding entertainment without exercise?" (27).

So, we get to the core: pulp fiction magazines are a menace because "they afford thrills" and require "no mental effort." To have a "thrill" is to have a somatic, embodied reaction. The hackles raise. The stomach knots. The jaw clenches. To "thrill" is to feel a sudden intensity of sensation—tactile, auditory, visual, olfactory, gustatory—or emotion such as horror, wonder, lust, anger, curiosity, and so forth. Accordingly, pulp fiction magazines require no "active perception" and they require "no mental effort" (27). If we take Forbes's criticism of the pulps as a typical version of many other criticisms leveled at the pulps, we understand that the threat these magazines pose is not just causing mental degradation but also moral and physical degradation on the level of the body.

Here the pulps become quasi-pornographic: such magazines are designed to engage the body, to evoke not reflective intellectual apprehension of aesthetic form and artistic convention but an embodied sensational and emotional thrill. This frame combines religious discourses against bodily pleasure as well as Enlightenment discourses that privilege detached

3. *A Real Weird Magazine*

reflection over emotion-based intuition. In other words, "the pulps" are sinful and atavistic in that they engage primitive somatic responses and pleasures rather than intellectual apprehension and reflection. The pulps are seen as just another contributor to a widespread decline of cultural sensibility. These cheap magazines animalize their readers by over-stimulating them into a state of spacious thoughtlessness and distraction by making them aesthetically slothful, unappreciative of fine art that should, necessarily, be mentally difficult, a sentiment that held wide stock in interwar literary culture. Even Lovecraft, an archetype for the idea of a high-art pulp fiction, corroborates Forbes's cynical hypothesis. For example, he wrote to the poet Reinhardt Kleiner in 1916 of his "reprehensible habit of picking up cheap magazines like *The Argosy* to divert my mind from the tedium of reality" (*Selected Letters* v.1 41). Seven years later, however, Lovecraft would be publishing in those very magazines.

Literary Art and Literary Artifact

Bringing together these two perspectives toward pulp fiction magazines—the nuanced/nonjudgmental and the reductive/judgmental—becomes useful for speculating about a cultural logic in print and literary culture in the early twentieth century and interwar period. This is an important process of change that comes to determine the way elements of the book and literary culture of the early twentieth-century were experienced within the pulpwood magazine business environment that produced *Weird Tales*.

In the late decades of the nineteenth century and into the early twentieth century, two entities were inextricably imbricated like clasped hands: (1) the disembodied, synchronic signifying structures that constitute literary artifacts and (2) the paper, ink, boards, and bindings that embodied them. The archive of literary art—narratives, poems, essays published as books, periodicals, or magazines—consisted of material substrates braided with immaterial structures of signification. However, these two entities underwent a kind of schism as publishing production expanded to hitherto unimaginable levels. The signifier of literary art (the abstract formal system) became disentangled from the material substance/artifact that embodied it (the literary artifact instantiated in ink and paper and bound between covers). From the interwar perspective, literature stopped existing dualistically in a more traditional sense as hybrids of (1) disembodied formal systems and (2) material substrata such as paper and ink. In certain strata of literary production, the formal systems of the language arts became disassociated with its media vehicle, its material substrate. In other words, literary works, particularly those figured as artistic ones, came to be expressed in this period as more or less incorporeal systems. The book could be closed and even burned, but the disembodied literary work could live on.

The formal rhetoric and cultural logic that determined the aesthetic value of the fiction published in pulpwood magazines are connected to this de-materialization of literary artifacts. As printing technology became more advanced and more print material was produced, low literature came to be perceived as soulless material goods, tumor-like masses of paper and ink circulating within economies not of cultural but of actual capital (e.g., *penny* dreadfuls, *dime* novels). Consequently, we can refer to many texts considered culturally degraded today with a reference not to an abstract idea like "literature" but to a concrete object like "pulp." For example, McCracken's account of the aesthetic of pulp fiction, titled *Pulp: Reading Popular Literature* (1998), rarely refers to pulp fiction magazines. Rather, his study of late-'90s romance novels, science fiction novels, fantasies, and mysteries downplays the historical and artifact nature of the term, the degree to which the materiality of low literature is foregrounded in its name. It seems McCracken understands the concept of pulp not as a historically and dialectically conditioned outgrowth of material and economic processes but as a transhistorical formal rhetoric. But it is important to emphasize that our ability to describe a certain quality of literature as a formless pile of decaying paper has important historical roots that carry significant ideological meaning and discursive consequences. Liquid and putrescent pulp has today become the opposite of "Literature"—an ideal, gloriously liberated from the body, incorporeal, soul-like. Pulp, on the contrary, is a taboo exuda, a corporeal slime, and therefore soulless and formless. In the realm of pulp fiction, materiality is ever present.

This full presence of materiality in pulp contexts goes far in explaining why in communities surrounding cultural productions genealogically linked to pulp fiction and pulp more generally—such as science fiction fanzines and conventions, comic book collecting, fantasy roleplaying games, and B-horror movies—the practice and ritual of collecting artifacts imbued with ritualistic significance—pulp magazine collecting, comic book collecting, trade paperback collecting, VHS collecting—is still widely prevalent. By a complicated discursive logic linked to value and function, the object, the artifact, has maintained its artistic aura and so has become a matter of deep concern in these communities. The most important point to emphasize here is how an acute awareness of the artifact nature of writing is an integral influence on the formal rhetorics that were produced by these pulp communities. In bibliophile, pulp collecting, and comic book collecting communities, it is sometimes implied that the literary artifact is symbolically parallel with the cultural logic that projects quality and value. The ideology that frames pulp works as degraded, as grotesque non-art, as ephemeral and formless matter that produces laziness, stupidity, and moral atavism, comes to influence the work, and the collector's value ideologically responds to this process of devaluation.

The Papery Ooze That Animalizes

Here is my thesis in the spirit of pulp sensationalism: by the 1930s, the most artistically ambitious pulp fiction writers, i.e., the *Weird Tales* Three, came to absorb the degradation projected onto them by the likes of Forbes, Mencken, Wilson, Pound, and several countless other literary elites. In their pulp ekphrasist works, works centrally—even obsessively—concerned with aesthetics, they formally and thematically embraced materiality, ephemerality, emotionalism, and narrative conventionalism. In other words, as a consequence of acknowledging and reacting to their interwar cultural devaluation, their prejudicial treatment, the *Weird Tales* Three sought to transform their work. Like the contaminated and polluted citizens of Innsmouth slowly but surely undergoing monstrous transformation from humans into aquatic Deep Ones, the pulp ekphrasist works of Howard, Lovecraft, and Smith, driven by hidden discursive logic fueled by elitist contempt, transformed from Literature to Pulp, from mere disembodied fiction to a papery ooze that animalizes.

Conversely, in other discourses of literature structured by an adversarial stance toward pulp literature, such as modernism, the incorporeal formal systems that constituted literature struggled vainly to enact an impossible task, to shed the material substrate that embodied them. Similar to Marx's spiritualized table that speaks and dances that he uses to demonstrate his notion of commodity fetishization, the formal system of literature struggled to become a thing without empirical substance, an essence without a body. Literature sought to become the enduring form liberated from the contingency, finitude, and vulnerability of paper and ink.

Coordinately, from the perspective of modernism historically situated elements like the material qualities associated with publication became incidental and irrelevant to the work as such, a cultural logic that clearly informed what would be called the "New Critical" methodologies for analyzing the formal dynamics of poetry. In a trick of self-hypnosis, for many literary elites, literature, thus, came to be understood as radically disembodied, ahistorical forms that endured, that were conceived as internally consistent "well wrought urns" fully realized for the most part outside of any extraneous contextual considerations. They existed as quasi-Platonic forms without bodies outside of time.

In the interwar period, degraded writing could be soulless, and the souls of sanctified books could flee pages and boards. Poems could live beyond their corporeal existence of paper and ink. Thus, with the increased sophistication and power of printing technology and industrial book and periodical production, marketing, and distribution, this schism of literature into (1) embodied ephemeral artifacts or pulp literature and (2) disembodied eternal formal systems understood in its apotheosis as modernism became acute. Moreover, degraded low works like those published in pulp fiction magazines came to be structured rhetorically by an acute awareness of its very own materiality and ephemerality. Sanctified works like modernist experiments in poetry and fiction were structured rhetorically by their unrealizable desire to cast off their material bodies and to rise to the level of immaterial essences, i.e., to become enduring forms out of time. Meanwhile, artistically ambitious pulp works embraced their own ephemerality and materiality fully in the form of a rhetoric of the gut that blasted the organ of the brain with wonder, horror, or tantalizing mystery.

3. A Real Weird Magazine

Opaque Versus Transparent Literature

In their the study of the periodical culture of modernism, Robert Scholes and Clifford Wulfman suggest that considering the table of contents of magazines that published modernist works will help, in part, to explain its difficulty: "Modernism was a self-conscious movement, in which works of art appeared together with manifestoes and critical exegeses. Modernism can almost be defined as those visual and verbal texts that need manifestoes and exegeses" (74). They go on to describe how modernist little magazines like *Poetry*, *The Dial*, *The Egoist* and *Blast!* published, alongside literary works, explanatory manifestoes and criticism. The little magazine not only introduced subscribers to new forms of modern art, but they also taught their subscribers how to experience modern art, taught subscribers how to read this new art, to see through its opacity.

Implied in this publishing practice is the notion of an art object that is bound up with explicating criticism. But this practice also implies an inverse idea, the concept of transparent art that appears in other places but that requires no explanation at all, that does not need to be published with criticism explaining how to read it. This is a self-evident literature that does not need to be explained. Though Scholes and Wulfman do not comment on this issue, the historically unique dynamics of modernism's rise and its subsequent cultural preeminence has effectively reified this "opaque art/transparent" binary. Modernism is difficult and requires criticism; pulp is easy and even the partially literate can read it. Unlike the experiments of Joyce or Beckett, pulp has no occult meaning that requires exegesis by a critic-priest.

This ideology of literature in modernity, a partial product of the publishing context of modernism, has resulted in many instances with the establishment of an invisible intellectualist prejudice that has become difficult for us to perceive: modernism requires explanation, needs to be scrutinized intensively, is incomplete without supplementary explicative texts. Moreover, the difficult literature of modernism is framed as representatively modern, more modern than this other kind of transparent literature that is easily and thoughtlessly consumed.

Unfortunately, this view is obfuscating. There is nothing like transparent or opaque literature from a theoretically rigorous perspective; moreover, there are no valid grounds to support the idea that opaque modernism is somehow more representative or authentically expressive of modernity than transparent pulp or conventional fiction. Though the rich traditions of a living and evolving modernism and the many canons derived from them are based on aesthetic principles intended to be consistent, it is appropriate in the spirit of continuing to regenerate those traditions to recall that all art medias require comparably sophisticated processes of interpretation and of decoding complex semiotic systems, and, to an extent, can be the subject of rich, thick description. From a rigorous perspective, the perception of this type of art as "opaque" and that type of art as "transparent" is less a description of the objective essence of the work in question and more a description of the ideological position and reciprocal reading strategies of the critic and artist connecting or not connecting.

The Print Culture Influences on Modernism

The periodical culture of modernism was only one of many complex elements that contributed to the difficulty of the experimental art of the early twentieth century, and the little magazine was not the only discursive space that produced modernism, other no less important spaces being, the café, the art studio, the museum, the little press, the salon, and so on. Traditionally speaking, scholars and historians of modernism and periodical culture choose to separate periodicals into two broad categories, the commercial magazine and the non-commercial, privately-published little magazine. This binary has been revised recently by scholars who offer a more nuanced and complex way of categorizing and delimiting the many periodicals of the era.

Past criticism of modernism suggest that the movement flourished in the Anglo-American context because it was given space in non-commercial, privately-circulated periodicals to avoid the influence of public taste that required conventionalism. Thus, magazines like Margaret

3. A Real Weird Magazine

Anderson's *The Little Review* and Harriet Monroe's *Poetry* are framed as non-commercial whereas larger circulation magazines like H.L. Mencken's *The Smart Set* or *Scribners* (called "slicks" because they were printed on glossy paper with expensive ink for the sake of advertisement spreadsheets) are framed as commercial. A consequence of modernist periodical studies has been the deconstruction of the unanalyzed assumption that the only authentic site of modernism was the little magazine

Little, Slick, and Pulp

Let's sharpen the discussion of little magazine versus slicks by reframing it from a binary to a tripartite structure, which would include (1) the non-commercial little magazine, (2) the commercial slick, and (3) the niche-market pulp magazine. Of the three types of literary periodicals, slicks and pulp magazines are assumed to be commercial enterprises, and so often the pulp magazine has been folded into the category of the slicks, their distinctiveness notwithstanding. Yet, there are important differences between pulp fiction magazines and slicks that need to be taken into consideration to adequately explain the pulp ekphrastic works of the *Weird Tales* Three and their aesthetic goal of vividly staging de-reification, i.e., rendering the ephemerality of the ordinary in literary form.

In addition to pulp magazines, conventionalized mass-appeal fiction and poetry was published in commercial slicks like *Scribner's*, *Cosmopolitan*, or *The Smart Set*. This type of advertisement-filled magazine was contemporary with and is often defined in contrast to the non-commercial little magazine of modernism. Slicks were commercial enterprises that delivered literature and art to consumers who wanted it along with advertisements, contents that were also part of the magazine's mass appeal. These magazines existed solely as commercial enterprises and secondly as occasions for the expansion of literary art (their marketing postures notwithstanding).

Unlike the literature published alongside advertisements in slicks, the literary works published in a typical issue of *Poetry* or *The Little Review* in the 1910s and '20s were the central justification for their existence as cultural and not commercial enterprises. The little magazine often existed as a result of a small coterie of subscribers or donations, and the manifestoes, criticism, book reviews, discussion forums that Scholes and Wulfman highlight pervaded these magazines—i.e., the corollary critical extensions that explain the difficult modern art—were coextensions of the poetry, discussion linked to the literature in the service of the literature.

In contrast, in a typical literary-themed slick magazine published in the same decade—e.g., *Scribner's*, *The Saturday Evening Post*, *Cosmopolitan*—the fiction or poetry printed is often equal with the journalism in different sections and the copious advertisements, sometimes occupying half of the magazine's pages. Put simply, the slick magazine often compared to and denigrated from the perspective of the little magazine did not exist to perpetuate and expand art but to produce profit for its investors. Such slick magazines were not primary sites of formal innovation or production. Instead, these periodicals were a medium for delivering conventionalized literature, a point driven home when it is considered that hitherto scandalous modernist works were published in slicks after they had been incorporated into the narrow conceptions of art characteristic of middlebrow readers.

The Pulpwood Magazine Defined

To compare the little magazine to the slick magazine is to consider only a small portion of the periodical culture that produced the little magazine and the modernism cultivated through it. Other medias are worthy of consideration, media formats that influenced and shaped interwar literary and art culture profoundly. Let us imagine a hypothetical type of magazine that delivers what appears to be transparent literature that requires no explanation at all. Not requiring serious intellectual labor or literary expertise, the literary works published in this hypothetical magazine satisfies with little effort. All who read it are experts and can execute valid judgments. Our thought experiment allows us to outline the pulpwood magazine with some accuracy. Indeed, as a business model and produced commodity, this was the source of the pulp magazine's economic viability: the centrality of fiction that utilized a conventional realist style that readers were familiar with, that readers could decode without the accompanying exegesis of a priest-critic. In its unpretentiousness, it interpellated readers as experts, as compeers.

Scholes and Wulfman focus on the continuity between the little magazines of modernism and the middlebrow, "mass," or commercial magazines like *Cosmopolitan*, *The Atlantic Monthly*, and *The Smart Set*, which they define in opposition to little magazines in terms of their larger subscription numbers and the large percentage of their pages turned over to advertisements. But, like other certain scholars, they say little of other periodical media pioneered at the time, particularly the popular all-fiction magazines of which *Weird Tales* is a prime though not typical example.

A Brief History of Pulp Magazines

Ubiquitous throughout North America and sometimes exported to Britain and other parts of Europe, the all-fiction magazine printed on pulpwood was not a "mass" magazine in that it was produced for everyone. By the interwar period, it had become a specialized commodity, marketed to a specific demographic, scientifically honed over the years for niche audiences with narrow tastes. Compared to slicks, it was similar to the little magazine of modernism in that its audience base was smaller and it garnered little if any revenue from advertisement. The ratio of fiction to advertisement in a typical all-fiction pulpwood periodical (*Weird Tales* is no exception) was very low compared to nearly half of the pages of a slick devoted to advertisements. But unlike little magazines, the pulp magazines were overtly commercial endeavors, business enterprises that highlighted their lack of advertisements as a marketing tactic.

Unlike the slick magazine, which marketed itself not only as a source of entertainment but as a technology of cultural or educational cultivation, the pulpwood magazine was an entertainment product. Unlike the little magazine, which frequently featured advertisements and non-aesthetic material like book reviews, editorials, discussion forums, cultural analysis, and so forth, the pulp fiction magazine was, in comparable terms, formally and rhetorically unvaried: it featured fiction and sometimes poetry and, for the most part, only a few pages devoted to advertisement and editorial correspondences or essays. Magazine historians should not discount the differences in structure, content, and business practices between pulp fiction magazines and middlebrow large circulation magazines, for there are many.

Carving up the periodical culture into "little," "slick," and "pulp magazines" does not evade the inherent reductivism of the extensive reading practices that shape scholarly accounts of popular literature. To get around this, we must closely examine a pulp magazine that contradicts the reductivist conclusions about this print archive. So, let's turn to the most highly-sought, valued, collected (and therefore enduring) pulp magazine of the pulp archive, that magazine that brought Lovecraft, Smith, and Howard together: *Weird Tales*. But before we examine *Weird Tales* and how it uniquely complicates assumptions about pulpwood magazines, we need some sense of the general history of the pulp archive. This will bring into focus how *Weird Tales* dialectically organized itself in response to the degradation of intensifying commercial literary production in the interwar period. Therefore, let us briefly go back to the origins of pulp fiction, to the newspaper and magazine publisher, Frank Andrew Munsey (1854–1925) and his weekly dime novel format magazine, *The Golden Argosy*, founded in 1882, which was not, strictly speaking, a pulp fiction magazine but is widely considered the Ur-source from which pulp fiction magazines derive.

The Origins and Evolution of Pulpwood Magazines

The Golden Argosy was a boys' adventure magazine that delivered miscellaneous writing for a juvenile audience, a large portion of its contents being serialized fiction. The magazine's earliest years were marked by financial trouble thus motivating Munsey to experiment with the format and intended audience of the publication. In 1888, having decided that an exclusively juvenile audience was too unreliable as a consumer base, Munsey dropped "Golden" from the title, seemingly considering *The Argosy* more mature in connotation. *The Argosy* continued to change steadily, but it was with the format changes in the December 1896 issue that it took on the appearance of what would later be considered a pulp fiction magazine. The December 1896 issue of *The Argosy* was printed on untreated wood pulp paper. It included no photographs or nonfiction articles. And it generally featured fiction in exclusivity. Besides some subsequent variations in size, the details of which are beyond the scope of this book, this basic print format would stay constant and be emulated by other publishers until the disappearance of pulp fiction magazines by approximately the mid–1950s.

From 1896 until 1906, all fiction magazines printed on cheap, wood pulp paper proliferated, and several publishers, seeing the financial success of *The Argosy*, followed Munsey's lead. In October of 1906 Munsey's company, once again leading innovation in the cheap magazine business, developed and published *The Railroad Man's Magazine*, which emphasized adventure stories featuring trains and railroads. This deceptively prosaic decision to focus on a specific narrative formula and theme, i.e., railroads and trains, would resonate with readers and become a commercial success, thus transforming the general audience pulp fiction magazine to the specialist pulp fiction magazine. Unlike the early general interest pulp fiction titles, these specialist magazines focused on more specific genres and audiences with narrower tastes. From 1915 onward, these thematically restricted pulps became ascendant. Titles such as *Detective Story Magazine* (1915), *Western Story Magazine* (1919), and *Love Story Magazine* (1921) demonstrate how the pulp fiction magazine came to be marketed with specific fiction reading interests in mind rather than a generalized readership.

The Founding of Weird Tales

Weird Tales was founded in 1923, and it is essential to remember that this was during a phase of maturity in the history of pulp fiction magazines.

By 1923, the pulp fiction magazine marketplace had assumed what many would consider its typical structure. Indeed, the cheap magazine marketplace had transformed into what would have been considered in common parlance "the pulps": cheap magazine titles focusing on specific topics printed on pulpwood paper that purchased the manuscripts of semi-professional writers on a cents-per-word basis. Of course, this is a reductive account of a multi-faceted world of popular fiction periodicals. For example, several professional writers published in the pulps, and general interest pulp magazines, such as *Blue Book* and *The Argosy*, were still available at newsstands alongside the other, now more common, special interest titles. Nevertheless, it is hardly arguable that by 1923 the pulps had matured, had become a recognizable and largely conventionalized cultural form.

Weird Tales, the literary context of the *Weird Tales* Three, should be viewed as a response to the conventionalized cultural form that pulp fiction magazines had assumed by 1923. Indeed, the founder of the magazine, J.C. Henneberger, stated as much, framing *Weird Tales* as a break with convention:

> Before the advent of Weird Tales, I had talked with such nationally known writers as Hamlin Garland, Emerson Hough, and Ben Hecht then residing in Chicago. I discovered that all of them expressed a desire to submit for publication a story of the unconventional type but hesitated to do so for fear of rejection. Pressed for details they acknowledged that such a delving into the realms of fantasy, the bizarre, and the outré could possibly be frowned upon by publishers of the conventional. [...] When everything was properly weighed, I must confess that the main motive in establishing Weird Tales was to give the writer free foreign to express his innermost feelings in a manner befitting great literature [Qtd. in Weinberg 3].

Weird Tales was a publishing enterprise that took what its founder interpreted as the inartistically conventionalized nature of the pulpwood magazine marketplace as a commercial and aesthetic opportunity. Stories of "unconventional types" were seen as unprofitable in the 1920s due to the absence of a hospitable marketplace, or loosely-defined marketplace. From Henneberger's perspective, writers wanted to treat the "realms of fantasy, the bizarre, and the outré" in pulp fiction but were unable or unwilling to do so due to overly restrictive editorial policies (Weinberg 3). Thus, his new magazine would provide pulp fiction writers a rare opportunity to experiment. This is an important distinction: rather than providing just another

3. A Real Weird Magazine

venue for an underrepresented genre of pulp fiction, say, for example, weird fiction or supernatural fiction, *Weird Tales*, at least at its beginning, was defined by two things: (1) a strategically ill-defined, less rigid editorial policy, and (2) a commitment to literary artistic ideals, if only as a marketing strategy.

S.T. Joshi speculates that "Henneberger founded *Weird Tales* not out of some altruistic goal of fostering artistic weird literature but largely in order to make money by featuring big name writers" (*I Am Providence* 451). This interpretation of *Weird Tales* as a mercenary, exclusively commercial, publishing enterprise is difficult to refute despite the attractiveness of the idea of the magazine as a unique bastion of artistic idealism at odds with a degraded interwar pulp fiction marketplace. *Weird Tales* did end up fostering a lot of literary art, the work of the *Weird Tales* Three being the obvious example. But it must be admitted that other pulp fiction magazines succeeded in giving writers geographically disenfranchised from the centers of literary culture the opportunity to publish what would later become canonical, or perhaps paracanonical, works, exemplars being *Black Mask* and the detective fiction of Dashiell Hammett and later Raymond Chandler. To what extent, then, is *Weird Tales* an exceptional pulp fiction magazine?

Is Weird Tales *Exceptional?*

Joshi's important reminder aside, there is evidence that irrespective of Henneberger's probable commercial motivations, hopeful writers, readers, and even editors related to *Weird Tales* as an ambitiously sincere artistic enterprise. Consider, for example, the first general editorial comment of the first issue authored by the first editor of *Weird Tales*, Edwin Baird: "Weird Tales is not merely 'another new magazine.' It's a brand new type of magazine—a sensational variation from the established rules that are supposed to govern magazine publishing" (180). In other words, *Weird Tales*, from Baird's perspective, was not just thematically different, i.e., just another specialist pulp fiction magazine like *The Railroad Man's*

Stories or *Western Story Magazine*, but rather structurally different, a magazine defined by the lack of thematically strict editorial constraints. Baird continues in the same editorial: "Our stories are unlike any you have ever read [...]. They are unusual, uncanny, unparalleled" (180). It is important to note that Baird is defining the focus of the magazine in negative terms, in what it will not be: a usual, pleasant, or ordinary magazine.

This is an important distinction: Baird does not lay out a set of themes that the magazine will treat. By way of contrast, consider the pulp fiction magazine, *Strange Tales of Terror and Mystery*, published as a competitor to *Weird Tales* from 1931 until 1933 by William Clayton, the same publisher who founded *Astounding Stories*, a famous science fiction pulp. In the inaugural issue of *Strange Tales*, the editor, Harry Bates, in an editorial titled, "Announcing Strange Tales," states, "We have wanted to bring out a magazine of this type ever since *Astounding Stories*, devoted to science fiction, made its successful appearance a year and a half ago (7)." Bates continues, sharing the miscellaneous plot elements of the stories the magazine will publish: "Vampire, leopard-men, voodoo, elemental, black magic—such stories are universally popular" (7). Unlike *Weird Tales* in 1923, which distinguished itself by its desire to publish works that refused categorization, *Strange Tales* in 1931 distinguished itself by outlining a category. *Strange Tales* in 1931 directs the thematic focus of its would-be writers and readers toward a specific thematic focus in the constraining fashion that *Weird Tales* initially defined itself against.

The Artistic Mission of Weird Tales

By framing *Weird Tales* as initially experimental in nature I do not wish to refute the idea that the magazine, as it evolved and developed, did not develop a distinctive focus on the supernatural, the horrific, and bizarre, or that it did not, by a complex discursive process involving writers, readers, artists, and editors, manage to engineer and thereby come to exemplify a new literary genre sometimes called "cosmic horror." To claim that *Weird Tales* was an experimental pulp fiction magazine is also not to

3. A Real Weird Magazine

refute that *Weird Tales* did not publish in its 279 issues ranging from 1923 to 1954 its fair share of literary ephemera. Indeed, some could plausibly frame *Weird Tales* as the originating point of a literary genre such as cosmic horror, and still others might point that out despite its self-branding as a literary artistic marketplace, it only occasionally published, in terms of literary quality, work above the level of a general pulp fiction fare.

Very few of the issues of *Weird Tales* contained literary criticism of a type highlighted by Scholes and Wulfman, although readers regularly demanded it. *Weird Tales* was an "all-fiction" pulpwood magazine, and one of its major selling points was its lack of extraneous material, including advertisement sheets. Unlike most of the publications we would call "little magazines," which typically devoted many pages to full sheet ads and classified pages, the pulp fiction magazine had very little space devoted to advertising and garnered little if any revenue from selling advertising space. This lack of advertisement can be explained by the business model associated with the marketing of pulp fiction magazines. For example, in the chapter "Behind the Scenes" of pulp magazine editor Harold Hersey's 1937 memoir, pulp advertisements are described in this way: "The advertising is the usual run-of-the-mill stuff taken on a contingency basis: not paid for until it pays for itself in results. Still, it does fill the second, third and back covers, and it looks professional [...]. Later on, if our circulation warrants it, we will be able to charge cash for advertising space" (17). *Weird Tales* was typical in this regard, foregrounding fiction over advertisements. Yet, like many modernist little magazines, *Weird Tales* published an important manifesto of goals, an account of aesthetic principles:

> The writer of a highly imaginative story intuitively knows of the existence of these things, and endeavors to search them out. He has an unquenchable thirst for knowledge. He is at once the scientist, the philosopher, and the poet. He evolves fancies from known facts, and new startling facts are in turn evolved from the fancies. [...] To the imaginative writer, the upper reaches of the ether, the outer limits of the galactic ring, the great void that gapes beyond, and the infinity of universes that may, for all we know, lie still further on, are as accessible as his own garden. He flies to them in the ship of his imagination in less time than it takes a bee to flit from one flower to another on the same spike of a delphinium [Qtd. in Weinberg 17].

In other words, *Weird Tales* sought to publish writers seriously concerned with an enterprise of art viewed as a form of knowledge production rather than mere commodity production. Is this manifesto merely a brand pose? Can we not ask the same question of similar modernist manifestoes?

Weird Tales *as Literary Context*

In the magazine's manifesto, the goal of the fiction of *Weird Tales* becomes defined in terms of cognition and knowledge building. The literature *Weird Tales* hopes to publish will offer a unique mode of thinking, of knowing invisible, secret things. It will function as an organ of perception, an x-ray device, telescope, microscope, and spectroscope, thereby offering access to the invisible phenomena. Furthermore, the scale of knowledge open to the *Weird Tales* writer is framed as inhuman, cosmic, and indefinable. There is an emphasis on speed: the *Weird Tales* writer knows these things through immediate intuition that comes at the speed of an insect's short flight from one flower to the other. The manifesto, "Why Weird Tales?," was not the only, isolated instance of framing exegesis for the stories included in the magazine. At the end of every issue, the editor, Farnsworth Wright, included a section titled "The Eyrie" which offered his reflections on the degree to which *Weird Tales* was living up to his stated goals. "The Eyrie" would also showcase readers' reactions to the stories, reactions he collated and abridged. Consider, for example, a passage from the April 1926 "The Eyrie" section:

> The stark school of realism insist[s] that true literature must be tied to the sordid experiences of everyday life. *Weird Tales* has answered these "realists" by presenting bizarre and outré stories that are among the gems of imaginative literature. Many of our stories are mere pleasant entertainment [...] but others are a very high type of literature [Wright 566].

Here is an acknowledgment of the low art cultural stereotype of pulp fiction magazines as commodity literature in the idea that some of the stories are framed as distractions. But in addition to Wright's posturing of humility is a serious assertion that much that the magazine was publishing was indeed literature, artistic objects with value in excess of their commodity value.

3. A Real Weird Magazine

As much as Wright's statement seems to confirm our cultural frame of the pulps as trash, we should guard against the assumption that pulp fiction magazines had then the lurid reputation they have now, a mythology established more after their disappearance from newsstands in the 1950s. Even at the height of their ubiquity, approximately 1935, this stereotype was vexed with many challenging it. For example, in a *New York Times* letter to the editor (September 4, 1935), pulp publisher A.A. Wyn writes in response to a negative article on the pulps. His description will allow us to experience some of the contemporary ambivalence toward the cultural status of pulp fiction magazines in circulation at the apex of their ubiquity. Writing as if he is speaking to the typical cultural elite, he states,

> You can't quite laugh at the 10,000,000 Americans who plunk down their hard-earned cash each month for their favorite magazine. And who knows what some future historian may say about the relative merits of the forests of pulp that go into the magazines and books of today? [Wyn 18]

For Wyn, the central issue of the questionable aesthetic status of pulp fiction magazines is not their essential badness, but their vast quantity, which necessarily precludes assessing anything other than the mere myth, a fiction—"the pulps"—that only outlines them, and vaguely so. Thus, Wyn cleverly draws upon another "mass media" to make his case: to speak of "the pulps" as trash is to say something like "the cinema is trash." Like the many films of the massive 1930s film industry, dismissing the majority of them as "mere entertainment" seems reasonable; however, to claim absolutely that all films are non-artistic commodities is not to allow the very real possibility that an occasional director's or actor's work will rise to the level of art.

The Artistic Authenticity of Weird Tales

Wyn's letter allows us to see how absolutist claims about the aesthetic inferiority of the pulps is an outgrowth of the same anti-modernity, the same anti-technological bias, the same prejudicial perspective that condemned film as an ephemeral attraction of modern development. Wyn is therefore prescribing a level of restraint to readers and reminding them that one or two pulp fiction magazines or pulp writers may, in fact, come to be seen in the future as artists.

Returning to "The Eyrie" section of *Weird Tales*, one sees that the genuine audacity of the editor, Farnsworth Wright, can be missed if we choose to read selectively his editorial from the perspective of traditional canons of modernism which would very likely though quite inaccurately frame *Weird Tales* as just another degraded mass publication aesthetically contaminated and compromised. More important than Wright's admittance that some of the stories published in his pulp are "pleasant entertainments for an idle hour," however, is his serious statement that some of the stories that Weird Tales publishes are "gems of imaginative literature," a "very high type of literature" (566).

The gem metaphor is particularly appropriate here. Precious gems are hidden deep underground in substrata rock and need to be looked for. Wright, like Wyn, was not naive about the wider, aesthetically undecided cultural frame of his commercial enterprise, the extent to which the all-fiction magazine published on pulpwood paper had a low cultural status. Yet, accounts of Wright published by *Weird Tales* writers describe an editor of keen aesthetic sensibilities who was a Shakespeare scholar, a music critic, and journalist before becoming a pulp editor. For example, one *Weird Tales* writer writes in a memoir of Wright, "He loved words, their flavor, likeness of sound balanced against unlikeness in meaning. He rolled words in his mouth as he would an old wine; he savored them, whether his or someone else's [...]. Prose, to him, needed rhythm, sonorous phrases; it needed balance and imagery, for he had the heart of a poet" (Qtd. in Weinberg 9).

This description of a language lover and literary aesthete does not sync with the myth of the inartistic and business-oriented pulp-fiction magazine editor brought into focus most sharply in Hersey's memoir, *Pulpwood Editor*. Of his decisions as an editor, he observes that financial culpability of the magazine as a business enterprise was prime: "I followed a simple rule: the magazine came first; as long as a successful writer, an artist or associate was happy with his work, I was happy to have him around, but no one was so important that he couldn't be replaced" (65). Of the various writers he had worked with over his long career, the arch-pulp editor Hersey frames those with artistic ambition as out of sync with the industry: "The professional has attained an objective state of mind about his work, the amateur still talks about that inspiration and individuality in self-expression which are so precious to the serious artist and so utterly worthless to the quantity writer" (70). For Hersey, the pulps were not a space for art, were in no way a cultural space that cultivated unique forms of knowledge or offered novel aesthetic experiences.

A Real Weird Magazine

Unlike Hersey, Wright seems to have believed that there was nothing essentially inartistic about the pulp fiction community his magazine was fostering. Unlike most pulp editors who struggled to find talented writers, Wright, who had a strong knowledge of literary history and a keen critical taste, found himself as editor of his pulp in the uncomfortable position of rejecting a work he thought aesthetically powerful but a commercial liability if published in *Weird Tales*. Consider a 1937 letter Smith wrote to H.P. Lovecraft in response to the writer's submission of the story "Through the Gates of the Silver Key":

> I have carefully read through THE GATES OF THE SILVER KEY and am almost overwhelmed by the colossal scope of the story [...]. But I am afraid to offer it to our readers. Many there would be, without any doubt whatever, who would go into raptures of esthetic delight while reading the story; but just as certainly there would be a great many—probably a clear majority—of our readers who would be unable to wade through it. [...] The story is so much more than a piece of fiction, and so far transcends not only the experiences of the readers, but even their wildest dreams, that they would have no point of contact with the ideas and thoughts presented in this opus [*Lovecraft Encyclopedia* 266].

The writers with artistic ambition who published in *Weird Tales* were not ignorant of the low cultural status of the magazine that was their primary market, and this is emphatically so in the case of the *Weird Tales* Three, who used their cultural devaluation as an aesthetic resource. The *Weird Tales* Three were occasionally ashamed of their affiliation with *Weird Tales* and sometimes considered their publication in the pulpwood magazine only a quasi-publication. They understood the improbability that their work would ever be considered art by anyone but themselves. Yet they conceived of themselves as artists despite cultural pressures trying to convince them otherwise: "The imaginative writer devotes himself to art in its most essential sense," writes Lovecraft in "In Defense of *Dagon*" (148).

Indeed, the literary efforts of the *Weird Tales* Three were darkened by a palpable sense of failure, and particularly so in the case of Clark Ashton Smith. Despite the conventional nature of their narrative style, they assumed they would be misunderstood and adopted a defensive posture toward their work. A 1937 letter from Clark Ashton Smith to R.H. Barlow, a close friend, correspondent, and companion of Lovecraft, appears indicative of the general relationship the *Weird Tales* Three cultivated with pulp marketplaces. Less than a year before Smith completely gave up writing fiction, he wrote of his frustrations with what he perceived as the incorrigible misunderstandings of readers, editors, and critics. He comments on how he struggles to continue to write: "I seem to have what psychologists call a 'disgust mechanism' [*sic*] to contend with: a disgust at the ineffable stupidity of editors and readers" (CAS Selected Letters 302). Compare this cynical statement with a letter from Clark Ashton Smith to H.P. Lovecraft postmarked December 10, 1929, only a few months into his attempt to write fiction as a result of Lovecraft's endorsements. Smith comments on the stories he found in pulp magazines he purchased to understand what the editors of the pulp fiction markets preferred. Of the work in *Science Wonder-Stories* and *Amazing Stories*, he writes, "I can see that if I am to make a real living out of fiction, I am in for a certain amount of quasi-hackwork" (CAS Selected Letters 105). Or consider a passage from a letter wherein Smith reflects on a story by Fitz-James O'Brien: "What would be the fate of this fine story if it were submitted to the *Atlantic* now for the first time?" (CAS Selected Letters 119). Or consider a letter where Smith writes of the publication of Lovecraft's work in *Weird Tales*: "I'd like to see them in a form more permanent and dignified than the pages of W.T." (*Dawnward* 160). Or consider further a dream, one Smith shared with Lovecraft on November 26th, 1929: "I wish there was a real weird magazine, with you [...] and myself on the permanent staff of contributors" (*Dawnward* 186).

Like the legendary beggar whose rude shelter is built on buried treasure, the *Weird Tales* Three were ignorant that, with *Weird Tales* and Farnsworth Wright, their dream was already realized.

4. Clark Ashton Smith and Artistic Form

A Brief Interlude Regarding Artistic Success

The conditions for artistic success vary. Additionally, some critics are uninterested in the ostensible success or failure of artists, viewing these ideas as too susceptible to ideological tendentiousness and corruption. Nevertheless, it is significant that certain works are successful or not, are recipients or not of projected, socially-sanctioned value. This projection of value can take many forms: preservation, the capacity for generating scholarly treatment, influence on later artists, and, perhaps most importantly, the capability for rendering knowledge.

The pulp ekphrastic work of the *Weird Tales* Three is successful on all these conditions and, specifically, the extent to which it succeeds in creating a strange kind of quasi-knowledge, i.e., an insight about the secret of history and very nature of the ordinary: the ordinary is ephemeral and modern history consists of an acute acceleration of change. From the perspective of the pulp ekphrasist works of Lovecraft, Howard, and Smith, like pulp paper, the ordinary decays over time; moreover, the pace of this disintegration accelerates in the condition of modernity to inhuman, even monstrous, levels. The sorcerers, aliens, unreal conspiracies, fictional bibliographies, sensorium-enhancing technologies, and shadow modernist works that permeate the pulp ekphrasist works of the *Weird Tales* Three, these all function to bring into the virtual ordinary of various story worlds an apocalyptic extraordinariness rendered as de-reification.

In the chapters that follow, I treat the *Weird Tales* Three individually, beginning with Clark Ashton Smith, proceeding to Robert E. Howard, and concluding with H.P. Lovecraft; however, along the way, I show how these writers' independent literary enterprises were also part of a collaborative enterprise, what I have been calling pulp ekphrasis, the use of modernist art to perceive the otherwise invisible accelerating pace of historical change. I begin with Clark Ashton Smith, a pulp writer intimately imbricated with what has been previously distinguished by some literary historians as the traditional context of modernism: the new poetry of the early decades of the twentieth century. Let us begin with the story of how Smith became a correspondent and literary co-laborer with Lovecraft.

Lovecraft in Cleveland

After refusing to visit friends or to leave New England for several years, H.P. Lovecraft uncharacteristically accepted an invitation to travel by train on July 30, 1922, to Cleveland, Ohio. He made this trip to visit his long-time correspondent, Samuel Loveman, and a lesser known group of writers, artists, and intellectuals. One of these intellectuals was Alfred Galpin (1901–1983), an academic philosopher and literature enthusiast who wrote for the Amateur Press Associations of which Lovecraft and Loveman were leading members. Through these associations, Galpin published one issue of a little magazine, *The Philosopher*, in December of 1920, which included the essay, "Some Tendencies in Modern Poetry." This interesting essay allows us to approximate the literary aesthetic tastes of Lovecraft's local literary milieu, the way many of his literary and artistic associates understood themselves as alienated from modern literature and art, an alienation that shaped their work in profound ways. Furthermore, it shows how poets like Carl Sandburg, Edgar Lee Masters, Amy Lowell (all of who are cited in the essay) and others were critiqued by Lovecraft and eventually, through association, by the *Weird Tales* Three as a discourse community. Although published before Lovecraft, Howard, and Smith would make contact, the following passage from Galpin's essay approximates the characteristic ambivalence toward modern poetry of the *Weird Tales* Three:

4. Clark Ashton Smith and Artistic Form

> What benefit, if any, may come then from this ephemeral fad? I doubt if anything substantial will result; but at least the great principle of the vividness, the necessity of the concrete detail, has been recognized. Seen through the transcending, the imaginative eye of the future, there is wonderful raw material for poetry here. [...] The present age is one of speculation rather than performance [Galpin 241–243].

For the *Weird Tales* Three, modernist art and poetry seemed to them a new and cohesive style that had no guarantee of endurance. Though they were alienated by this new style, like Galpin, they were fascinated and enthralled by it to the extent that it had engineered new techniques for emphasizing "the great principle of vividness" and the "necessity of concrete detail" through "dreaming into semi-consciousness" (241). Like Galpin, the *Weird Tales* Three intuited the rhetoric of modernist poetry as outlined in the three principles by Ezra Pound in his "Retrospect," published in a 1918 collection of criticism, *Pavannes and Divagations*:

1. Direct treatment of the "thing" whether subjective or objective.
2. To use absolutely no word that does not contribute to the presentation.
3. As regarding rhythm: to compose in sequence of the musical phrase, not in sequence of a metronome [5].

The three phrases Galpin uses in his essay to characterize the technical "tendencies" of modern poetry conform to Pound's three principles quite neatly: "vividness" suggests "direct treatment"; "concrete detail" suggests streamlined diction; and "semi-consciousness" suggests the preference for organic rather than artificial rhythm. Galpin, Lovecraft, and Loveman's theory of modernist poetry anticipated later descriptions quite accurately.

Poetics of the Weird Tales Three

Though the pulp ekphrastic fiction of the *Weird Tales* Three has captured the imagination of readers more than their poetry, treating selections of their poetry obliquely reveals how their more enduring fiction is influenced by a highly-theorized poetics. The *Weird Tales* Three's techniques and themes regarding poetry were an inverse of Imagism, a preference for the "indirect treatment of the thing" and a thematic focus on ephemerality and the organic over the eternal and mineral. In contrast to Pound's emphasis on novelty and concreteness, they preferred traditional and conventionalized forms and metaphysical abstraction. The opening line of a sonnet published by Lovecraft in *The Providence Journal* in April of 1930 repudiates the principles as outlined by Pound above as well as his famous injunction to poets to "make it new": "I never can be tied to raw, new things" ("Background" 92).

For Lovecraft, Howard, and Smith, the modernist literary image, a powerful literary artifact pioneered for holding in stasis the phenomena of the unfolding present, was simply impotent in the face of the awesome eternity and cosmic scales that often concerned them. But there are important qualifications that will be considered in fuller detail later, such as the ambivalence imbued onto literary modernist technique by the *Weird Tales* Three, an ambivalence that does not exclude a level of morbid fascination.

Lovecraft's Discovery of Clark Ashton Smith

While visiting Cleveland for over two weeks, Lovecraft stayed at Galpin's residence and spent much of his time mingling with a literary circle associated with the poet, Hart Crane, and the amateur journalist and bookseller, Samuel Loveman. This was a horizon-expanding experience for the provincial Lovecraft, who now found himself being introduced, via Loveman and Galpin, to writers, composers, watercolorists, and architects. Sometime during this visit, he was introduced to Crane's modernist poetry, particularly his poem "Pastorale," of which he composed a parody titled, "Plaster-All," an exaggeration of Imagist poetic technique that ridicules what Lovecraft thought was the pretentious idea of a "Cleveland intelligentsia."

4. Clark Ashton Smith and Artistic Form

Though Lovecraft was not impressed by the literary productions of the Cleveland poetry scene centered on Hart Crane, he nevertheless discovered an obscure poet while visiting the Midwest who would come to deeply influence him. This obscure poet, Clark Ashton Smith (1893–1961), however, had emphatically not followed Pound's three principles or what Galpin called "the great principle of vividness" and the "necessity of concrete detail" (241). By the time Lovecraft discovered Smith's book of poetry, Smith had effectively become a hermit, and he had, by the *annus mirabilus* of literary modernism, turned away from the literary world, although he had published his poetry in the teens alongside modernists in *Poetry* magazine and other periodical venues associated with modernism. Lovecraft would rekindle Smith's literary ambitions, not as a poet but as a "pulp ekphrasist."

Wanting to thank Lovecraft for his visit, Galpin entrusted to him Smith's rare volume of poetry printed in 1912 by A.M. Robertson's San Francisco based Philopolis Press, *The Star-Treader and Other Poems*. At the time, Lovecraft was not familiar with the Smith's work. This is how the title poem, "The Star-Treader," begins:

> A voice cried to me in a dawn of dreams,
> Saying, "Make haste: the webs of death and birth
> Are brushed away, and all the threads of earth
> Wear to the breaking; spaceward gleams
> Thine ancient pathway of the suns [...]
> ["Star-Treader" 30].

In its emphasis on abstraction, formal meter, and symbolism, his poem brazenly violates all of Pound's principles.

Clark Ashton Smith's Cosmicism

Smith's cosmic imagery stirred Lovecraft. After reading "The Star-Treader," Lovecraft wrote Smith a praise-filled letter and inaugurated a literary correspondence that would last the rest of his life and result in Smith's transforming himself from an obscure poet to an artistically dubious pulp writer and, later, a legendary figure in the popular genres of science fiction, fantasy, and supernatural horror.

After introducing himself as a friend of Loveman's (Smith was already a correspondent with Loveman), Lovecraft praises Smith: "What a world of opiate phantasy and horror is here unveiled, and what an unique power and perspective must lie behind it!" (*Dawnward* 35). Lovecraft admires the poet's "cosmicism," the extent to which his poetry turns away from the ordinary to concentrate wholly on the extraordinary or what Smith referred to elsewhere as "the sublimity and vastness of the stars and star-spaces" (CAS Selected Letters 5). This is the opposite of that field suggested by the term "concrete detail" that Lovecraft's friend, Galpin, identified as central to modern poetry's innovations.

Lovecraft and Smith shared reverence for these cosmic themes. Five months before discovering Smith, Lovecraft wrote a polemic essay for a privately-printed amateur magazine titled "A Confession of Unfaith," where he reflects on his atheism. A passage from this essay illuminates the extent to which his philosophical and theological perspectives were similar and complimentary to Smith's: "My attitude has always been cosmic; and I looked on man as if from another planet. He was merely an interesting species presented for study and classification. I had strong preferences and partialities in many fields, but could not help seeing the race in its cosmic futility as well as in its terrestrial importance" (536). In this passage, Lovecraft reveals how his literary work emerges from a perspective tied to a cosmic scale and a cynical attitude toward the modern society viewed as ephemeral. To an extent, it is the inverse of what Galpin identified as modern poetry's distinctive qualities: "concrete detail" is discarded and *terra firma* is thrown into relief by the vastness of a star-field.

In discovering *The Star-Treader and Other Poems*, Lovecraft had found a literary compeer who grasped the aesthetic potential of the astronomical perspectives revealed by modern science. But before exploring the pulp ekphrastic works that were produced by Clark Ashton Smith and published in *Weird Tales* partly as a result of his relationship with Lovecraft, let us briefly turn to his past, when Smith was not yet a member of the *Weird Tales* Three who fictionalized modernism but instead was a precocious modern poet who, from a traditional literary perspective, was participating in modernism production proper.

4. *Clark Ashton Smith and Artistic Form*

Smith as a Modernist Curio

In his *A History of American Magazines* (1968), Frank Luther Mott focuses for a chapter on a "flagship" little magazine of Anglo-American modernism, Harriet Monroe's Chicago-based *Poetry*, the magazine remembered as Ezra Pound's organ for introducing the American reading public to the poetry movement he engineered. Beginning his historical sketch, Mott reflects on the large number of important poets whose work appeared in Monroe's magazine. He asks, "How many of the poets represented in the half-century of this magazine's publication should be mentioned in a brief history such as this?" He answers, "It seems a pity to neglect any of them, but most poets' tapers are blown out early, of course. Anyone running down the average table of contents, even if he is fairly well read in the books and magazines of the times, will recognize little than half the names" (237).

In other words, some names are recognizable to us by virtue of the 1930s era mythology of literary modernism cultivated by accounts of modernism like Edmund Wilson's *Axel's Castle* (1931), Malcolm Cowley's *Exiles Return* (1934), and Stephen Spender's *The Destructive Element* (1935). Other names, however, are not. Indeed, the many poets who fade into the table of contents alongside the usual suspects of modernism are a kind of pulpy excess, are so many weeds strangling twentieth-century Anglophone modernism that need to be cut back as a first principle.

Reflecting on this mass of obscure names productively troubles the boundary marking divisions that literary historians have engineered over the years to understand the vast and multi-layered archive and discourse that is the Anglo-American literary culture of the early twentieth century. This sublime archive includes not only the literary work and criticism initially promulgated in non-commercial little magazines published out of Chicago, New York, the Left Bank of Paris, and London—a methodologically attractive proposition from the perspective of the traditional literary historical narratives. It also includes pulp fiction magazines, nationally distributed slick magazines, newspaper journalism, privately-printed volumes, private journals, literary correspondences, and much more. Magazines like *Poetry* are very useful to literary historians because of their ability to domesticate, in its excess, a cognitively recalcitrant archive; however, as Mott reminds us, even these magazines obscure an underlying excess. To approach the archive as "the magazines of modernism" is not narrow enough. These magazines, it seems, are only useful inasmuch as later critics "filter" them for posterity, tag the enduring and flower-bearing perennials and mark the unidentifiable weeds.

Perhaps returning to the third issue of *Poetry*, the December 1912 issue, will illustrate Mott's thesis, will confirm via a quick scan of its table of contents the worthiness of the high reputation of the magazine and its famous editor, who, as early as 1919, H.L. Mencken referred to as the "mother superior" of "the New Poetry Movement" ("New Poetry" 48). Featuring five poems by William Butler Yeats and a taste-establishing review by Ezra Pound, this third issue of the magazine indeed confirms the magazine's reputation as a primary site of academic modernism's emergence.

But what of the other, shadowy poets featured in this third issue of *Poetry*? We have been considering one of them: Clark Ashton Smith, the poet Lovecraft discovered in Cleveland a decade later, in 1922. Despite a brief cameo here on the main stage of Anglo-American modernism, Clark Ashton Smith figures as a central writer in the history of the popular genres of science fiction, fantasy, and the supernatural.

The Aesthetically Nourishing Obscurity of Clark Ashton Smith

Elsewhere, Clark Ashton Smith has been called the legend of pulp science fiction. Yet, here he is in the same table of contents as William Butler Yeats and Ezra Pound. This unique point of contact between what would later be constructed as the high of modernism and the low of science fiction, fantasy, and supernatural horror in the years leading up to the Great War and the interwar period represents to me an important point of departure, a penultimate moment before modernism that would

4. Clark Ashton Smith and Artistic Form

violently purify itself by exorcizing cosmic writers like Smith and exiling them into pulp fiction magazines like *Weird Tales*. Arguably, Smith accepted this exile in *Weird Tales* because of Lovecraft's influence. His association with *Weird Tales* surprisingly afforded the poet who would become a pulp fiction writer a rare vantage point, the unique ekphrastic perspective of an apostate: in his pulp fictions, Smith would fictionalize actual modernism as so many shadow modernist works that function like sensorium-expanding technology that ultimately reveal the ephemerality of the ordinary and the cruel acceleration of change that defines modern history.

From the perspective of traditional histories of modernism, to consider Smith is to consider a failure, a rear-guardsman who was initially honored by publication in *Poetry* but who was unable or unwilling—as tastes and styles in poetry changed and an aesthetic of productive destruction to dominate—to avoid censure and eventually the indifference of the world of twentieth-century Anglophone poetry. From a traditional literary-historical perspective, Smith's career is a story of rejection by the mainstream poetry establishment, of finding himself artistically out of sync with Chicago, New York, London, and Paris and increasingly frustrated by his fruitless attempts to disseminate his art, to publish it, to gather income from it. His is the story of becoming an obscure outsider, a subject position he exaggerated, romanticized and adopted for rhetorical purposes. This brief entry in his commonplace book demonstrates Smith's attempt to rationalize his rejection and to twist it into a positive element of his aesthetic project: "There are poets whose obscurity consists in the fact that they perceive analogies and correspondences too remote or arcanic to be discerned by others" (*Black Book* 47). Consider his criticisms of Harriett Monroe's editorial choices. Writing to his mentor, George Sterling, in July of 1913, he wrote, "Miss Monro[sic] has been 'infected' by Ezra Pound, who is rabid for a 'new form,' and she is letting poetry [sic] go by the board" (CAS Selected Letters 93).

Because of his early artistic pretensions and his subsequent public failures, the arc of Smith's poetry career literalizes the aesthetically productive alienation from and antagonism to modernism that vitalizes the pulp ekphrastic work of the *Weird Tales* Three I study. Unlike his *Weird Tales* peers, Smith could easily be considered a modernist to the extent that he published alongside those who would become modernists in later accounts. Smith was initially praised as a contributing modern poet in the same significant venues that published those who would become the main characters of modernism. Unlike other *Weird Tales* writers who orbited, reacted to, and were morbidly fascinated by, but did not directly intrude into what might be considered, strictly speaking, the scene of modernism, Smith satisfies all conditions for direct inclusion in the canon of modernism. Nevertheless, Smith's most significant contributions to genre fiction come into focus after modernism, in the late 1920s and 30s, when, in order to resolve his ambivalent enthrallment to the new art and literature, he forsook poetry and took artistic nourishment from the obscurity his aesthetic iconoclasm had brought upon him.

Smith, a Modernist?

One might argue that Smith should be considered a modernist, his distinctive pulp fiction context notwithstanding. Indeed, considered within such a frame, we might commit Smith as a modernist based on his social orbit, such as his correspondence with H.L. Mencken and Harriett Monroe, and the perceived radical novelty of his poetry when it was first published. However, to frame Smith as a modernist would obscure the extent to which his poetry was sharply at odds with modern movements. Consider, for example, this statement from a 1922 review of Smith's second book of poetry, *Ebony and Crystal*, titled "Boy Publishes More Poetry" and published in the *San Francisco Examiner* in December, two months after Eliot's *The Waste Land* appeared in the inaugural issue of *The Criterion*: "A volume more at variance with the spirit of the poetry world today would be hard to conceive of" (20). Though Smith orbited modernism in both print context and social network, it is nevertheless his thematic content that distinguishes him most sharply from traditional, and reductive, descriptions of modernism.

To demonstrate this, let us compare Smith's treatment of form with that of a hyper-canonical modernist like T.S. Eliot.

4. Clark Ashton Smith and Artistic Form

T.S. Eliot and Strangely Behaving Matter

T.S. Eliot's *The Waste Land* famously imagines organic life as strange animated matter. In the specific case of human matter, life is vividly rendered as an aware and feeling "handful of dust" (56). The multi-faceted, alien narrator of the poem attends to humans with perceptive intensity to understand the source of its embittered vitality and the strange nature of its striving. Through the process of reading the poem and looking upon human life through the gaze of the alien narrator, the species we are members of is defamiliarized. Or, to use science fiction theorist Darko Suvin's term, vitalized human matter is cognitively estranged, productively transformed into a contingent and decaying formation of matter that we can ponder largely uninfluenced by ordinary habits of perception or preconceptions about what counts as normal (Suvin). For example, consider the speaker's, identified at this point in the poem as Tiresias, description of sex between a typist and a clerk:

> The time is now propitious, as he guesses,
> The meal is ended, she is bored and tired,
> Endeavors to engage her in caresses
> Which still are unreproved, if undesired.
> Flushed and decided, he assaults at once;
> Exploring hands encounter no defense;
> His vanity requires no response,
> And makes a welcome of indifference
> [*The Waste Land* 63].

Here the male clerk is imagined as having a psychological interior whereas the female typist is psychologically inscrutable. The clerk believes the typist is bored and tired after the meal and that he will entertain her by caressing her body. She does not respond to his caresses, but the clerk is not concerned with this indifference and even interprets it as a signal to satisfy his sexual desire.

This rendering of the clerk, the typist, and their sexual activity is less an aesthetic disrobing of social ideology, the quasi-scientific description of a biological activity, i.e., disenchantment of human sexuality; instead, Eliot's rendering is a creative gesture, an aesthetic contortion via alien perception. Courtship and sex have become strange here because they are impressed upon an alien sensorium, one the technology of the poem allows us to identify with.

In this way, Eliot renders organic life as strangely-behaving matter throughout the poem. And he inaugurates his extended rendering beginning with the question that opens the second stanza of the "Burial of the Dead" section: "What are the roots that clutch, what branches grow / out of this stony rubbish?" (55). Addressing the reader hailed as an alien who does not identify as human, the narrator answers this question thus: "I will show you fear in a handful of dust" (56). From the absolute alterity of the narrator's perspective, a compression of organic matter appears to the simulated alien sensorium as a contingent formation of dust dissolving that knows fear. Humanity is a mysterious formation of matter, an organic excrement of the mineral earth that is swiftly passing.

Enduring Versus Ephemeral Form

What appears to unite the modernist Eliot and the pulp ekphrasist Smith is their preoccupation with the mystery of organic life rendered as strangely-behaving matter animated by disembodied form. But what distinguishes them is their view of the role of the disembodied form, i.e., the principle of organization that structures matter, interacts with matter to produce a contingent and ephemeral vitality. How is it that, when configured in such a way, a handful of matter can fear for a time? How can—to borrow an image from Smith's poem "The Hashish Eater—or—the Apocalypse of Evil" "the light as of a million million moons" come together in a temporarily stable pattern to constitute a face that sighs in pain before passing into oblivion (29)?

Both of these otherwise disparate writers' works are animated by the central question of the contingency, ephemerality, and endurance of matter shaped by form, but their understanding of the power of form distinguishes them sharply. For Eliot, form endures; for Smith, form is a temporary and strange effect that produces the untruthful illusion of stasis.

4. Clark Ashton Smith and Artistic Form

Eliot and the Impossibility of Pure Form

We can begin to illuminate Eliot's fascination with enduring form, his theory of form and its relationship to matter, by demonstrating that the poet finds no value in the idea of form autonomous of matter, i.e., what Ortega y Gasset might term "dehumanized" poetry or art. For Eliot, there can be no form without matter and no matter without form.

Eliot's understanding of form's inextricable relationship with matter can be brought into focus via contrast, by briefly treating as a foil, the ideas of Wassily Kandinsky, who, in his 1912 pamphlet, *Concerning the Spiritual in Art*, argues polemically that the apex of artistic innovation is to engineer a pure form without matter. Citing contemporary art's apparent sympathy toward abstract form and its correspondent similarities to so-called "primitive art," Kandinsky claims that all art is united by a "similarity of ideals," animated by desire to "express internal truths," and thus should "renounce [...] in consequence all consideration of external form" (1). For Kandinsky, pure art is pure form; the most truthful and faithful art is one that has shed its body absolutely.

We engage Eliot's aesthetic theory through poetry; thus, his theory of form and its dependence on matter, in direct refutation of Kandinsky's, comes through in his 1921 essay, "The Metaphysical Poets." In this essay of literary history, which Eliot claims treats how poetry changed "between the time of Donne or Lord Herbert of Cherbury and the time of Tennyson and Browning," Eliot establishes his theory of the "dissociation of sensibility" (64). He describes it in this way:

> The poets of the seventeenth century, the successors of the dramatists of the sixteenth, possessed a mechanism of sensibility which could devour any kind of experience. [...] In the seventeenth century a dissociation of sensibility set in, from which we have never recovered; and this dissociation, as is natural, was aggravated by the influence of the two most powerful poets of the century, Milton and Dryden [64].

Eliot goes on to describe a pattern of aesthetic degeneration whereby poetry became either excessively formalist and mineral, on the one hand, or excessively emotional and organic, on the other; rigorous formal discipline in poetry, allegorized in "Tradition and the Individual Talent" later as mineral, a sliver of oxidized metal, became, according to Eliot, discursively incompatible with the organic passion of the Romantics. Contrasted against Kandinsky's ideal of art as pure, disembodied form, Eliot's comments here outline his theory of form: form is, or should be, inextricably bound up with matter; to take his allegorical logic to its conclusion, vital form is an alloy of the organic and inorganic, an eros of carbon and silicon.

Form and Matter

For Eliot, and for Smith, form and matter have an inextricable relationship. They cannot be unbraided. But the pulp ekphrasist and modernist's philosophical correspondence can be tested and contrasted, and doing so produces valuable insights, namely, a principle for distinguishing discourses in modernism that centers on ephemerality, endurance, form, and formless matter.

For Eliot, the function of aesthetic form is to make otherwise ephemeral patterns of organic matter endure, to make them transcend their contingency and finitude. "These fragments I have shored up against my ruins," the alien narrator states at the end of *The Waste Land* (69). Eliot expresses here a faith in aesthetic form and its ability to preserve, in a way, the ephemeral and contingent organic patterns that we are.

Not so for Smith, who treats the apparent endurance of aesthetic form as a sinister illusion and organic form as ephemeral. In doing so, Smith articulates a discursive boundary thematically differentiating their two incompatible views of form. This can be demonstrated by considering closely one of Smith's works of pulp ekphrasis.

"Ubbo-Sathla," the Illusion of Formal Endurance, and Formlessness

Published in July of 1933 in *Weird Tales*, Smith's "Ubbo-Sathla" relates the story of a writer living in interwar London, one Paul Tregardis, and

4. Clark Ashton Smith and Artistic Form

his discovery in a curio shop of a mysterious sculptural work of shadow modernism, described in this way: an "orb-like" "milky crystal," "about the size of a small orange," "slightly flattened at the ends, like a planet at its poles," and "with an intermittent glowing in its heart, as if it were alternately illumed and darkened from within" (223). Tregardis is strangely awestruck by this "milky crystal," and his puzzlement is intensified by "a dawning sense of vague and irrecognizable familiarity, as if he had seen the thing before under circumstances that were now wholly forgotten" (223). He takes the crystal home, analyzes it in the privacy of his study, and something strange happens:

> By imperceptible degrees, there stole upon him a sense of dreamlike duality, both in respect to his person and his surroundings. He was still Paul Tregardis—and yet he was someone else [...] without surprise on the part of Tregardis, the process of re-identification became complete. He knew that he was Zon Mezzamalech, a sorcerer of Mhu Thulan, and a student of all lore anterior to his own epoch [224–225].

As the story proceeds, we learn that the form of Paul Tregardis was merely a dream-vision, a contingent illusion, emerging from the meditations of a sorcerer, Mhu Thulan, who, aesthetically immersed in scrutinizing closely the formal contours of another orb, has mentally simulated a previous life. Put another way, the ephemeral form of Tregardis, the interwar London he seemed to live within, his life as a writer: all of this was an aesthetic effect of Mhu Thulan's reading of the strange orb.

However, this story continues to bloom. Another frame is provided, eclipsing the previous one: we learn that Mhu Thulan and his crystal were, like Tregardis, also the result of another aesthetic experience and therefore mere illusory form. As the sorcerer dwelling in his tower fades away, another, stranger narrative eclipses that contingent, ephemeral situation. We learn that the sorcerer, Mhu Thulan, too, was a mere formal effect of a shadow modernist art object, the product of an act of reading, except in this wider frame the simulated reader has been replaced by the titular slime monster, the horrible and formless Ubbo-Sathla, described in this way: "The formless mass that was Ubbo-Sathla reposed amid the slime and the vapors. Headless, without organs or members, it sloughed from its oozy sides, in a slow, ceaseless wave" (228). What aesthetic object is this slime monster reading? A slab of "star-quarried" stone described in this way: "About [Ubbo-Sathla], prone or tilted in the mire, there lay the mighty tablets of star-quarried stone that were writ with the inconceivable wisdom of the pre-mundane gods" (228).

Compare closely the enduring "fragments" rendered in Eliot's *The Waste Land* as contrasted against the fecund yet formless and decaying hyper-organic mass of Ubbo-Sathla frothing over the star-quarried slab of stone. Braving this strange comparison brings into focus an intriguing discursive formation centering on endurance and ephemerality, organic contingency and inorganic permanence: for Eliot, enduring aesthetic form animates the dust, vitalizes like the breath of a creator god; thus, poetry becomes something like a soul. For the pulp ekphrasist Smith, who has deeply understood the dream of modernism, however, the enduring aesthetic form is something more sinister: an illusion poisoned by secret finitude. An inorganic testament to eternity, it expresses a lie. An impotent memorial, the "star-quarried slab of stone" functions as a terrible index of eternity that reveals our ephemerality, contingency, finitude, and vulnerability in a monster-haunted cosmos. In "Ubbo-Sathla," the shadow modernist work of art is being swallowed and deformed by formlessness apotheosized.

5. The Failure of Clark Ashton Smith

Anti-Modernism in Context

The general idea of Smith's, Howard's, and Lovecraft's antagonism toward and distaste of modernism is not a particularly unique or notable sentiment in the years leading up to the Great War and those of the Interwar Period. Modernism's ability to shock and disgust is legendary. Furthermore, a kind of anti-modernist sentiment arose along with the first symptoms of what we might call modernist formal experimentation in literature and the other arts. It was a literature and art premised by the destruction of older forms and modes and could not help but evoke negative responses. In terms of literature, we can perceive the beginnings of anti-modernism in something as early as the charged correspondence between a frustrated H.G. Wells and a dismissive Henry James; and the fire has become a conflagration by the time we come to the despicable "Entartete Kunst" or "Degenerate Art Exhibition" in Nazi Germany (Munich, July 19th, 1937–November 30th, 1937). But with the pulp ekphrasist works of Smith, Howard, and Lovecraft, we have something more than reactionary ire. We have in the pulp ekphrastic work of the *Weird Tales* Three a corpus of art that evolves in reaction to modernism and that seeks to fictionalize modernism, to virtually instantiate it with previous rhetorics of sensational literature, and, in doing so, comes to grasp, with its core rhetoric, its unique appeal, and its prosthetic utility: the enduring non-representational and dehumanized form theorized by Ortega y Gasset as the discursive goal of modernism reveals the secret of modern history articulated simply as the accelerating ephemerality of the ordinary.

The *Weird Tales* Three take as their initial starting point an idiosyncratic but nevertheless sincere vision of what modernist art does: in becoming an enduring, dehumanized, and non-mimetic form that endures, it throws into horrible focus that which does not endure, i.e., everything else. Unlike the widespread parodies of modernism published in newspapers and middlebrow magazines of the time, and unlike the widely publicized censorship attempts and indignant disavowals of modernism that have linked sexual licentiousness with it, Smith, Howard, and Lovecraft go beyond unsophisticated repudiation in order to engage in ekphrasis and so artistically project onto a distorted and ultimately fictional shadow modernism their fears and hatreds concomitant with their identification as stewards of a threatened European aesthetic tradition.

Clark Ashton Smith, a modernist poet who became a pulp writer, analogizes in his high to low career arc and literary outsider posturing the central themes and formal concerns of the pulp ekphrasis of the *Weird Tales* Three. His career offers a lens through which we can understand the genealogy of the formal rhetoric produced by the *Weird Tales* Three's vexed relationship with modernism. Below I briefly relate Smith's early career as a poet publishing alongside modernists. I then conduct close readings of his key pulp ekphrastic fictions published in *Weird Tales* and related venues to demonstrate how Smith's particular version of shadow modernism functions to reveal the ephemerality of the ordinary.

Smith's Fictional Art

Through a process of exchange consisting of sharing tropes and narrative structures as well as correspondence with fellow *Weird Tales* writers, Smith, like Lovecraft, transformed his critical reading of modernism into a central concern in pulp fiction.

In Smith's pulp ekphrastic stories about shadow modernism, experience and sensation are always a terrible excess and consciousness is a protective filtering of that excess. For Smith, sensory organs hold off and order the unbearable strangeness that is reality, a reality that is always rapidly changing. Moreover, in Smith's stories of shadow modernist art objects, shadow modernist artists, and experiences of shadow modernist art, the boundary separating human beings from the being of the aesthetic object is dangerously unstable. Humans become art objects and art objects achieve consciousness. In this way, Smith's fictionalized aesthetic experiences consist not only in the confrontation of an experiencing subject with an animate aesthetic object, but it is also a moment when those distinctions collapse, and artist becomes mere matter, and art becomes conscious. In Smith's pulp ekphrasis stories, aesthetic experience is an excess that derives from the "short circuiting" of the filtering function of the senses, a short circuiting the abstract art of shadow modernism is designed to produce. Moreover, the experience of shadow modernist art is fictionalized in Smith's work as too much sensation that ultimately results in the dissolution of the ordinary.

Clark Ashton Smith and George Sterling

We must briefly establish such how Smith found himself publishing in *Weird Tales* where he had once published in Harriet Monroe's celebrated *Poetry*. This story of his transformation from a modernist poet into a pulp ekphrasist begins with his "discovery" in 1907 by another poet, George Sterling (1869–1926). From the perspective of traditional canons of twentieth-century poetry, Sterling is a regionalist poet who, outside of California, never achieved wide visibility. He was a close confidante of Ambrose Bierce, Robinson Jeffers, and Jack London, and other California-based intellectuals and artists. He was the leader of a respected and publicly supported California-based literary circle, of which Smith was a member. Additionally, as book reviewer, public-relations spokesperson, literary critic, and poet, Sterling consolidated and promoted the work and art of a coterie of journalists, writers, and artists geographically centered upon the famous Bohemian Club of San Francisco. Accordingly, Sterling promoted Smith in this way.

Sterling's poetry, rarely reprinted, is worth further analysis; however, it is Sterling's role as literary mentor to Smith and not as poet that is significant. Like Smith, Sterling had initial success as a poet, was published in *Poetry* alongside key modernists, but would later fall out of fashion. Sterling brought Smith into the literary world by promoting him and helping him to publish. But being out of sync with modernism himself, he also contributed to the Smith's identification as a literary outsider. Consider an excerpt from a review of Sterling's poetry by Harriett Monroe, published in *Poetry* in the March of 1916 issue of *Poetry*:

> Already the young poet's brilliant but too facile craftsmanship was tempted by the worst excess of the Tennysonian tradition: he never thinks—he deems; he does not ask, but crave; he is fain for this and that; he deals in emperies and auguries and antiphons in casual throes and lethal voids—in many other things of tinsel and fustian, the frippery of a by-gone fashion [302].

By November of 1926, with a series of rejections behind him, Sterling's career as a poet had become stifled. On November 4th, 1926 Clark Ashton Smith tried to raise his mentor's spirits by writing in a letter predicting that tastes in poetry would turn toward Sterling's exotic, extramundane themes: "The present orgy of materialism will exhaust itself sooner or later" (CAS Selected Letters 94). His efforts to improve Sterling's spirits proved ineffective. Two weeks after this letter was written, Sterling committed suicide by taking cyanide.

The Origin of the Smith and Sterling Alliance

Briefly highlighting Smith's early relationship with Sterling emphasizes how a distance from modernism, a posture of being disconnected from contemporary literary, was a central part of Smith's identity as a writer, and this ambivalent identification with high literature and it's repudiation shaded Smith's later pulp ekphrasist works. Smith's early modernism is largely forgotten because Smith deliberately distanced himself from it. Smith is remembered today by genre-fiction writers such as George R.R. Martin, Neil Gaiman, and China Mieville as a major artistic

5. The Failure of Clark Ashton Smith

influence, a key figure in contemporary traditions of genre fiction. But when Smith is recalled in these contexts, his early career as a poet publishing alongside Yeats and Pound is often a mere footnote, a literary historical curio. Nevertheless, it was through the establishment of an early correspondence with the rejected poet Sterling—who aspired to be an artist and never a pulp hack—that Smith began to enter any public notice at all.

Smith attached himself to Sterling and his career, and he saw in him a mentor and a model. Their relationship, documented throughout their long correspondence starting January of 1911 and lasting until Sterling's suicide, consists of Sterling harshly critiquing Smith's poetry as too morbid, Smith praising Sterling's poetry, and Sterling suggesting lines of reading and literary periodicals to consider for publication. Also, both lament what they see as the declining tastes in poetry as a result of the rise of materialism. Despite his harsh critiques of Smith's work, Sterling was convinced of Smith's poetic genius from the beginning. When the unknown Smith sent Sterling manuscripts of his poetry, Sterling, in an uncharacteristic move, responded: "Your work is [...] so much above the average of what comes to me from stranger and friend, I have ventured to make a few comments and suggestions [...]. I think a bright future awaits you" (CAS Selected Letters 19). Sterling used his literary contacts to promote his friends who were writers, and he did this for Smith with particular gusto. He spoke highly of him to his publishing contacts, secured for him interviews with writers such as Robinson Jeffers, Jack London, and Ambrose Bierce. Additionally, Sterling worked closely with a local printer, A.M. Robertson, on behalf of Smith to bring out his first volume of poetry in 1912, *The Star-Treader and Other Poems*. And he promoted this volume intensely, sometimes excessively so. For example, Ambrose Bierce, writing to the editor of a California newspaper, *Town Talk*, complains about a series of promotional pieces authored by Sterling in which Sterling falsely attributes praise of Smith's poetry to Bierce: "In nearly all of these eulogies I find myself credited with praises I never uttered" (288). He continues in a more sober register, however, stating of Smith's work, "It seems to me uncommonly good work and a promise of better work to come" (289).

Here Bierce highlights an element of Smith's persona that influenced much of his early work: his youth and its promise. Smith's first book of poetry, *The Star-Treader and Other Poems*, was published in 1912 when Smith was only nineteen. And in the literary columns of many prominent

California newspapers, it received many positive reviews, with many reviewers comparing Smith's poetry to Keats and Tennyson and other romantics. Consider the headline of a front-page article on Smith published in San Francisco's leading daily newspaper, *The Call*, August 2, 1912: "Boy Is Poetic Genius; Lonely Sierras Inspire Muse." Other California publications lavished Smith with praise. He was a literary celebrity for a time, confirmed, to an extent, by the fact that *The New York Times* reviewed his book of poetry in January of 1913. Unbiased by regional pride, however, New York's assessment of Smith's poetry was more balanced. Compare the *New York Times* headline to the headline of the above cited San Francisco newspaper: "A YOUNG POET: He Has Quality, but Also the Faults of Youth."

Smith's Failure as a Poet

The eventual consensus of the literary establishment was that Smith's first volume suggested a successful career to come. This success never materialized. Smith's start resulted, of course, in his publication in *Poetry* and later publication in H.L. Mencken's *The Smart Set*. But his success and favor in the modern poetry scene was short lived. His publication of poetry in nationally prominent magazines became scarce after 1912, with rejections from the *North Atlantic Review* figuring prominently in his correspondence with Sterling. His promise, like Sterling's, did not come to fruition. Smith, like Sterling, continued to write poetry, but no one would publish it, a proposition confirmed when it is considered that by 1925 Smith had been forced to publish at his own expense additional volumes of poetry through regional presses. The Book Club of California published *Odes and Sonnets* in 1918. But in 1925, having failed to secure the interest of another commercial publisher, Smith self-published *Ebony and Crystal* and *Sandalwood*. These books did not sell nor did they receive much critical attention. Throughout the rest of his life, Smith complained to his *Weird Tales* correspondents about stacks of unsold books stored under his bed. In 1937, to a correspondent, a fellow writer considering self-publication, Smith offered this bit of cynical advice: "The fewer you print, the more

5. The Failure of Clark Ashton Smith

the collectors of 1987 will pay for a copy of the volume" (CAS Selected Letters 312).

Smith's failure as a poet significantly influenced his art and came to structure much of the fiction he published in *Weird Tales*. But he did not consider the possibility that his work was objectively flawed. He chose instead to blame the materialistic spirit of the age and a reading public that did not understand his work. Throughout his correspondence with Sterling and his shared experience of rejection, Smith developed a theory to explain the problem of modern literature in terms of its earthly preoccupations, the degree to which it turned away from such large issues as the vastness and emptiness of the cosmos and the strangeness and mystery of existence in order to focus instead on gossip, sexual titillation, introspective psychology and sociology, or what Smith cynically referred to as "the social upheaval of the ant-hill" (CAS Selected Letters 14). This statement of principles Smith wrote in his commonplace demonstrates his anti-human thematics: "The poet should, with unerring vision, distinguish the eternal from the ((topical)) ((secular)) temporary, and maintain a glacial purity uncontaminated by the latter" (*Black Book* 47, "(())" denotes crossed out words). Or consider a letter to his mentor Sterling in July of 1913: "So many present-day writers are like the diseased beggars at the gates of Eastern cities, exposing their sores to public pity and benevolence" (CAS Selected Letters 21). Smith's language of contamination, purity, and disease suggests that same anxiety of contamination attributed elsewhere to high modernists, who perceived commercialism, popular appeal, and bourgeoisie tastes in art as a contaminate. In Smith's case, however, contamination is not based on elitism and populism but on the "insignificantly human" and "profoundly cosmic." For Smith, the issue is scale, scope, and the aesthetic potential of acknowledging humanity's existential situation from the widest possible perspective.

Damn the Planet

If excessive introspection was part of modern literature's sin, the other half was its social focus, its propensity to dwell upon social and political issues, concerns Smith casually dismissed to Sterling in 1915: "Damn the planet, anyway—it's only fit for the habitation of hogs, who enjoy rooting" (CAS Selected Letters 26). And earlier, in 1912: "The thing called civilization, as the history of the past shows conclusively enough, is only a dog chasing its own tail" (CAS Selected Letters 10). Smith's rejection of modernism can be succinctly conveyed in a statement that appears in one of his letters to Benjamin De Cessares, a New York–based journalist who had favorably reviewed Smith's poetry: "There are more things in heaven and earth than are dreamt in phallicism or psychoanalysis" (CAS Selected Letters 87). Writing to thank a journalist who, in a rare turn, positively reviewed his poetry in 1913, Smith sums up his criticisms succinctly: "Poetry, particularly work like mine, which is so far removed from the everyday interest of the immense bulk of mankind, stands in little danger of being overestimated in these days" (CAS Selected Letters 18).

Despite Smith's apparent indifference here to the lack of estimation secured by his poetry, in other letters he reveals anger at what he imagines as a genuine misunderstanding on the part of magazine editors and critics. In response to rejections by Harriet Monroe and additional failures with the *North Atlantic Review*, he complained to Sterling in September of 1912, "I wish there were a hell for magazine-editors and their public, in which, for a few hundred thousand years, they could be made to see themselves as you and I see them" (CAS Selected Letters 17). Perhaps all of Smith's frustrations with the literary world that rejected him is present in this statement written by Smith to Sterling in one of the earliest letters of their vast correspondence, October 6, 1911: "I am astonished to find how few really grasp the sublimity and vastness of the stars and star-spaces" (CAS Selected Letters 5).

Lovecraft and Smith and Artistic Destruction

Ten years later, Smith met one of those few in Lovecraft. Originally, these writers exchanged fiction manuscripts and unsold volumes of poetry,

5. The Failure of Clark Ashton Smith

having no hope (or even ambition) of making their work public in any further way. However, when Lovecraft learned about the proposed founding of *Weird Tales* from J.C. Henneberger (it was not founded until 1923), he immediately wrote to Smith about it in November of 1922 in the following note: "One need not be ashamed to write or draw for such magazines—Poe & Bierce, I believe, used to write for any old thing" (*Dawnward* 39). For Smith, publishing in a pulp magazine like *Weird Tales*, a self-styled artistic pulp, could be conceived romantically, as a kind of grotto where the cosmic artists of the period could retreat.

In *The Star-Treader and Other Poems*, Smith turns away from humanity to contemplate mysteries as a mystic. The speakers of his poems lament their corporeality, their essential rootedness to the mundane, and they long to shed their bodies, their very materiality. They desire to disincarnate fully—to spiral apart, to fuse with the stars. Furthermore, what Lovecraft refers to in "A Confession of Unfaith" as the "cherished pomps and prides" of human civilization, Smith symbolically obliterates, a destruction he thematizes by morbidly reflecting on the beauty, truth, and creative potential of wanton destruction. Consider this passage from Smith's poem, "Nero," where the sadistic Roman emperor gazes on the city of Rome as it burns: "Destruction hastens and intensifies / The process that is Beauty" ("Nero" 49).

To draw back from human civilization and gaze on it from an inhuman, cosmic perspective is a philosophically destructive gesture, a violent disrobing of human conceits, the destruction of the ordinary by juxtaposing it with cosmic scales. For the narrator of Smith's poem, there is something essentially beautiful, cathartic, and even truthful about nihilistically blotting out the whole of Roman civilization, "the toil of many men, / The consummation of laborious years" ("Nero" 49). From the inhuman, cosmic perspective of astronomy, this symbolism parallels precisely the fate of all earth life depending on the brief life cycle of a modestly sized star that is burning out. In Smith, Lovecraft had found a poet who was audacious enough to confront the "opiate phantasy and horror," the "unique power and perspective" of the implications of astronomy. In other words, Lovecraft had found a kindred thinker who was willing to consider all human civilization, politics, morality, the totality of human concerns and, to use Smith's language, "the social upheaval of the ant-hill" (*Dawnward* 35; CAS Selected Letters 14).

The Periodical Context of Smith and Lovecraft

There was more to endear the obscure Smith to Lovecraft: as a poet, Smith was a failure, an unfashionable reject that no "respectable" magazine (for Lovecraft, read "aesthetically compromised magazine") would dare publish. Unlike the fashionable Hart Crane, who Lovecraft had just met—who had, incidentally, recently been published in the June 1922 issue of *The Dial*—alongside Santayana, Lawrence, Yeats, Picasso, Aiken, Hesse, Pound, Clark Ashton Smith was absent from the all-poetry magazines of the day. Smith's absence from *The Dial*, *The Little Review*, *Poetry* and similar magazines would have practically confirmed for Lovecraft the superiority of the California poet's poetry, its philosophical maturity and aesthetic elitism.

Less than a year after Smith and Lovecraft began their correspondence, Smith wrote to Sterling to describe the founding of *Weird Tales*, when Lovecraft secured for Smith an invitation to publish verse. Smith appeared in the fifth issue of the magazine with two original poems, and from then on, until 1928, he appeared in the magazine intermittently. In addition to selling his poetry, he also sold illustrations and translations of French poetry to the magazine. For example, the August 1930 issue of *Weird Tales* features three of his original translations of prose poems by Baudelaire.

Although Smith kept up his correspondence with Lovecraft and other *Weird Tales* writers throughout the twenties, he continued to focus on poetry and drawing. He considered the writing of prose a low art form. For example, writing a month before Sterling committed suicide (October 11, 1926), Smith commented on the fact that his mentor had been writing essays instead of poetry: "Too bad you have to write prose. It's a beastly occupation" (91). This prejudice toward prose persisted until 1928 when he finally considered trying to write fiction and publish it in *Weird Tales*, as evidenced by a letter he wrote to Lovecraft on March 20, 1928, where he shares story ideas: "One of my conceptions concerns a man who takes a stroll on Boulder Ridge, the long, rambling, volcanic moraine on which I live, and suddenly finds that he has lost his way, and is wandering in a strange nightmare country" (*Dawnward* 157). This letter would herald

5. The Failure of Clark Ashton Smith

Smith's first short story sale to *Weird Tales*, a story titled "The Ninth Skeleton," a story that reveals Smith's early preoccupation with the abstract idea of aesthetic form and its capacity to render occult knowledge about the ordinary.

"The Ninth Skeleton"

The protagonist of "The Ninth Skeleton" is a slightly veiled Smith, a young artist in love seeking his love in the wilderness. A large portion of the pulp ekphrastic work published by the *Weird Tales* Three features artists, poets, writers, or sculptors as their protagonists. Smith's stories are no exceptions. Like Smith, the protagonist lives in the Auburn countryside in a cottage. Smith's companion at the time, Genevieve K. Sully, is fictionalized in the story as the protagonist's fiancé, Guenevere.

The narrative itself is not complex. It relates a brief journey in the woods and an encounter with a strange art object. The main character walks through the woods, which become increasingly beautiful. The sight and smell of them intensify to unbearable levels. Eventually, the intense sensory experiences are too much for the protagonist's inflamed senses to bear, and the environment seems to change, to transform from painful beauty to absolute horror: "The sky had now grown so dark that the whole scene took on a semi-nocturnal aspect, and made me think of a doomed world in the twilight of a dying sun" (15). In Smith's first story published in *Weird Tales*, we have a nod to the ephemerality of the ordinary. Reeling and disoriented because of the sensory overload, the narrator stumbles upon a statuary garden of enduring forms: huge stones that resemble "headstones and funeral monuments" (15). The stones convey a sense of "awful antiquity": "It was hard to believe that life and death could be as old as they" (15). Written on the stones are indecipherable, alien characters of no known language. The narrator describes them succinctly thus: "About them was a hoariness and mystery and terror of incomputable Eld" (15).

"Mystery." "Terror." "Incomputable." Alien. Undecipherable. In Smith's first story, we have a quasi-exhibition of shadow modernist art objects that transcend time and give those who view them access to the ephemerality of the ordinary. After the protagonist stumbles into the garden of strange stones, he has a supernatural experience heralded by a series of strange sounds: "I turned and listened; there was something in these sounds that served to *complete* the demoralization of my unstrung nerves; and monstrous fears, abominable fancies, trooped like the horde of a witches' sabbath through my brain" (15, emphasis mine). Here the horror, which begins as intense aesthetic beauty, is terminally experienced by the protagonist as "complet[ing]" something (15). In other words, the horror here consists in the uptake of knowledge.

Here, as elsewhere in the pulp ekphrastic work of the *Weird Tales* Three, the flesh of the brain is foregrounded over the immaterial mind. Later *Weird Tales* writers develop this theme and will collapse the subject and object distinction by dwelling on animate yet profane matter. Moreover, they portray a "knot" relationship between subject-perceiving aesthetic objects and the objects they view; in this way, both the subject experiencing art and the aesthetic object blur in essence, ontologically mix, so that the aesthetic can be said in these stories to consist of not merely of an interpretant and an enigmatic sign being interpreted but rather as a necessary fusion of the two.

A strange inversion takes place. Human beings are reduced to the status of base material: brains, meat, skeletal structure, dust. And the aesthetic object is quickened, de-objectified through association with consciousness. Thus, the many instances of the animated aesthetic object—e.g., a moving statue, a glowing painting, a world of poetic vision made manifest—in juxtaposition to a symbolic human being reduced to its base material sub-structure—e.g., a spattered brain, a mutilated body, a rotting corpse—can be viewed as important moments in *Weird Tales* where the space of the ordinary, structured by clear distinctions between subject and object, collapses. A Venus infused with baleful energies that smashes the human brain to paste; a supernaturally charged ring of stones that vibrate out a keening that "troops through," penetrates, and ultimately destroys brains are kindred allegories, occurrences that can only happen outside of the space of the ordinary after the literary effect of reality has been violated.

5. The Failure of Clark Ashton Smith

The End of the Story

Nearly two years passed before Smith published fiction in *Weird Tales* again, in the May 1930 issue with his story, "The End of the Story." This strange tale is set in a fictional province of eighteenth century France, Averoigne, in the year 1789. It relates the story of Christophe Morand, a young law student, who, traveling through the province, comes to stay at a Benedictine abbey, a stay that results in his dream-journey into a world of abstract art.

"The End of the Story" is a re-imagining of John Keats's ekphrastic poem, "Ode on a Grecian Urn." Keats was a poet Smith admired. As in Keats's "Ode," the story is an ekphrastic description of the timeless world of classical mythology, figured as an eternal space of infinite beauty. In the story, the Benedictine abbey Morand visits is distinctive for its grand library. The books are described as works of art: "There were innumerable monkish copies of antique authors, bound in wood or ivory, with rich illuminations and lettering that was often in itself a work of art" (23). Here is emphasized another dimension of the aesthetic object as it appears in *Weird Tales*: its function as a totalizing intellectual and even cartographic technology. Here the archival range of the artistic library is vast, spatially and temporally. It juxtaposes pre-historicity with antiquity, the western world with the eastern. And as the story unfolds, the library-as-aesthetic-object comes to function as a cognitive prothesis like many of the shadow modernist art objects rendered in the pulp ekphrastic works of the *Weird Tales* Three.

Morand's attraction to the beautiful library intensifies, and so he begins perusing the volumes. While doing so, he discovers a strange but curious book, "a thin volume with plain untitled binding of dark leather" (23). The comparably unadorned book anticipates the logic of aesthetic abstraction and anti-representation followed by the *Weird Tales* writers. It is the "abstract" and enduring dehumanized art object that has shed its mundane origins, its concrete qualities, that is fictionalized as the most powerful, the most dangerous to the space of the ordinary. Dis-embodied qualities such as color, shape, and acoustic vibrations not linked to any material, concrete origin source: such ontologically-vexed entities are later fictionalized in other pulp ekphrastic stories as horror-invoking, intensely beautiful, and yet painfully alluring. They are also harbingers of the de-reification rendered in fiction as rhetorically engineered violations of the literary effect of reality. There are many instances where characters literally hurl themselves into the body of these abstract aesthetic essences, such as in Smith's "The City of the Singing Flame" (*Wonder Stories*, July 1931) to die in ecstasy. Another example is in Lovecraft's *At the Mountains of Madness* when a character is pulled into a curve. Therefore, a richly-illuminated tome bound in wood or ivory adorned by mimetic representations is less dangerous in the context of the pulp ekphrastic works of the *Weird Tales* Three than a comparably more abstract tome, one that participates in the primal form of "book," i.e., a simple black-boarded quarto.

The Abbot who has invited Morand into the abbey notices the young man's attraction to the abstract book. He warns him that to read this strange book is to imperil his soul. But the allure of the book is too much for Morand. He is overwhelmed by curiosity: "I could not have denied the desire which forced me to take from the drawer the thin volume with plain unlettered binding" (26). Sneaking into the library late at night, he reads the book.

The volume contains a story, which as it is related becomes an embedded narrative. The story handwritten in the book is about a Count who, while wandering in the forest near the abbey Morand is reading in, encounters a goatish satyr in the woods. The satyr tells the Count that in the ruins of a castle not far from the abbey, in the caverns beneath it, "in places far underground, like the hell your priests have fabled, there dwells the pagan loveliness, there cry the pagan ecstasies" (27). The satyr disappears and the Count, heeding the satyr's story, seeks out the ruined castle. When he finds it, he descends through a triangular flagstone and down a flight of stairs into darkness. But here the story ends, the volume being only six pages long. It is left unfinished.

Entering the Story

Morand is stirred by this story, by its referential relationship to the abbey within which he reads. He longs to know "the end of the story."

5. The Failure of Clark Ashton Smith

There are two frames here blurring together: (1) the virtual world that narratively frames the story of Morand and (2) the virtual world of the story written in the black book that Morand becomes immersed in as he reads. Typical of the shadow modernist art objects of the pulp ekphrastic works of the *Weird Tales* Three, the fragmentary story of the count, like the abstract book that embodies it, stirs Morand, evokes in him an intense attraction: "The curiosity I had felt concerning the contents of the manuscript was now replaced by a burning desire, a thousandfold more powerful, more obsessive, to know the ending of the story" (27). Driven by his desire, Morand does something quite strange: he takes the Count's story as fact and steps into the sub-story's plot by following in the footsteps of the Count. Morand locates the ruined castle and the triangular flagstone, and he, like the character in the fragmentary story he has read, descends into the shadowy depths of the ruins. In this way, the frame separating fiction and fact in the world of Morand has collapsed. Walking through darkness into brilliant light, Morand finds he has come to another land, a dimension that can only be described as an abstract and eternal realm of infinite beauty: there is a laurel grove and a marble palace "gleaming with onyx and polished porphyry"; the grass is described as "more lustrous than emerald velvet" (31; 30).

The beauty of the strange land is so intense that Morand wonders if he can psychologically withstand it. He reports being "drowned in a sense of ever-growing ecstasy" (30). The central spectacle of this world is a woman, described as an "antique Venus" whose "movements were all as effortless and graceful as those of the serpent" (31). Morand is struck by her beauty and he falls into her arms. They make love, and then he loses consciousness. Morand then wakes up to a strange scene: he is not in the world of abstract beauty any longer but is lying on a dirt floor beneath the castle; additionally, the Abbot—who has followed him—is coming into the room shouting Latin spells. The beautiful Venus, with whom Morand has fallen in love flees in horror. Then the Abbot informs Morand that the Venus, disenchanted of illusion, is in fact a demon discussed in ancient mythology. Nicea's beauty, he continues, is merely an illusion: "If you could behold her as she really is, you would see, in lieu of her voluptuous body, the folds of a foul and monstrous serpent" (33). The story ends with Morand reluctantly leaving with the Abbot, but he feels regret. He cannot resist returning to the castle to find Nicea against the Abbot's warnings. His fate is sealed.

Like Keats's "Ode," Smith's "The End of the Story" is a story of a love set in a timeless world of mythology; however, Smith calibrates Keats's ekphrastic vision. For Keats, the image of the lovers frozen in passionate pursuit depicted on the Grecian urn represents a world of immortality and eternal beauty. The speaker of the poem longs for this world because, unlike mundane existence, this mythological world is beautifully unchanging and so fortified from the disintegrating influence of time. Furthermore, the speaker longs to enter this eternal world and to adopt an immortal mode of being like those of two lovers whose "wild ecstasy" will not diminish but will go on forever.

Smith is undecided and ambivalent toward this prospect, painted in this story with several strokes of horror. In this story Smith has fictionalized the timeless world of the aesthetic, an inescapable realm of absolute and eternal novelty. Nicea, the Venus-nymph depicted here, is represented as a coil of serpentine folds that spiral around a victim in order to sap his life energy, to reduce him to a husk. The result of a human visiting the aesthetic world for Smith is to invigorate the aesthetic object as the expense of the human. The balefully intelligent, alien entity waiting at the center of the web of the shadow modernist literary work is indeed absorbingly beautiful, too beautiful, and is vampirically vitalized and given agency by the human who comes to serve as a morbid form of fuel. The enduring art object—in this case a Venus statue—attains a kind of transgressive subjectivity; however, the human experiencing the virtual art object, who heeds the siren song of the pure aesthetic object, often takes on the object-like ontological status of that the art object has shed. The human becomes matter, not only a bloodless corpse but a formless ooze of putrefied flesh that passes away before the enduring timelessness of the aesthetic object that reveals the ephemerality of the ordinary.

Vampiric Art in "The Devotee of Evil"

Like Lovecraft and Howard, Smith focuses his attention on this theme of shadow modernism's vampirism. To an extent, we might say that in his

5. The Failure of Clark Ashton Smith

pulp ekphrasist stories, Smith tells this same story recursively. This artful retelling and revision of the same story is part of the pulp technique. For example, Smith develops his unreal shadow modernist works in a later story that the *Weird Tales* editor, Farnsworth Wright, rejected. Originally titled, "The Satanist," and later titled, "The Devotee of Evil," the story relates the story of Philip Hastane, a fantasy novelist, and his brief relationship with a mad man, Jean Averaud, an artist/engineer who creates a musical instrument with which he channels a kind of "black radiation" which is pure evil. This radiation is ultimately the cause of his demise. When he is bathed in it, it transforms him into a piece of grotesque art, a statue of black obsidian.

Smith's first mention of the story seems to be in a letter to Lovecraft on April 2nd, 1930: "'The Satanist' won't deal with ordinary devil-worship, but with the evocation of absolute cosmic evil, in the form of black radiation that leaves the devotee petrified into a sable-image of eternal horror" (CAS Selected Letters 110). A synopsis also appears among his papers, in which he states, "A devotee of absolute cosmic evil, who finally evokes (pure) evil in the form of a black radiation that leaves him petrified into a (...) image of eternal horror..." (Strange Shadows 157). Most interesting is the description of the musical instrument that brings about the "black radiation." The narrator, Philip Hastane, first describes the monstrous library Averaud has been studying from, a chimeric hodge-podge of science, mysticism, and art": They were an ungodly jumble of tomes that dealt with anthropology, ancient religions, demonology, modern science, history, psychoanalysis, and ethics" (155). This strange library, like the library in the Benedictine Abbey of "The End of the Story," prefigures the intellectually totalizing power of the musical instrument Averaud has created, an engineering project ostensibly derived by his esoteric studies. Later, the room where the instrument is stored is described as a strange triangular concert hall: "The chamber was large, triangular in form, and tapestried with curtains of some sullen black fabric. It had no windows" (157). The narrator goes on to describe the instrument:

> There were many wires of varying thickness, stretched on a series of concave sounding-boards of some dark, unlustrous metal; and above these, there depended from three horizontal bars a number of square, circular, and triangular gongs. [...] A small, hammerlike instrument hung opposite each gong, at the end of a silver wire [158].

Averaud begins to play the instrument: he strikes the triangular gongs with hammers and produces a horrible shadow modernist music: "I felt as though a flood of finely broken glass was pouring into my ears" (159). The music increases in volume and it ultimately causes a strange, visual manifestation: "A vertical shaft of faint shadow, surrounded by a still fainter penumbra, was forming in the air" (159). The music becomes unbearable. It begins to agitate Hastane's mind and threatens to drive him mad. The narrator describes his experience of the music in terms of de-reification, of the ephemerality of the ordinary: "My very sense of space was distorted and deformed as if some unknown dimension had somehow mingled with those familiar to us. There was a feeling of dreadful and measureless descent" (159).

The Evil of the Abstract Form

When the narrator states, "my very sense of space was distorted and deformed," he articulates the ephemerality of the ordinary succinctly (159). At the height of this experience, Averaud stops playing the instrument, releasing Hastane from his torturous revelry. Averaud explains to the horrified Hastane that the shaft of black shadow is a kind of pure, concentrated evil, and that the purpose of the musical instrument is to channel this pure evil sound. This is a clear enunciation of a thesis that runs through the pulp ekphrastic works of the *Weird Tales* Three as regards the aesthetic object and the condition of its production in modernity: as art purifies itself, as it becomes more and more an abstract and dehumanized form, it becomes more evil to the extent that it is more timeless, more enduring. And the enduring, eternal form, untouched by time, reveals the ephemerality of the ordinary by throwing into contrast the fluidity, contingency, and finitude of the world as seen through the myopic human perspective. Translated into an ethical/moral context, such an insight into the radical liquidity of human normativity might result, the *Weird Tales* Three warn, in nihilism, the disrobing of human conceits, a point grimly expressed by Conan the Cimmerian in Robert E. Howard's "Beyond the Black River"

5. The Failure of Clark Ashton Smith

(*Weird Tales* 1935): "Civilization is unnatural. It is a whim of circumstance. And barbarism must always ultimately triumph" (100). In other words, the ordinary is ephemeral. Reality is a fragile stasis that will pass away. As aesthetic objects shed their organic, psychological, social, and historical contents and become abstract, dehumanized forms, they become more evil because their previously hidden endurance becomes visible; their endurance thus reveals the experience of the ordinary as ephemeral. In a literary context, it formally renders this thesis by staging the unraveling of the literary effect of reality, a virtual analog of the ontological stability we mistakenly perceive that masks eternal flux and strangeness: the parameters of time, the cartographic projections of space, these distinctions between subject and object, are shattered.

For Smith, Howard, and Lovecraft, as their shadow modernist art objects shed their earth-focused representational dynamics and turn away from the human world to approach that realm of pure enduring form and abstraction—e.g., an incorporeal shaft of insubstantial color, a few beats of sound, a curve—they reveal the structuring, ordering function of the literary effect of reality. Consequently, the aesthetic object purged of earthly origins shines out in many forms, characteristically minimalist: a sphere, a cube, a cone (gilded in a mirror sheen surface), color unfettered to a substance, a refrain of music, a square of blank canvas, an almost imperceptible dance of the body. And the pure aesthetic object is fictionalized as inhuman, demonic, as absolutely dangerous, a herald of ultimate doom. When we put the book down, the literary effect of reality is shattered; bleary eyed, we see our reality, our actual ordinary reality, as less stable than before.

Smith, like Howard and Lovecraft, takes the ephemerality of the ordinary as an aesthetic first principle. Anti-scientific, anti-religious, and anti-philosophic, it is effectively an acute awareness that all is passing away, and rapidly so, a view Smith articulates in a penseé he recorded in his commonplace book: "All human thought, all science, all religion, is the holding of a candle to the night of the universe" (*Black Book* 50).

This is the dark insight that the pulp ekphrastic works of the *Weird Tales* Three seek to reveal through the lens of the non-representational, abstract form, i.e., the shadow modernist art objects they develop together. Pure form rendered vividly brings into focus absolute formlessness.

6. The Cultural Alienation of Robert E. Howard

The Reputation of Weird Tales

In his 1937 memoir *Pulpwood Editor*, Harold Hersey decries a low business tactic used by pulp magazine publishers looking to capitalize on the success of their competitors: "It is a common practice [...] in the pulpwoods, to eye a successful magazine venture, then bring out one almost exactly like it in title and make-up. [...] A neat trick in layout is duplicated by a rival editor, a new department idea given the sincerest form of flattery, and a fiction theme or set of characters emulated elsewhere" (10). By describing this business tactic, Hersey identifies an oblique way for speculating about the commercial success of *Weird Tales*, largely inaccessible to us today due to a lack of records. From the year it was founded in 1923 and throughout the rest of its existence, *Weird Tales* was known to be in a precarious financial state, a commercial history meticulously and dramatically related by pulp historian John Locke in his *The Thing's Incredible: The Secret Origins of* Weird Tales. Locke's history ends after the first two years of the magazine's tumultuous commercial history; so, in order to briefly speculate about its subsequent commercially viability, we must consider partial and symptomatic evidence. For example, even after 1924, when the magazine becomes, arguably, commercially stable, it continued to pay its writers "on publication" rather than "on acceptance," a business practice that made it look to professional pulp writers as an unstable market for manuscripts. Accordingly, there were reports from *Weird Tales* writers in letters of checks not honored by banks

6. The Cultural Alienation of Robert E. Howard

and requests from the editor and business managers for patience. For example, Robert E. Howard, writing to Farnsworth Wright in May of 1935, complains about his poverty and *Weird Tales's* financial troubles: "To a poor man the money he makes is his life's blood, and of late when I write of Conan's adventures I have to struggle against the disheartening reflection that if the story is accepted, it may be years before I get paid for it" (Collected Letters v. 3, 307). Furthermore, a key part of the magazine's retrospective legend recounted by knowledgeable collectors is an emphasis on how *Weird Tales*'s readership was very small compared to mainstream magazines but nevertheless committed to buying the magazine every month.

To generalize, *Weird Tales* was a magazine that catered to the tastes of a small, specialized readership, and therefore had but tenuous commercial viability.

Because it did not cease publication until the end of the pulp era (approximately 1952), we might assume that, as a business enterprise, it made some kind of a profit. This ambivalent vision of a financially-troubled *Weird Tales* needs to be juxtaposed against extensive surveys of pulp fiction magazines that generalize about the all-fiction periodicals of the interwar period, framing them as nothing but commodities, as business enterprises without any aesthetic authenticity. Perhaps contradicting the inaccurate vision of *Weird Tales* as a non-commercial enterprise authentically committed to aesthetic concerns over mere profit, it cannot be denied that the magazine engendered what might be considered success, a few years of if not financial viability then at least a higher aesthetic reputation, a phenomenon expressed by the establishment of an imitator title. This period of success can be marked as beginning with an important publishing event in July of 1931, when one of the editors employed by the largest pulp fiction magazine firm, The Clayton Group, released the following statement in *Writer's Digest*, the trade journal of pulp fiction magazine publishers, writers, and editors: "The Clayton Group is now buying stories for a new magazine to be devoted exclusively to material of the weird type. In it we welcome stories of the occult, weird, ghost, supernatural, vampire, voodoo, obi, werewolf, reincarnation, mystic, psychic kinds" (Qtd. in Lichtblau 63). Clayton was publishing a new magazine, an obvious imitation of *Weird Tales*. It was called *Strange Tales of Terror and Mystery*.

Some Symptoms Regarding the Reputation of Weird Tales

Its first issue of *Strange Tales* appeared in September of 1931, and it featured one story from Clark Ashton Smith, "The Return of the Sorcerer." But despite publishing some *Weird Tales* writers (a common pulp practice was to imitate a title and then "scoop" writers who famously published in the title being imitated) the imitator of *Weird Tales* failed. That *Strange Tales* was not successful (it ran for only seven issues) is less significant than the fact that it suggests that *Weird Tales* had, by 1931, developed a reputation for commercial viability. What kind of reputation? Consider, for example, H. Bedford Jones's 1931 editorial for *The Author and Journalist* where he highlights what he sees as the perverse growing in popularity of weird fiction in the pulp fiction marketplace: "The oddest phenomenon of recent magazine history is the group that goes in for so-called weird or amazing stories. [...] The popularity of this type of magazine is a sad reflection upon the mentality of the reading public" (38). In spite of Jones's assessment, there were only two magazines in 1931 specializing in "weird fiction": one was *Weird Tales*, and the other was its short-lived imitator, *Strange Tales*. Jones's characterization of *Weird Tales* as perverse echoes some of the same charges leveled at literary modernism. Despite the *Weird Tales* Three's deliberate anti-modernism, the magazine they were publishing in was being viewed by the public in a similar way as the modernists who had come before: transgressors who flouted convention in the name of art.

We can sharpen this speculation about the reputation *Weird Tales* was developing by turning to another piece published in *The Writer's Digest* related to the Clayton Group's decision to imitate *Weird Tales* with *Strange Tales*. A month after Clayton's announcement, an article appeared in *The Writer's Digest* titled, "The Psycho-Mystic, Horror, and Weird Story Field" by a pulp writer named Joseph Lichtblau. The article identifies and describes a new fiction market. Lichtblau writes,

> With the advent of the new Clayton magazine, *Strange Stories* [...] I feel this article should be of the most timely interest to you who have really fertile imaginations. In the past, Weird Tales offered a rather limited field for psycho-mystic,

6. The Cultural Alienation of Robert E. Howard

occult, weird, ghost, supernatural, vampire, vodoo, obi, werewolf, reincarnation, mystic, psychic stories since other magazines did not use them [63].

The purpose of articles like the one written by Lichtblau published in *The Writer's Digest* is to model for pulp writers how to write for specific types of markets. In his article outline, Lichtblau describes in detail what he imagines are the essential narrative tropes of this specific "psycho-mystic" market. He offers example narratives, and in this way emphasizes *Weird Tales's* discursive focus on issues of art, artistic creation, and the character of the artist. This following example evidences that Lichtblau had read *Weird Tales* and demonstrates the magazine's focus on the fictional and supernatural art object:

> A widower buys a statuette of a woman that resembles his dead wife. In life, she had been modest, so virtuous that she even refused him his marital rights! He gloats over the statuette; manhandles it sadistically; feels he is getting a giant revenge on his dead wife because that nude statuette is so defenseless in his salacious hands. In the in end, it falls down on his head and kills him! [65–66].

Lichtblau is quick to point out that the conventionalism of good triumphing over evil is not essential for publication in this strange magazine: "In Weird Tales, however, evil can 'put it all over' good, and your stories will never offend the editor! So long as your yarns horrify the reader to a satisfying extent, fascinate, mystify him and make him shudder, you can go as far as you like, it seems" (66). Lichtblau ends his analysis of the "psycho mystic" market in preparation for Clayton's new *Strange Tales* by describing the current market. He ends his article with a warning to "pulp hacks" who do not consider aesthetic standards or technique in regard to *Weird Tales*: "Weird Tales, however, demands a much better style; some of the yarns are written so impressively and in such a 'high brow' manner, that one wonders how talented authors could contribute for 1c per word on publication which is the rate for acceptable stories of this periodical" (67). In other words, *Weird Tales*, the magazine of Lovecraft, Howard, and Smith, had, by 1931, developed a reputation of literary artistic excellence.

Lichtblau was correct to wonder about the financial viability of the artistic writers publishing in *Weird Tales*, the way the aesthetic concerns did not seem to sync with the financially constrained conditions of pulp fiction production. By June of 1931 many specialists in the pulp fiction magazine world were taking notice of *Weird Tales* and were raising an eyebrow about its aesthetic pretensions. Its reputation was growing, and the commercial failure of its imitator, *Strange Tales,* suggests that *Weird Tales*'s reputation was not merely due to its thematic focus but instead its literary quality. But this early 1930s growth of *Weird Tales*'s artistic reputation must be qualified by its less flattering appearance to some readers: it appeared not as a legitimate business enterprise finally worthy of notice by pulp publishers but as a strange publication, a perversion, a sign of the "atavism" of the American reading public. For example, in 1929, before *Strange Tales* was launched, Farnsworth Wright felt compelled to defend *Weird Tales* in *The Writer's Digest.* Responding to a description of *Weird Tales* that appeared in the journal, he states,

> It seems that the descriptive line, "It carries the most ungodly stories a starved writer in a garret could concoct," gives a false impression to the readers of the The Writer's Digest as to the quality of our stories [...]. We admit that the stories in Weird Tales are different from those in other magazines, but to call them "the most ungodly stories a starved writer in a garret could concoct" gives an unfair and misleading impression [82].

For Wright, *Weird Tales* needed defending in 1929 from a growing number who were noticing it and understanding it not in terms of aesthetic authenticity but of sensational spectacle, a mode of misunderstanding comparable to the earliest reactions to modernism. The extent to which *Weird Tales* catered to a specialized, even strange audience, was becoming part of its identity. Thus, it became known as a specialized market for promoting the weird in fiction, and in this way can be somewhat validated as operating against the simple commercial logic of the pulp marketplace.

Robert E. Howard and Weird Tales

Weird Tales's commercial troubles may have been briefly alleviated in the early 1930s due to its growing reputation for strangeness, sensationalism, and literary quality. And it is significant to note that this success parallels a sustained period of heightened productivity and regular correspondence between the *Weird Tales* Three. One of these writers, Clark Ashton Smith, has received treatment already. The second writer, Robert

6. The Cultural Alienation of Robert E. Howard

E. Howard, youngest of the other two writers by nearly two decades, is the focus of this chapter.

Robert E. Howard's first contribution to *Weird Tales* appeared in the July 1925 issue. He was eighteen years old. The story he published was titled "Spear and Fang," an action adventure story featuring a prehistoric barbarian who fights a proto-human. In spite of Howard's publication in the magazine in 1925, he did not make contact with Lovecraft until 1930, when he was twenty-four; and shortly after contacting Lovecraft, Lovecraft put him in contact with Clark Ashton Smith, establishing an informal literary triumvirate.

Robert E. Howard's significant contributions to the pulp ekphrastic enterprise of the *Weird Tales* Three did not begin in earnest until approximately 1930, when he began corresponding with Clark Ashton Smith and H.P. Lovecraft regularly. These two ambitious writers (as well as other *Weird Tales* writers they introduced to Howard) stirred the young Howard and increased his literary ambition. Through Lovecraft and Smith's mentoring—direct and indirect—Howard became an essential member of the pulp ekphrastic enterprise that distinguishes *Weird Tales* as an important archive of twentieth-century literary history.

Brief Interlude

Before proceeding to treat Howard in depth, let me briefly reiterate my overarching argument. I have asserted that H.P. Lovecraft, Clark Ashton Smith, and Robert E. Howard were responding in much of their fiction to broad and contemporary stylistic trends in literary and artistic history, i.e., that much of their pulp fictions are ekphrastic renderings and fictionalizations of modernism generally understood as it appeared in the interwar period to those external to its discursive context. Moreover, I have been arguing that Lovecraft, Smith, and Howard's pulp ekphrasis, their response to modernism, can be characterized as an acutely ambitious aesthetic project in and of itself. A major feature of their pulp ekphrastic works, I argue, is the combination of literary realism with virtual aesthetics to dramatically stage the ephemerality of the ordinary, a project practically executed by the dissolution of the literary effect of reality. To the extent that the *Weird Tales* Three technically formalize in their pulp ekphrastic works the theme of the ephemerality of the ordinary, their work expresses a radically conservative ethos toward the process of modernization: they view modernity as a catastrophe, as a process of cruelly accelerating change that heralds an approaching crisis.

H.P. Lovecraft, Robert E. Howard, and a Philological Debate

In March of 1924, *Weird Tales* published H.P. Lovecraft's "The Rats in the Wall," and six years later, following an established pulp market practice of reprinting stories praised by readers, Farnsworth Wright chose to include it again in the June 1930 issue. "The Rats in the Walls," a tale of a haunted English castle, is considered H.P. Lovecraft's most conventional "gothic" tale. It features all the typical material of the gothic horror: drafty castle corridors, mounds of skeletons, piles of grinning skulls, secret compartments, a black cat, rats, haunted grottos, and a series of hereditary sins. This story has been framed by many as a deliberate and even academic pastiche of the classic gothic tales Lovecraft had been studying when he wrote "The Rats in the Walls" for a different scholarly project, his long critical history of supernaturalism in literature titled *Supernatural Horror in Literature*. Lovecraft's study begins by citing some of the key tropes he identifies as essential to the gothic tale and that incidentally appear in his "Rats in the Walls"—e.g., "secret murder," "bloody bones." It is an intriguing incongruity that he criticizes these tropes here as too traditional and, to some extent, historically exhausted for writers of horror considering he was, at the time, writing a story that utilized them:

> The true weird tale has something more than secret murder, bloody bones, or a sheeted form clanking according to rule. A certain atmosphere of breathless and unexplainable dread of outré, unknown forces must be present; and there must be a hint expressed with a seriousness and portentousness becoming its subject,

6. The Cultural Alienation of Robert E. Howard

of that most terrible conception of the human brain—a malign and particular suspension or defeat of those fixed laws of Nature which are our only safeguard against the assaults of chaos and the daemons of unplumbed space [1043].

Although Lovecraft identifies these tropes as exhausted, he nevertheless uses them in "The Rats in the Wall."

Central to this gothic story's construction of a "certain atmosphere" as described by Lovecraft above, is the protagonist's supernatural and mystical exploration of the prehistory of Britain. At the end of the story, after the protagonist has undergone a supernatural reversion into a past consciousness, he screams a sentence in Gaelic: "Dia ad agaidh 's as aodann ... agus bas dunach ort!" (396). In ending the story this way, Lovecraft obliquely, and perhaps unintentionally, engaged in a stale anthropological debate. By having the final language uttered by the supernaturally reverting protagonist in Gaelic, Lovecraft seemed to stake his allegiance to a theory in anthropology that the Gaelic people preceded the Cymric people in Britain. But Lovecraft made this decision not out of a polemic commitment to any anthropological theory or partisan idea but out of simple exigency: he did not have access to the Cymric language. He did, however, have a Gaelic phrase at hand in a short story he owned, Fiona Maccleod's "The Sin Eater." He decided on Gaelic because of convenience. But he lamented this decision in a letter to his friend in 1923, another *Weird Tales* writer, Frank Belknap Long: "The only objection to the phrase is that it's Gaelic instead of Cymric as the south-of-England demands. But as with anthropology—details don't count. Nobody will ever note the difference" (Qtd. In *Freedom* 7). When the story was published in 1924, no one noticed this distinctive use of Gaelic. However, when "The Rats in the Walls" was reprinted in 1930, someone did, in fact, notice this subtly distinctive stroke. This was the twenty-four-year-old *Weird Tales* regular contributor, Robert E. Howard.

Howard was intrigued by this because Lovecraft's use of the Gaelic suggested his adherence to a discredited theory of the Celtic origins of the British people, a theory debated by historians and philologists; thus, Lovecraft's incidental adherence to this controversial theory would have struck a polemic tone to informed ears. The young Howard was intellectually committed of his Irish heritage and was attracted by the idea that Celtic elements could claim a more primary place in terms of British language and culture than Germanic ones. And so, he wrote to the editor of

Weird Tales, Farnsworth Wright, asking if he knew Lovecraft's stance on this controversial issue. Referring to the climax of Lovecraft's "The Rats in the Walls" (in which the protagonist, who has atavistically reverted to his earliest "ancestral self," speaks Gaelic) Howard writes, "I note from the fact that Mr. Lovecraft has his character speaking Gaelic instead of Cymric, in denoting the Age of the Druids, that he holds to Lhuyd's theory as to the settling of Britain by the Celts. This theory is not generally agreed to, but I scarcely think that it has ever been disproved [...]" (Collected Letters v.2, 42–43). Wright forwarded the letter to Lovecraft, who responded personally to Howard. Consequently, a correspondence that would last the rest of Howard's six remaining years began on a scholastic footing.

Lovecraft and Howard

Surveying their correspondence suggests that Lovecraft was intrigued by the young Howard, who he saw as a series of rich paradoxes. Lovecraft circulated Howard's letter to his correspondents and in this way brought the young writer into contact with other writers who would enrich his work. In an October 1933 letter to his philosopher friend, Alfred Galpin, Lovecraft summarizes his view of Howard in this way:

> Robert E. Howard is an interesting Texas character; only 27 years old, yet as full of the reminiscent lore of the old Southwest as any grizzled cattleman of the 1870's [...]. He has an odd, primitive philosophy—hating all civilization [...] & regarding the barbarism of the pre–Roman Gauls as the ideal form of life. He writes fiction purely for money, hence his more or less stereotyped catering to popular trends. Once in a while, though, he unconsciously achieves a very genuine power in his depictions of ruins, catacombs, & cities redolent of unholy antiquity & blasphemous elder secrets [Letters to Galpin 193–94].

To the Anglophile Lovecraft loyal to what he understood as the apex of culture represented by Ancient Greece, Republican Rome, and England's Georgian period, Howard seemed a curious enigma: the youth was an intellectual who spurned intellectuals, a writer who was embarrassed by his sedentary trade of writing, a bodybuilding roughneck who brewed his own illegal beer and boxed in illegal prizefights yet spent much of his time

6. *The Cultural Alienation of Robert E. Howard*

stooped over a typewriter writing poetry and pulp stories. Here was an audacious writer who engaged in hours of reading to quote Shakespeare, Keats, and Browning in order to criticize the *vita contemplativa* and celebrate the *vita activa*. Lovecraft's observation, "he *unconsciously* achieves a very genuine power" succinctly sums up Howard (194, my emphasis). Lovecraft and Smith thought deeply about their technique and philosophies and deliberately deployed them through the nuanced engineering of precise rhetorics of short fiction; Howard, however, though undoubtedly thoughtful, was more spontaneous and vital and at least posed as one who eschewed excessive theory.

Robert E. Howard and Popular Culture

Robert E. Howard's influence on many elements of popular culture is unquestioned; however, his troubled and intriguing relationship with the elite culture of the 1920s and '30s and his reaction to modernism is rarely explored because many are quick to assume that no significant relationship exists. This gap is in large part due to the fact that, in terms of his work's popular cultural dissemination, very few associate his specific pulp fiction productions in *Weird Tales* with the widespread cultural tropes they brought about through their influence. For example, many in and outside of the Anglophone context are aware of the *Dungeon & Dragons* roleplaying game and the video games it influenced; of the fantasy imagery of Frank Frazetta's Howard-inspired paintings that adorn so many Howard-derived fantasy novels; however, few would connect these elements with an aesthetically sophisticated ekphrastic treatment of an elite artistic culture like modernism.

Currently, Howard's contributions to popular culture eclipse his status as a literary artist and critic. Jonas Prida, in his introduction to *Conan Meets the Academy: Multidisciplinary Essays on the Enduring Barbarian*, makes a distinction between the literary work and art of Robert E. Howard and "the figure of Conan in popular culture," and I think this distinction is very appropriate (1). But this important qualifying distinction means we should proceed carefully. Howard only lived to 30; he committed suicide in 1936, and so his relatively scant yet influential literary output has been overshadowed by the cultural productions that were broadcast from it and based on it, such as comics, films, roleplaying games, video games, and so forth. Clearly delineating Howard and his literary work from the popular culture productions that he influenced is a first principle for any critical treatment of the writer as a pulp artist.

The Intellectual and Artistic Context of Robert E. Howard

One could plausibly argue that Howard was one of the only intellectuals in his rural community and was therefore looked upon with suspicion by his uneducated neighbors as peculiar. In spite of the fact that he made his living writing, he was a committed athlete and glorified frontier living. Unlike Lovecraft and Smith, who reluctantly came to write for and publish in *Weird Tales* after long periods of elite literary activity in the 1900s, 1910s, and early 1920s (Lovecraft in private publications, Smith in poetry magazines), Howard's work as a pulp writer entailed his first (and last) participation in professional literary culture. Although Howard unapologetically adopted the stance of the mercenary pulp writer who wrote first and foremost for financial remuneration, he was nevertheless a sensitive poet, a voracious reader, and an amateur philosopher who corresponded widely when he could about literary topics, literary technique, politics, philosophy, and current events with many learned people. His engagement with literary and art culture in rural Texas during the oil boom era is an intriguing incongruity that contributes significantly to his worldview and literary output that encapsulated it. Indeed, the central theme of Howard's work is contact between high and low culture, the "elitism" of literary modernism and the "sensationalism" of pulp writing. The barbarian wielding his sword against the decadent sorcerer always participates allegorically in the tension inherent in the pulp writer reflecting on the elite writer, philosopher, artist, and intellectual.

6. The Cultural Alienation of Robert E. Howard

Aside from publishing juvenilia in small high school publications, correspondence circles, and in his hometown's local newspaper, publication in *Weird Tales* was, for Howard, not a mark of cultural degradation that embarrassed but was rather a validating accomplishment. Unlike many modernists like T.S. Eliot, Ernest Hemingway, and Virginia Woolf—who lived in centers of culture such as Paris and London and interacted with the apotheosized of literary, artistic, and philosophic culture—Howard lived in the small Texas frontier town of Cross Plains, which did not have a public library. Cross Plains did not boast its first radio station until 1922, and in 1919 had a population of 1,500 (Finn 44). From the perspective of this town, publication by a magazine firm based out of Chicago was indeed a mark of cultural distinction, one Howard's unique cultural circumstances made even more extraordinary. Aside from the books Howard was able to purchase during trips to metropolitan centers, he relied on pulp fiction magazines for his reading material and for education as a writer. Unlike Smith and Lovecraft, whose contacts in San Francisco and Providence and relationships with successful writers and artists of the day contributed to their cultural knowledge, Howard's culture and views were the product of his own eclectic, self-guided reading, not out of self-adopted iconoclasm but out of physical necessity. If, perhaps, Lovecraft and Smith cultivated their cultural and aesthetic iconoclasm with intentionality, Howard's aesthetic and the cultural productions broadcast from it became out of step because of his social and cultural context.

Unlike Smith and Lovecraft, who were arguably able to retreat from the forces of history and modernity into an insulated fantasy world, the ephemerality of the ordinary connected to modernity that they so often thematized as evil in their work, Howard experienced modernity and the ephemerality of the ordinary firsthand as an intense shock, one that penetrated his everyday life directly and acutely. He lived in rural Texas during the oil boom years. This important biographical experience can only be glimpsed by drawing a stark distinction between Howard's early life traveling around rural parts of Texas (1906–1919), with the latter part of his life, when his family settled in Cross Plains, Texas (1919–1936). The son of a traveling frontier doctor, Howard often writes in his correspondences about his earlier residential movements. Consider this brief autobiographical sketch he wrote for himself at 15 years old as part of a composition assignment:

> I was born in Peaster, Texas, a small town not far from Weatherford, in January 1906, at an early age [...]. After a few trips, moves and other adventures which I will pass over as I was too small to take notice of them, I found myself in Seminole, Texas, just forty miles this side of the New Mexico Border. This was prairie country—extremely so. Water was scarce there; too scarce, so we moved to Bagwell, Texas, which is between Texarkana and Paris. That part of the country where we lived used to be part of Arkansas. It is all piney woods there, and every time I smell the pine scent I get homesick ... [Qtd. in Finn 29].

As a child, Howard's life was predominantly rural in nature. Though Howard's father and mother frequently changed residences during his youth, the family chose to settle in Cross Plains in 1919. In less than two years, however, the town population had increased significantly due to the discovery of oil. Howard lived in an "oil boom" town and this experience influenced his literature significantly. For example, this passage from an October 1930 letter he wrote to H.P. Lovecraft demonstrates the impact of these living conditions on Howard: "I've seen old farmers, bent with toil, and ignorant of the feel of ten dollars at a time, become millionaires in a week, by way of oil gushers. And I've seen them blow in every cent of it and die paupers" (*Freedom* 91).

The Geographical Distinctiveness of the Weird Tales *Three*

Thus far, the pulp ekphrastic enterprise of the *Weird Tales* Three has been presented as a cohesive artistic enterprise; accordingly, because of the cultural degradation projected onto it, the pulp ekphrastic enterprise of the *Weird Tales* Three uniquely renders modernism through distortion and fictionalization because of the alienated vantage point connected to this degradation. Additionally, by briefly considering Howard's unique intellectual context here, we see how part of this distinctive perspective attributable to the *Weird Tales* Three derives from their geographical as well as cultural alterity. Consider Howard in rural Texas; Lovecraft in Rhode Island; Smith in the Sierras; Wright in Chicago: keeping in mind the extent to which this geographical profile is highly distinctive from the geographical profile of traditional "monolithic" definitions of modernism sharpens the uniqueness of the *Weird Tales* Three and their pulp ekphrasis. It suggests that many of its unique discursive dimensions derive from its spatial distance from what have been considered traditional geographical hubs of modernist culture, hubs such as New York, London, Paris, Berlin, Rome, and Vienna. *Weird Tales* is not only in the shadow of modernism because it is a commercial magazine printed on disintegrating paper by writers unacknowledged by the cultural elite; it is also in the shadow of modernism because of where it comes from: places beyond the metropolitan centers that have traditionally produced culture and art.

7. Robert E. Howard and Rendering the Real and the Unreal

The Distinctiveness of the Weird Tales *Three*

From the perspective of the communities that have contributed greatly to the endurance of the *Weird Tales* Three's literary legacy—e.g., horror film, fantasy roleplaying games, comics, death metal music, video games, etc.—Clark Ashton Smith, H.P. Lovecraft, and Robert E. Howard may seem different on the level of theme, hardly elements of what I am arguing is a cohesive aesthetic enterprise of pulp ekphrasis. For instance, Smith is a literary curio remembered today by the genre writers and pulp collectors. Lovecraft has been taken up by horror film enthusiasts. Howard has a strong presence in comic book collecting communities due to his influence on the superhero genre. Indeed, the work of the *Weird Tales* Three persists through popular culture as autonomous traditions but rarely together as a unified aesthetic project and never as representatives of the apex of the pulp aesthetic.

To an extent, the thematic distinctiveness of these writers is undeniable, and emphatically so if the fiction of H.P. Lovecraft and Robert E. Howard are compared and contrasted. For example, the typical protagonist of Lovecraft's stories is an erudite scholar who follows the thread of various enigmatic texts and symbols to come to a level of certainty about a secret, horrific truth. With their emphasis on parlor-room reflection, textual scholarship, and nuanced detection, Lovecraftian horror narratives seem to have little in common with the fantasy action tales that anchor Robert E. Howard's fantasy legacy. Howard's pulp ekphrastic fantasies feature protagonists in the more heroic tradition of epic narratives. This fantasy adventure is arguably more somatic than intellectual; swords flash, blood sprays, enemies scream, and the hero ultimately triumphs by action rather than sustained reflection and the process of detection. But what unites these apparently disparate types of pulp ekphrasis are the way they are both centered on hostile and creative reactions to modernist and elite culture.

Sword and Sorcery and Anti-Intellectualism

Just as the Lovecraftian protagonist recoiling in horror from a shadow modernist art object represents an ekphrastic engagement with elite culture figured as horrible, Robert E. Howard's trope of "barbarian warrior" versus "sorcerer" represents a comparable cultural logic. Several of Howard's action stories that feature supernatural elements and pre-modern settings have come to be seen as inaugurating a sub-genre of particularly American fantasy fiction termed "sword and sorcery," a genre generally celebrated for its ideological populism and anti-intellectualism, moral ambiguity, and proletarianism.

And if suspicion of intellectualism and the centrality of violence and action are key elements of Howard's sword and sorcery fiction, the supernatural as menace is another essential one. For example, when the fantasy writer, Fritz Leiber, wrote in April of 1961 a letter to the editor of the newly established fanzine devoted to fantasy fiction, *Amra*, he coined the term "sword and sorcery " to refer to the specific kind of fantasy fiction pioneered by Howard in the 1930s. In doing this, Leiber significantly frames the "supernatural element" as an essential component of the Howardesque "sword-and-sorcery story": "The word sorcery implies something more and other than historical human witchcraft, so even the element of an alien-yet-human world background is hinted at" (21).

Howard's most enduring characters in the sword and sorcery genre are fighters who solve problems with fists, steel, and gunpowder. Howard's enduring characters like Conan the Cimmerian, King Kull, and Solomon Kane are violent sword, axe, and pistol-wielding warriors who fight against the supernatural and often take as their antagonist supernatural enemies framed as compromised by virtue of their occult knowledge, a knowledge that is the source of their supernatural power and evil.

This acute level of anti-intellectualism in Howard's sword and sorcery fiction was first observed and articulated publicly after Arkham House, an independent publisher founded to preserve Lovecraft's and other *Weird Tales* writers' legacies, released the first hardcover anthology of his fiction, titled *Skull-face and Other Stories*. H.R. Hays, a celebrated translator of Pablo Neruda's poetry, reviewed this expensive, small circulation book for *The New York Times* on September 29th of 1946. Hays titled his review, "Superman on a Psychotic Bender," and his review is negative. He nevertheless begins by complimenting Howard's writing, stating, "The stories are written on a competent pulp level (a higher level, by the way, than that of some best sellers)" (167). He then goes on to psychoanalyze Howard and diagnoses him as a schizophrenic. Moreover, he frames Howard's fiction as perverse wish-fulfillments of the "semi-literate" of the industrial age: "Howard's heroes were [...] wish-projections of himself. All of the frustrations of his own life were conquered in a dream world of magic and heroic carnage" (*The New York Times* 167). The enemies of Howard's sword and sorcery characters are a campy distortion of actual cultural elites like Hays, typically intellectual and elite figures: sorcerers, politicians, rogues, and poets who leverage the supernatural and their access to secret archives to threaten the freedom of the roving barbarian (or Texan). Indeed, Howard's sorcerers are slightly-veiled allegories for the elites of the interwar period who often projected barbarism onto the culturally and geographically marginalized.

Robert E. Howard and High and Low Art

What commentators on Howard's fiction have yet to discuss in depth is the surprising extent to which Howard's sword and sorcery stories thematize the tense and antagonistic relationship between low art and high art in the early decades of the twentieth century. The Howardian barbarian figure, in this view, is a kind of avatar of the pulp writer, the nonintellectual proletarian writer who is in agonistic relation with the elite writers of the day. In the naked barbarian's bringing of steel against the magical elements of sorcerers we can glimpse, once again, a pulp ekphrastic rendering not of actual modernism but a strategic distortion, a shadow modernism.

As Andreas Huyssen and John Carey have argued elsewhere, this alienation of the intellectual world of culture from the fictional "masses" became exaggerated in the early decades of the twentieth century with the unfolding of "the great divide." Indeed, critics and historians of interwar literature and culture have documented and analyzed how artists, writers, and other cultural elites took an adversarial stance toward what seemed from their perspective inauthentic commodity or mass culture. What has not been documented is the inverse of this, the adversarial stance taken by populist writers like Howard who wrote thrillers for the pulps. Accordingly, the *Weird Tales* Three experienced this cultural alienation acutely and were even artistically nourished by it to the extent that they internalized it and thematized it in their fiction. In the case of Howard's sword and sorcery characters, the archetypical violent warrior or barbarian confronting the sorcerer or rogue spinning magic is nothing less than the pulp writer reacting to the alienation inherent in a confrontation between experimental art and the discursively uninitiated.

Robert E. Howard and Modern Writers

In a December 1932 letter to H.P. Lovecraft, Robert E. Howard expressed his adversarial stance toward "modern writers" this way:

> I think yourself and Jim Tully are the only ones whose work will endure; among the writers now living, I mean [...]. As for Dreiser, Sinclair Lewis, Louis Bromfeld, Ben Hecht, Sherwood Anderson, F. Scott Fitzgerald, George Jean Nathan,

Floyd Dell, Mike Gold—three ringing raspberries for the whole mob [...] [*Freedom* 510].

Lovecraft responded to Howard with a 22-page letter that ranged in topic: the politics of Texas, theories of animal phobias, and anecdotes about his travels to New York to see what he called "shrieking attic murals" and "modernistic atrocities" at the Museum of Art. In addition to these topics and many more, Lovecraft turned, of course, to modern literature, and when he did so, he took on the voice of a seasoned mentor. To the twenty-seven-year-old pulp writer, Lovecraft (then 42), responded: "You are certainly a bit hasty and unjust in giving a blanket condemnation to thoughtful writers like Dreiser, Lewis, Hecht, Bromfield, O'Neill, Anderson, etc. These are really the greatest writers [...] for they are the only ones who try to understand people and present them as acting from the deep hidden motives which truly animate them" (*Freedom* 532). Lovecraft goes on to criticize several popular writers: "They represent people as acting from fictitious motives which do not exist, and distort the whole pattern of life and human nature in the direction of artificial convention and childish oversimplification" (532). And Lovecraft concludes his scolding of Howard by defending H.L. Mencken, a critic he condemns elsewhere. These two pulp writers' debate about the merit of modernist literature in America troubles stereotypical notions of commercial pulp fiction and those who write it. More importantly, it further brings into focus how Lovecraft, Howard, Smith, and other *Weird Tales* writers understood the contribution to literature by modernist writers. They were aware of their literary and artistic innovations. Howard's dismissal of them as "wet smacks" does not mean he has not reflected deeply about them.

More important is the way the *Weird Tales* Three came to understand the contributions of modern writers as connected with something that can be termed their "realism." Lovecraft scolds Zane Grey (and in this way, scolds many of his pulp fiction peers) for their lack of realism, their unskillful habit of representing their characters as "acting from artificial motives." For Lovecraft, the value of literary modernism is connected to its psychological realism and not its technical and narrative innovations. As a pre-eminent fantasist, Lovecraft's emphasis and praise of the real might appear as an incongruity; however, his emphasis on authentic renderings of the real in literature nevertheless maintains consistency with his mature theories of supernatural literature.

7. Robert E. Howard and Rendering the Real and the Unreal

Rendering the Unreal Authentically

At first glance, this argument for literary value based on a principle of realism seems a curious thing for a fantasist like Lovecraft, a writer most see as committed to the unreal, to deploy; however, Lovecraft is promoting realism not in terms of a narrow representation of what actually exists. The realism that Lovecraft values is based on subtle philosophical condition, the degree to which the effect of reality produced by the literary work is rhetorically effective. For example, in the opening of his *Supernatural Horror in Literature* wherein Lovecraft appeals to the science of psychology to justify a rhetoric, formalism, and above all artistic and literary quality of the "weird tale," by which he means the literature of the supernatural:

> The oldest and strongest emotion of mankind is fear, and the oldest and strongest kind of fear is fear of the unknown. These facts few psychologists will dispute, and their admitted truth must establish for all time the genuineness and dignity of the weirdly horrible tales as a literary form. Against it are discharged all the shafts of materialistic sophistication which clings to frequently felt emotions and external events [...] [1041].

In this semantic context, we might consider Lovecraft, Howard, and Smith literary realists (with important qualifications). This is because of the extent to which their representations, their "mimeses," their rhetorics of fiction, focus on rendering as rhetorically impactful confrontations with the unknown and violations of the "materialistic sophistication," of the literary effect of reality. The aesthetic victory condition of the unreality of the *Weird Tales* Three's fantasies is to make strange the ordinary worlds rhetorically rendered by conventional literary realism, to expose the degree to which the artifice of narrative orders an otherwise unknowable chaos.

Pulp Ekphrasis and the Problem of the Real

Lovecraft and Smith influenced Howard and Howard influenced them in return. Near the end of his life, Howard was writing of his Conan the

Cimmerian character using the term "realism." In Howard's 1935 letter to Clark Ashton Smith he refers to Conan the Cimmerian, fighter against of sorcerers and demons, as his most realistic creation:

> It may sound fantastic to link the term "realism" with Conan; but as a matter of fact—his supernatural adventures aside—he is the most realistic character I ever evolved. He is simply a combination of a number of men I have known, and I think that's why he seemed to step full-grown into my consciousness when I wrote the first yarn of the series [Collected Letters v.3, 367].

For the *Weird Tales* Three—despite their distaste for modern art and literature—one of the thematic elements that frustrated and vitalized modernism was its narrow hewing to the real as a theme. Curiously, this artistic commitment to the real, to realism as an effect of artifice, sometimes serves as an occasion for recognizing the similarities between their own artistic enterprise and modernism's: "The bare truth about the nature of things may be more fantastic than anything any of us have yet cooked up," writes Smith to Lovecraft (*Dawnward* 458). But despite their acknowledgment of the real as a valid object of artistic treatment, the *Weird Tales* Three more often ridicule it as the focus of the unimaginative writer and artist, as in Smith's cynical letter to a fan in May of 1932: "The nearer people are to the animal, the feebler their powers of imagination and abstraction. That's why realism is so popular to-day" (CAS Selected Letters 178). Regrettably, they seemed incapable of considering seriously how a committed realists' emphasis on the ordinary might be viewed as a Sisyphean struggle to re-enchant the disenchanted in a historical context like modernity that is so hostile to enchantment.

Realistically Rendering the Unreal

How do we reconcile this tension between (1) a celebration of the real as worthy of artistic and imaginative investigation and (2) a denigration of the real as unworthy material for art? For the *Weird Tales* Three, and emphatically so for Howard, this tension is resolved through his contradictory efforts to "realistically render the unreal." Howard explores this contradictory idea in a September 1930 letter to Lovecraft by way of clumsily critiquing certain supernatural horror stories:

> The fault I find with so many so-called horror-tales (particularly including my own) is that the object of horror too swiftly becomes too solid and concrete. It takes a master of the pen, such as Machen and yourself, to create a proper SUGGESTION of the unseen and unknown horror. [...] When a writer specifically describes the object of his horror, gives worldly dimensions and solid shape, he robs it of half its terrors [*Freedom* 50].

The realistic rendering of the unreal Howard appropriately struggles to describe to Lovecraft can be paraphrased as a writer's sincere attempt to describe something that gives an aesthetic effect through the process of its failure. In other words, the realistic rendering of the unreal is when a writer makes the failure of signification bear an aesthetic charge. The very strategy of "realism," in this context, is made strange and defamiliarized.

Staging the Failure of Literary Realism

The conventionalism of literary realism, the way it is deployed as a narrative strategy by writers and interpreted routinely by readers, becomes a condition of aesthetic potential for the *Weird Tales* Three, and specifically for Lovecraft. In addition to his uncharacteristic defense of modernism, it is in that same December 1932 letter to Howard quoted above that Lovecraft outlines the faults of those whom he terms the "superficial writers": these writers "reproduce conventional situations" and evoke "facile emotions" with "tricks of glamour" that are "thoughtlessly repeated" in adherence to "convention" (*Freedom* 532). Put simply: non-exceptional pulp writers are critiqued because they take the technique of realism for granted and fail to aesthetically trouble it. The literary effect of reality they produce is produced naively, is marred by a representation of the ordinary as ordinary. Although he does not specifically speak of technique, Lovecraft faults Zane Grey and other conventional writers like him because of their conservatism in literary technique. And Lovecraft, troubled by a sense of his own artistic inferiority linked to his cultural marginalization, does not leave his own work out of this harangue:

> As for my own junk—let me warn you that it does not merit classification as literature at all. I try to keep it above the pulp-magazine average—but it is not even within striking distance of the solid and permanent merit represented by Poe, Machen, Blackwood, Dunsany, James, and de la Mare [*Freedom* 533].

But Lovecraft did not rely on conventionalized and unconvincing literary realism to a fault. Instead, Lovecraft tests the limits of this technique and so, at least in the virtual worlds of his stories, allows his readers to test the limits of consensus (conventional) reality. For example, "The Colour Out of Space" is one pulp ekphrastic work that vividly demonstrates the results of Lovecraft's experimental combination of conventional literary realism with the logic of abstract aesthetics of modernism. It is the story of a color falling into a farm, and, because of this color, the farm disintegrates over time, literally dissolves into slime.

This tale of the reality of a farm disintegrating over time allegorizes Lovecraft and the *Weird Tales* Three's assault on conventionalized literary realism, the way they incorporate the non-representational aesthetics of modernism into modernism in order to create an irresolvable tension that produces a descent into formlessness.

Testing Realism in Post Oaks and Sand Roughs

In their long correspondence, Lovecraft often assumes Howard has no concern for literary technique, and he was mistaken when he did so. The technical problem of representing reality in literary language was one Howard focused on specifically, although the works where this focus is most clear were not viable for pulp marketplaces. In fact, Howard wrote an entire novel in which he experimented with the form of the novel to see how far he could represent ordinary reality. While struggling in the early 1920s to secure regular pulp magazine markets for his sensational mid-fiction of barbarians fighting sorcerers, Howard composed an experimental novel titled *Post Oaks and Sand Roughs*, which his autobiographically-inspired protagonist describes as "a realistic account of the drabness, and sham of small town life, the futile and abortive gropings of humanity" that

7. Robert E. Howard and Rendering the Real and the Unreal

has "no plot, no sequence, no moral" (*Post* 141; 110). Howard never attempted to sell this experimental novel or to publish it in his lifetime, and it appeared for the first time in 1990. For Howard, *Post Oaks and Sand Roughs* was strictly a technical experiment. Significantly, Howard considered the novel a failure.

Post Oaks is interesting for the degree to which it showcases a famous pulp writer of fantasy, science fiction, and supernatural horror dealing directly with the technical problem of representing reality with literary form, representing the ordinary, with only the technique of conventionalized realism at hand. Howard's formalization of the ordinary takes the shape of a virtual space hostile to human beings due to its terrible propensity to recede before the sensorium, to reject the perceiving touch of the sensorium. As a writer popularly known for his weird and fantastic tales of "sword and sorcery," this unpublished novel's sustained meditation on the inability of literary language to convey reality is a consistent yet logical coextension of the pulp ekphrastic enterprise of the *Weird Tales* Three. Where the *Weird Tales* Three typically establish a solid literary effect of reality and then stage its technical horizon, i.e., stage de-reification by dramatizing confrontations with abstract forms, *Post Oaks and Sand Roughs* questions the possibility of representing ordinary reality at all.

In this novel, the ordinary is fictionalized as a hostile space because it rejects the mental touch of the protagonist's sensorium. It is dangerous for the protagonist to find himself in the space of the ordinary because being in this space depresses experience, drains it of value. Consider a vivid demonstration of how the ordinary is fictionalized in this memoir.

Some context: the protagonist, Steve Costigan has secured employment as the aide to a geological researcher. His job is to hold a rod while the geologist picks up rocks in the desert. Consider the narrator's description of this job:

> There was no breeze, and the sun, glancing from the bare rocks of either side made the basin a veritable hell. A strip of mesquite flaps shimmered near him; beyond lay a plowed field. Crossing the mesquite flat, Steve was almost overcome by thirst and heat [...]. As he emerged from the stunted mesquites, he saw a small, warped, unpainted house and directed his steps in that direction to ask for a drink of water. As he approached he saw two women shelling beans on the porch and several small children crawling about the yard, bare-headed and nearly naked of body seeming as impervious to the terrible heat as the green lizards sunning on the rock fences. Steve wondered at this [*Post* 44–45].

Here the desert refuses Costigan because he is not adapted to its ecological demands. This is so because his perception of the desert is formalized in negative terms. The literary images that constitute the description are not entities as such but bring into focus rather negative traces that only partially refer to—that only begin to outline—the existence of things. There is "no breeze," the rocks are "bare" (44–45). The bright sunlight "glanc[es] from the bare rocks" and the "mesquite flaps shimmer." There is a field that is "plowed," but it is yet to be sown with seed. There is an "unpainted" house. The children are "naked." The paint and clothing are missing. The cool breeze is missing. The moss and grass on the rocks are missing. Furthermore, the field is distorted by glancing light. The world recedes before the sensorium of Costigan, who tries to grip phenomena with his sensorium but cannot.

The Receding Ordinary in Post Oaks and Sand Roughs

As this example demonstrates, in the ordinary world of *Post Oaks and Sand Roughs*, ordinary phenomena disrupt perception by receding before the sensorium; thus, strictly speaking, Costigan never becomes conscious of the desert. Further, ordinary phenomena yield to perception in such a way that the illusion is given that sensation happens. Costigan appears to see things. But close inspection of the passage reveals that he sees nothing. That is what makes the ordinary so strange in this novel: Costigan appears to see it, but it is actually invisible. The narrator describes Costigan's encounter with the women and children of the unpainted house in terms of an experience that has not been consummated, a vivid demonstration of what must be cumbersomely referred to as the "visible invisibility" of ordinary phenomena: "The children halted in their prattle to stare at him, silent and roundeyed. The women continued their work, gazing at him with no gleam of interest. He was nothing in their lives" (45).

Written using the technique of conventionalized realism and executed by Howard to consider specifically the technical problem of representing the ordinary world of rural Texas, a gloss of the writing might result in it being designated a text valuable only to the "extensive" eye of the antiquarian rather than a literary scholar. But "intensive" scrutiny of the style reveals it to be deliberately banal, a deliberate troubling of a conventional literary realist technique. In short, *Post Oaks and Sand Roughs* formalizes the failure of realism, the establishment of the literary effect of reality by executing a troubled realist technique. It constructs an uninteresting world with representational strokes not intended to bring into focus details or achieve a convincing rendering of reality but instead intended to test the limits of that technique through formally instantiating an aesthetic lack of commitment to detail.

This is not minimalism in the manner of Ernest Hemingway or Raymond Carver, which isolates the essential elements of a narrative and skillfully curtails supplemental detail in order to intensify form and theme. It is instead a deliberate attempt to formalize scene, character, and action in a marked negative register to thereby hold out for contemplation formlessness as such, the failure of the literary effect of reality, and the ephemerality of the ordinary. The oppressive barrenness that surrounds Costigan is echoed elsewhere in the novel in a description of "Lost Plains," the fictionalized version of Howard's own hometown, Cross Plains, Texas: "He glanced at Lost Plains, the long, dusty main street, the huddle of small, drab brick buildings and the rambling frame structures all dozing like hags in the sun" (*Post* 60). He goes on to describe his alienation from this community: "He twitched his shoulders. Here he had no friends. He was a jest, an eccentric" (*Post* 60). Like the desert homestead idly lingering uninterestingly in the middle of the desert beneath a harsh sun, Lost Plains is drab, dusty, nondescript, and equally hostile to Costigan.

The Unreal Ordinary of Lost Plains

In juxtaposing the barren desert with the community of Lost Plains, the character of Steve Costigan becomes an occasion for the author to link a theme with his technical challenge of representing reality: the inability to connect with reality (theme) combined with the inability of the author to represent it in literary form (technique), i.e., as a phenomena that can be gripped by the virtual sensorium of the protagonist parallels the physical and social alienation that defines the desert and Lost Plains. Costigan's physical pain—his heart palpitations, his thirst, his dizziness—anticipates his emotional pain derived from his alienated situation in town. Costigan's inability to perceive the ordinary, to grip it with his sensorium (i.e., the inability of the writer, Robert E. Howard, to represent ordinary reality with substance) echoes the detachment he feels from his community that derives from his anxiety about his profession as a writer. Unlike the women shelling beans on the porch or the children playing in the mud, both of whom are portrayed as being adapted to the dryness and the heat of the desert, Costigan is portrayed as an ecological outsider, an alien entity. He is equally a social outsider in Lost Plains, a point which is drawn starkly in the author's description of Costigan's job as a pharmacy soda jerk: "All day he would dash back and forth behind the fountain, which he had grown to hate, serving drinks and waiting on customers [...]. At night he staggered home to fall into his bed and sleep the sodden sleep of utter exhaustion. He went to bed fatigued and awoke fatigued" (95).

His attempt to engage in his community's economy and work life here fails on two levels. It results in the disintegration of Costigan's body and the discouragement of his spirit. Recalling the description of the desert cited above, Costigan's work at the soda fountain is equally nondescript. The author does not begin by relating the nature of the work. He chooses, instead, to describe it negatively, in terms of what it pushes out of Costigan's life, namely, the activities related to his intellectual pursuit as a writer. As the description unfolds, as the narrator turns to the details of laboring at the pharmacy, Costigan's work as a soda jerk is sketched, only faintly outlined: he "dashes back and forth behind the fountain" (95). He does "many things he was not paid to do" (95). Although the author does not dwell on the concrete details of Costigan's work, which, like the barren desert, is somewhat invisible in terms of literary rendering, the author nevertheless depicts the effects of the ordinary work on Costigan: like the intolerable desert and the indifferent dwellers in the barren homestead, his employment as a soda jerk confirms, both physically and spiritually, how unfit to the ordinary he actually is.

7. *Robert E. Howard and Rendering the Real and the Unreal*

Nourishing Violence in Post Oaks and Sand Roughs

For Howard, the failure of *Post Oaks* taught him that he could not execute a literary effect of reality vital enough to authentically represent his ordinary. His representation of the ordinary as hostile space thus expresses a technical and thematic thesis, an artistic acknowledgment of limits. Moreover, Costigan's failed attempts to occupy and perceive the ordinary thematizes this technical problem. The author imagines the ordinary as an indescribable, invisible space that threatens Costigan both physically and spiritually. But he contrasts this space with an alternative one, one that cannot be described as ordinary at all: an extraordinary arena defined by nourishing violence.

Focusing on how Howard represents this extraordinary space in *Post Oaks* begins to explain the writer's prevalent use of fictional acts of violence in his pulp ekphrastic works of sword and sorcery. Aestheticized violence is an essential part of Howard's contribution to the pulp ekphrastic enterprise of the *Weird Tales* Three. More than a mere plot device, Howard's aestheticized violence is part of his mode of literary representation. For Howard, violence is part of establishing a successful and enduring literary effect of reality.

The extraordinary space that appears in *Post Oaks* is the back hall of a large icehouse where Costigan retreats from the ordinary at night to engage in the transgressive activities of drinking beer and participating in prizefights with oilfield workers. Consider the author's description of the icehouse: "Steve came into the ice plant one night when a strange excess of nervous energy fired him and kept him moving in spite of the fact he had toiled all day with no food since breakfast, and should have been terrifically weary" (102). Costigan is hypnotically drawn to the icehouse at the fringes of the Lost Plains community. His attraction to this place seems to be in response to his need for spiritual as well as physical nourishment. He quickly begins participating in the fights held there. Consider a description of one of these prize fights, and particularly focus on the extent to which the invisible quality of the author's description of Costigan's work and experience in the desert contrasts here with the deliberate perceptual intensity. Here violence helps the writer solve the technical challenge of establishing a literary effect of reality:

> Yells merged crazily, and the entire building seemed to sway and whirl like a dervish. Steve's lips were cut deeply and his mouth was full of blood. His brain was dazed, and still Bill's gloves crashed against his head and jaw. An instant's clarity—as through a mist he saw the frenzied yelling faces, Bill crouched like a jungle beast before him, motionless for a brief instant as he gathered himself for one terrific blow [...]. Steve reeled, the blood gushing from his mouth to mingle with the sweat on his chest. And in the fleeting instant before the fighting commenced again, Steven knew life, fierce, red, and vibrant. God, this was his element! To fight, to kill, or to be killed, here in this hell-hot, smoke-laden atmosphere with a gang of roughnecks screaming oaths and obscenities and shouting for his slaughter [104].

Unlike the silent, windless desert that rejects the touch of his sensorium, the icehouse room is represented by phenomena with vivid qualities that rush and overwhelm. It is pervaded by sound, movement, color, and emotion. The building "whirl[s] like a dervish" and "yells merge crazily" (104). Furthermore, the people who are in this space focus on Costigan. Unlike the people in the desert and the community of Lost Plains—who are indifferent to Costigan—the roughnecks and fighters cannot see anything but the youth: they shout for his slaughter as Bill lands blow after blow. Struggling through the barren desert and laboring behind the soda fountain both harm Costigan on a spiritual and physical level, and like these two experiences, participating in the prize fight does indeed seem to result in at least physical harm. However, the physical violence fictionalized here is distinct from any actual violence that you or I might experience. Here is a healing type of violence that is not constructed by the author as painful and diminishing but as nourishing, as contributing to the literary effect of reality: it is physically invigorating and spiritually renewing while, at the same time, it occasions the establishment of the literary effect of reality. Consider the description of Costigan's feelings and reflections after the fight is over:

> Steve felt jubilant in a strange manner. His mind was clear now, and the blood raced through his veins. He felt no bad aftereffects from his terrific battle and decided that his heart was as sound as ever. No weak heart could have withstood the strain. He sighed deeply and with relish and glanced up at the stars which seemed somehow less cold, more friendly. He laughed [106].

Howard's more widely-known pulp ekphrastic sword and sorceries, framed as fantasies, are in fact concerned with the dynamics of the literary effect of reality in their central essence, with rendering the unreal realistically. Moreover, the pulp ekphrastic fantasies of the *Weird Tales* Three are concerned with literary renderings of the unreality of reality, of being artistically true to the radical agnosticism expressed transparently by Smith in a September 1933 letter to August Derleth: "One who keeps an open mind and is willing to admit that all things are possible, but accepts either the dogmatism of material science nor the revealed religious or system of theosophy" (CAS Selected Letters 221). Put another way, the *Weird Tales* Three's literary artistic enterprise is neither ideologically nor artistically partisan to representing the real or the unreal but something different and difficult to describe, a breathless acknowledgment that the real is beyond description.

Strangeness Like a Blow to the Face

Post Oaks taught Howard that to use conventional realism to formalize ordinary experience precludes the establishment of the literary effect of reality. Realism, for Howard, can only be used to formalize extraordinary realities, and in the rural barrenness of Cross Plains—the context that would provide material for treatment in fiction—extraordinariness seemed to have been difficult for Howard to discover. His insight, brought to him through a sincere struggle with literary realist technique and its limits, is one shared with Lovecraft and Smith: Merely ordinary experience cannot be rendered authentically because such realities, from their perspective, are mere effects of a temporary domestication of a more profound and ascendant strangeness. In other words, ordinary experience is too strange and requires extraordinary literary techniques.

Select passages in this novel are also important to the extent that they show Howard learning how to use violence to establish the literary effect of reality. The lesson Howard learned regarding the technical affordance of aestheticized violence can be seen in a Conan story published in *Weird Tales*, March of 1933, titled "The Tower of the Elephant." The opening of this story demonstrates how violence came to be part of Howard's representational technique, his shadow modernism, his hybrid technique of (1) establishing the literary effect of reality and then (2) violating it. In the final sentence of this opening Howard has adapted fictional violence to his representational technique:

> Along the crooked, unpaved streets with their heaps of refuse and sloppy puddles, drunken roisterers staggered, roaring. Steel glinted in the shadows where wolf preyed on wolf, and from the darkness rose the shrill laughter of women, and the sounds of scufflings and strugglings. Torchlight licked luridly from broken windows and wide-thrown doors, and out of those doors, stale smells of wine and rank sweaty bodies, clamor of drinking-jacks and fists hammered on rough tables, snatches of obscene songs, *rushed like a blow in the face* ["Tower" 59, my emphasis].

Kull as Violent Critic

Howard's Conan the Cimmerian stories are his most widely known contributions to *Weird Tales*. These stories participate in the pulp ekphrastic enterprise of the *Weird Tales* Three and are technical exercises for establishing and then dramatically violating the literary effect of reality.

Howard's Conan the Cimmerian stories have an interesting artistic genealogy that, properly traced, clearly reveals that these apparent pulp fantasies are actually technically self-aware works with a surprising concern for realism in the spirit of historical fiction. Before Howard created the character of Conan the Cimmerian, he first authored stories of another, lesser-known barbarian, King Kull. Like many of the manuscripts he sent to *Weird Tales* that were rejected by Farnsworth Wright, Howard excused their failure to sell by considering them "experiments," which they were.

In the Kull story "experiments" we can glimpse an early yet inchoate element of the pulp ekphrasis that emerges in the work the *Weird Tales* Three. In Howard's Kull stories, shadow modernist works are fictionalized as enduring forms of dangerous art and monsters. Kull's engagement with shadow modernism is unique in that, allegorically speaking, it represents a violent form of criticism: the monster of art is generally attacked, defeated, and then forced into yielding up fragments of cosmic knowledge, i.e., the ephemerality of the ordinary. Put simply, Kull violates art and plunders the secrets it contains. His violence is a critical, interpretive gesture.

Howard's Kull stories are experiments because, except for "The Shadow Kingdom" (*Weird Tales*: August 1929), "The Mirrors of Tuzun Thume" (*Weird Tales*: September 1929), and "Kings of the Night" (*Weird Tales*: November 1930), none of the rest of the Kull manuscripts sold to professional marketplaces, and many of them were left unfinished (though they were posthumously anthologized and even "finished" by other enthusiastic fantasy and science fiction writers in the 1960s). Commentators have observed how Kull is the literary progenitor to Howard's most commercially successful and most popularly recognizable character, Conan the Cimmerian. The idea that Kull was a sort of embryonic Conan is confirmed when we consider that the first Conan the Cimmerian story, "The Phoenix in the Sword"—published in *Weird Tales* in December of 1932—was a rewriting of the last Kull manuscript, a story titled "By This Axe I Rule" (which *Weird Tales* rejected).

This transformation of the final Kull story into the first Conan the Cimmerian story, and its subsequent acceptance by Wright at *Weird Tales*, implies an important point: the unconventional Kull was conventionalized, to an extent, and so became Conan the Cimmerian. Relative to the vast pulp fiction market that *Weird Tales* was but a minor part of, the Conan the Cimmerian stories delivered on the promise made by the magazine's title: the journeys of Conan the Barbarian were, indeed, weird to the average reader; however, relative to the fiction published in the magazine, the character of Conan the Cimmerian was comparatively conventional: a warrior travels into strange and shadowy tombs and fights animated art objects.

Kull, however, seems to have been too weird for the magazine's editor and readers. Seen in the correct light, the character of Kull, though he became Conan, after a fashion, was quite different, even radically different, than the character he would become. It is not overstatement to say that Kull is a non-normative, anti-social figure: he is a racially indeterminate, apparently asexual, sedentary, paranoid, and cynical rather than curious. He is future-negating and at violent odds with the political and social order he ostensibly rules. This is not a typical male pulp protagonist. We can see in the Kull character and the journeys he undertakes Howard the experimentalist, deviating from pulp formulas and testing new artistic possibilities (and consequently suffering the economic consequence of a rejected manuscript).

Kull and Demonic Art

Howard's primary narrative form in the Kull stories is adventure. Though the plot devices change in each story, a general adventure narrative pattern does come into focus as Howard recursively hones the pulp ekphrasis delivered by the Kull stories. In the Kull stories, Kull is generally forced to go on a journey and confronts an art object or monster that is supernatural. Hazards and trials tend to emanate from the art object. Eventually, the art object is either destroyed or yields an insight depicted as a totalizing perspective in the form of a fragmentary map of the cosmos. The truth Kull learns is always as awesome as it is simple, another paraphrase of the ephemerality of the ordinary: material existence is essentially ephemeral, and ephemerality is actually endurance, a thesis captured succinctly by the speech offered to a dying Kull by a shadow creature which exists out of time in the published fragment, "The Striking of the Gong":

> There are worlds beyond worlds, universes within and without universes [...]. Your barbarian brain clutches at material actualities [...]. You are part of that great ocean which is Life, which washes upon all shores, and you are as much part of it in one place as in another, and as sure to flow back to the Source of it, which gave birth to all Life. As for that, you are bound to Life for all Eternity as surely as a tree, a rock, a bird or a world is bound [130].

In the Kull experiments, the monster of art is typically violently destroyed, its power diminished; however, as Howard masters the formula of the Kull stories, his theme comes into focus, and the art object becomes, predominantly, a source of wisdom, although the wisdom it offers is always the same doctrine. To begin to make a case for these claims, consider one of the earliest Kull story experiments closely, "The Screaming Skull of Silence," which relates the outcome of Kull's search for a mythical castle and his struggle with a demon who is imprisoned within it.

7. Robert E. Howard and Rendering the Real and the Unreal

The Screaming Skull of Silence

In seeking out a mythical castle, we can glimpse the emergence of an important macro-narrative pattern coming into focus that structures many of the pulp ekphrastic works of the *Weird Tales* Three, such as Lovecraft's "Call of Cthulhu": a protagonist, inspired by a fragmentary work of art, confronts and explores an architectural art object or grotto—a temple, a tower, a castle, a house, a tomb. This architectural art object is generally figured as living or animate. The architecture then interactively responds to the explorations of the protagonist, and thereby yields up its secret contents: a series of artistic spectacles and eventually a monstrous work of art. This is the labyrinth of secrets, the maze, the dungeon, that yields aesthetic objects and reacts to the explorer as a subject with agency. The many architectural art objects explored by protagonists of the pulp ekphrastic works of the *Weird Tales* stories can be seen as allegories for quasi-art museums. In a significant number of the *Weird Tales* stories I study, to be inspired by art to visit a castle, to plunder a tomb, to enter a deserted city, to burglarize a temple, is also to visit an art museum and to engage in ekphrasis, and so uncover a horrible secret.

In this story, Kull the King is told a myth by a courtier that concerns a strange castle, "The Skull of Silence," where the necromancer Raama imprisoned a demon of silence. Kull, motivated by boredom and driven by arrogance to prove his worth, desires to seek out "The Skull of Silence" to confirm the myth's truth. Here Kull engages in a kind of literary criticism similar to that engaged in by Morand in Clark Ashton Smith's "The End of the Story." Stirred by the myth, Kull decides to enter into it, to seek out material referents of the story in spite of the qualification offered by his courtier: "All is illusion [...] all outward manifestations of the underlying Reality, which is beyond human comprehension, since there are no relative things by which the finite mind may measure the infinite. The One may underlie all, or each natural illusion may possess a basic entity. All these things were known to Raama, the greatest mind of all ages [...]" (119). He interrupts the courtier's speech this way: "'Enough.' Kull gestured impatiently. 'Raama has been dead so many thousands years that it wearies me to think on it. I ride to find the Skull of Silence; who rides with me?" (119).

Kull eventually discovers that castle and thereby confirms the reality of the myth. Importantly, the castle is described in terms of a monster: "They halted before the castle that crouched there like a dark monster [...]" (121). When Kull approaches the main portal of the castle, he discovers a strange art object, a gong of an indeterminate and perpetually shifting color: "But Kull could not be sure of the color for to his amazed stare it changed and shifted, and sometimes his gaze seemed to be drawn into great depths and sometimes to glance extreme shallowness" (123). Kull strikes the gong and thereby releases the demon, the "soul of all silence" (122). The strange monster is described in vague and obscure terms, as a sense-experience, a kind of negative music:

> Silence spreading out over the earth, over the Universe! Men died in gibbering stillness; the roar of rivers, the crash of seas, the noise of winds faltered and ceased to be. All Sound was drowned by the Silence. Silence, soul destroying, brain shattering—blotting out all life on earth and reaching monstrously up into the skies, crushing the very singing of the stars! [123]

Realizing, to his horror, that he has released the demon of silence upon the world, Kull thinks quickly and seizes the nearest weapon at hand: the mallet and the gong he used to release the demon from its prison. Kull begins to beat the gong and quickly realizes it is sound that hurts the demon of silence. In a cosmic "battle of the bands," he fights the demon with the percussion emanating from the gong:

> Back and back and back—and back. Now the wisps hovered in the doorway and behind Kull men whimpered and wallowed to their knees, chins sagging and eyes vacant. Kull tore the gong from its frame and reeled toward the door [...]. The whole Universe should have halted to watch a man justifying the existence of man-kind, scaling sublime heights of glory in his supreme atonement [124].

Kull continues to strike the gong and drive back the demon of silence. Eventually, he drives the demon deeper into the castle. Kull's moment of triumph is worth citing at length for its strangeness, for the unique way it formally negotiates the sense-based contradictions that tend to structure Howard's portrayals of the supernatural. Here the literary effect of reality is violated explicitly because Howard attributes action to a quality: "Now the Silence writhed in a dark corner and shrunk and shrunk. Again, a last blow! All the sound in the Universe rushed together in one roaring, yelling, shattering, engulfing burst of sound! The gong blew into a million vibrating fragments! And Silence screamed!" (125). Inspired by a myth, having jour-

7. Robert E. Howard and Rendering the Real and the Unreal

neyed to an art museum-grotto, King Kull confronts a kind of negative music, a demon of silence. Despite the struggle, Kull does succeed by force of will to preserve the ordinary, although it comes close to dissolving. Consider the moment when Kull initially confronts the demon of silence: "The silence entered Kull's soul; it clawed at his heart; it sent tentacles of steel into his brain. He clutched at his forehead in torment; his skull was bursting, shattering" (122). Despite the threat of the demon, however, Kull survives the battle. The ordinary world survives, is protected from universal strangeness, by "a man justifying the existence of man-kind" (124).

8. Cthulhu Is Beautiful

Modernism and the Science of Art

In his 1948 essay examining modern novels, "Technique as Discovery," Mark Schorer, a literary scholar and *Weird Tales* contributor, distinguishes these works by their awareness of the importance of technique over subject matter. In this essay, Schorer celebrates the novels of canonical modernists like James Joyce, Ernest Hemingway, and Virginia Woolf and equally censures contemporary novelists such as H.G. Wells and James Farrell, of whose writing he complains, "His prose is asked to perform no service beyond communication of the most rudimentary kind of fact" (82). For Schorer, and for many American critics coming to celebrate the literary experiments of modernism in academic contexts in the 1940s, what distinguishes the modernist novel is how it expresses a preeminence of technique, a technique that supplemented, renewed, estranged, and grew out of the subject matter centering the narrative.

Schorer concludes his essay with a prescription for novelists of the future derived from surveying the modernist novels of previous decades: "What we need in fiction is a devoted fidelity to every technique which will help us to discover and to evaluate our subject matter, and more than that, to discover the amplifications of meaning of which our subject matter is capable" (83). The important term here is "discover."

For many critics like Schorer, a key component of understanding the formal novelty of modernism is acknowledging not only its formal difficulty but also its unique rhetoric and technique as a form of knowledge creation, i.e., its "research" quality or epistemic nature. The many dis-

8. Cthulhu Is Beautiful

courses around literary and other aesthetic techniques perpetuated in the little magazine culture that generated modernism should not be understood as the product of a single genius who propitiously came upon a unique method. Rather, they should be understood as a specialized, professional, almost collaborative discourse requiring the labors of both innovating artists and knowledgeable critics. From a traditional perspective, the typical modernist artist seems anti-social, like a host, as figured by Malcolm Cowley, being deliberately rude to his guests (i.e., readers); but from the perspective of the magazine archive, what could the many pages devoted to manifestos, critical exegeses, and criticism signify, if not a desire to build knowledge, even scientific knowledge collaboratively? Was modernist literature a collaborative enterprise? Schorer thinks so.

The idea that young Anglo-American artists of the first three decades of the twentieth century were able to experiment with aesthetic form because of the concurrent emergence of a receptive, even scientific criticism is not a difficult hypothesis to test, but to do so rigorously would require the methods of historiography. One can imagine a survey of the little magazine archive specifically devoted to quantifying the percentage of writing devoted not to making public the new artistic experiments but to interpreting them. The task of accumulating and analyzing such quantitative data becomes more possible with the development of digital software for these kinds of tasks, but the absence of such data in the past has rarely stopped literary critics from making strong claims. It will not stop me here from making at least a weak one: we might glimpse this scientific dimension of the enterprise of modernism by treating two salient texts: (1) a vision of modern criticism and (2) a vision of modernist artistic production offered by two key figures of the movement, H.L. Mencken and T.S. Eliot.

Considering Schorer, we must ask: was modernism a collaborative, quasi-scientific enterprise aimed at producing knowledge?

The Artistic Catalysis of Eliot and Mencken

In a 1919 essay titled "The Criticism of Criticism of Criticism," H.L. Mencken deploys a scientific metaphor to explain the role of the art critic:

"A catalyzer, in chemistry, is a substance that helps two other substances to react. For example, consider the case of ordinary cane sugar and water. Dissolve the sugar in the water and nothing happens. But add a few drops of acid and the sugar changes into glucose and fructose. Meanwhile, the acid itself is absolutely unchanged" (9). He explains his metaphor in this way: "This is almost exactly the function of the genuine critic of the arts. It is his business to provoke the reaction between the work of art and the spectator" (9–10). Looking at the logic of this metaphor reveals that, for Mencken, the function of critical-catalysis is to unweave the work of art, conceived here as a quantity of dissolved sugar. The art critic functions as a disassembler, breaks down the work of art into its base elements.

Mencken's essay resembles T.S. Eliot's famous scientific metaphor in his "Tradition and the Individual Talent," also published in 1919, in which he considers not the critic but the artist-poet as a chemical catalyst, a shred of pure platinum, and the art object as a combination of oxygen and sulfur dioxide. Eliot writes, "The combination takes place only if the platinum is present; nevertheless the newly formed acid contains no trace of platinum, and the platinum itself is apparently unaffected; has remained inert, neutral, and unchanged" (94).

Although both critic and artist are conceived here as chemical catalysts, they function in that capacity in distinct ways. For Eliot, the artist-catalyst combines elements; for Mencken, the critic-catalyst takes these bound elements apart. And yet, in spite of the inverse ways they function as catalysts, both are unaffected by the chemical reaction they bring about. For Mencken, "the acid itself is absolutely unchanged" (10). For Eliot, the shred of platinum "is [...] unaffected; has remained inert, neutral, and unchanged" (94).

These complementary texts add up to a compelling vision of modernism as a scientific enterprise from which participants keep detached as objective agents. Through the lens these essays provide, modernism appears as a collaborative enterprise between emotionally-detached artists and critics working together on a project that seems, on the level of emotional valance, scientific in tone. Indeed, the artist-catalyst and critic-catalyst appear more like scientists committed to art as to empirical research, engaged in what Schorer calls a process of "technique as discovery" to engineer what Viktor Shklovsky terms the "device" of art, a device that functions to renew experience, to estrange it like a sensorium-enhancing prosthesis. And like scientists committed to an objective knowledge above all, Eliot's and Mencken's descriptions imply a cabal of modernist researchers—critics and artists—anxious about contaminating their project by becoming too emotionally invested.

The Modernist Enterprise and the Production of Knowledge

Such a comparison to science is a widespread motif in canonical accounts of modernism published in 1930s, when modernism was being critically consolidated, as when Edmund Wilson writes in 1931, "There is something akin to the scientific instinct in the efforts of modern literature" (295). However, when we fully register that this widespread rhetoric of modernist art's resemblance to scientific endeavor was perpetuated by artists and philosophers ill-equipped to take fully into account the actual complexity of science, let alone to compare it to art, it becomes less persuasive. As a non-scientist, one may talk at length about chemical catalysis; but as a literary critic, the most one can say with confidence is that science is concerned with creating empirically verifiable knowledge of the physical world. Is this correct? If this is the case, what is the artistic analog?

If we take the vision of modernism as a kind of science of art seriously, is it productive to ask what kind of knowledge it seeks to create? What is the body of knowledge that modernism as a science is contributing to?

This is where Mencken's and Eliot's metaphors, exposed as ideology, stop being useful, and where we need to turn elsewhere for an answer or at least a shadowy outline of an answer. And we can find a fresh perspective of the "scientism" of modernism in the unlikeliest of places, particularly in the pulp ekphrastic works of the *Weird Tales* Three.

Gazing at modernism through the lens of their pulp ekphrasist works, we see that Howard, Smith, and Lovecraft saw, apprehended, and theorized the scientism of shadow modernism clearly in a way similar to Wilson, Mencken, and Schorer. Unlike them, however, these pulp writers would be able to theorize the knowledge produced by the science of modernist art not by discussing actual but virtual modernism, a sensationalized and strategically distorted shadow of it. Like Benjamin's mysticism, the *Weird Tales* Three's fictional modernism was oblique and speculative, a strategic distortion of modernism, but nevertheless revealing in its assessment about its capacity for producing knowledge about the secret nature of modern history.

Is it any surprise that a community deriving from a publication like *Weird Tales* animated by the artistic ambitions of Lovecraft produced an audacious personality like William Lumley, a one-time contributor to *Weird Tales*? Lumley could go further in sensational belief than the *Weird Tales* Three, Eliot, Wilson, and Schorer in viewing modern artistic activity as a strange science, as an enterprise capable of producing empirically verifiable knowledge: "We may think we're writing fiction, and may even (absurd thought) disbelieve what we write, but at bottom we are telling the truth in spite of ourselves" (*Lovecraft Encyclopedia* 159).

Lumley's overstatement aside, the idea of artistic practice as a collaborative and scientific enterprise, a knowledge-creating or epistemological undertaking, like scientific research, figures prominently in the pulp ekphrastic works of the *Weird Tales* Three, and emphatically so in the work of H.P. Lovecraft

H.P. Lovecraft and the Occult Knowledge of Art

The idea of art as a search for occult knowledge is explored by Lovecraft early in his writing career in works published in the amateur publications that pre-dated *Weird Tales,* and later in his career, alongside *Weird Tales* publications, in the fan magazines produced by fans of *Weird Tales*. For Lovecraft, artistic enterprise is a form of knowledge seeking, and the strange knowledge art produces is delivered to the inquiring person through emotional rather than intellectual understanding. An affect like horror or wonder or dread is not, for Lovecraft and the *Weird Tales* Three, a neutral tingling of the nerves but is rather a signal, a fragment of a larger symptom to be interpreted as significant. Thus, the shadow modernist art

8. Cthulhu Is Beautiful

objects created through this enterprise are somatic technologies, prostheses, for apprehending the ephemerality of the ordinary. In this way, the prime symbol of the artistic object for Lovecraft and the *Weird Tales* Three is the unconventional book that stirs the body, the non-mimetic or para-mimetic sculpture that incites dread, and that reminds the person who reads it (or looks upon it) that his or her ordinary reality is an ephemeral domestication of universal strangeness. These symbols coalesce into the image of the key or book of occult lore, a series of metaphors Lovecraft draws on in his sonnet series, *The Fungi from Yuggoth*.

This theme of shadow modernist art objects as tools that stir the body and thereby deliver occult knowledge about the ordinary is one of Lovecraft's central themes, one that the writer dwells upon and hones throughout his productive years—one that he returns to over and over in an attempt to master it, to polish and sharpen the symbols needed to express his vision not of a fantasy world per se but of the ephemerality of ordinary reality.

Lovecraft's description of the artist's mission in an essay defending the writing of weird fiction published in the amateur press associations demonstrates his partisan commitment not to fantasy but to art-as-fantasy:

> The imaginative writer devotes himself to art in its most essential sense [...]. He is the painter of moods and mind-pictures—a capturer and amplifier of elusive dreams and fancies—a voyager into those unheard-of lands which are glimpsed through the veil of actuality but rarely, and only by the most sensitive [...]. Most persons do not understand what he says, and most of those who do understand object because his statements and pictures are not always pleasant and sometimes quite impossible ["In Defense of Dagon" 148].

Lovecraft understood his role as an "imaginative writer" to be a devotee of "art in its most essential sense," an enterprise he understood as a scientific search after strange knowledge that entailed voyaging into "unheard of lands" (148). In this way, his repeated fictionalizations of shadow modernist art, artists, and aesthetic experience as scientific investigations into the unknown nature of the ordinary reveals his resemblance to the very modernists he fictionalized, modernists who also understood art not as the subjective expression of deep feeling but as a collaborative pioneering of a technique designed to make experience strange, a strangeness domesticated by the bourgeoisie art they debunked.

"The Call of Cthulhu" and the Sublime

Few works in Lovecraft's corpus demonstrate more clearly the writer's penchant to fictionalize the formal technique and historical movement of modernism as a science for producing occult knowledge of the ordinary than "The Call of Cthulhu," published in *Weird Tales* in July of 1927. This story exemplifies the typical pulp ekphrasist narrative characteristic of the mature works of *Weird Tales* Three in that it combines both a conventional nineteenth-century realist technique with unreal objects that index and bear, as formal structures, the rhetoric of the aestheticism of modernism. Put another way, "The Call of Cthulhu," like many other pulp ekphrasist works of the *Weird Tales* Three, fictionalizes techniques of modernism and thereby represents them in a virtual world as so many unreal objects so that they can be examined through a series of narrative events. They often appear as a formless fragment of aesthetic production, a non-representational aesthetic object purged of all of its signifying, referential, or mimetic dimensions. In the case of "The Call of Cthulhu," this object is an almost unpronounceable jumble of letters: Cthulhu fhtagn.

"The Call of Cthulhu" is structured around the narrator Thurston's report of his recently-murdered uncle, George Gammell Angell's, papers on the "Cthulhu Cult." At the story's beginning, Thurston has already come to his conclusions and understands the horror they signify; however, he withholds his conclusion and takes the reader through his piecing together of the various texts and documents that add up to his conclusion. His first paragraph strikes the tenor of the sublime, a highly theorized aesthetic category that, according to classical accounts like Immanuel Kant's and Edmund Burke's, results from a confrontation with the boundlessness, lawlessness, and chaos of primordial nature:

> We live on a placid island of ignorance in the midst of black seas of infinity, and it was not meant that we should voyage far. The sciences, each straining in its own direction, have hitherto harmed us little; but some day the piecing together of dissociated knowledge will open up such terrifying vistas of reality, and of our frightful position therein, that we shall either go mad from the revelation or flee from the deadly light into the peace and safety of a new dark age [21–22].

"Terrifying vistas," "seas of infinity": these phrases suggest the sublime as it is generally understood. However, it is essential to recall that the sublime, as understood by thinkers like Kant and Burke and as defined by obscurity, vagueness, and indefiniteness, cannot be present here when figurative and metaphorical logic of "deadly light" is taken into consideration, as well as the extent to which the incapacities of the human mind, i.e., ignorance, is framed as mercy, as the canceling foil for such an experience.

In traditional contexts, the sublime is typically connected not to the known but the unknown. In the opening paragraph of "The Call of Cthulhu," in contrast, the source of horror and terror is that which is known, illuminated, and correlated, and so is an inverse of the sublime. For the *Weird Tales* Three, the science of shadow modernism is not terrifying to the extent that it reveals human ignorance, the untranscendable horizon of human knowledge. In their pulp ekphrastic works, Lovecraft's particularly, a kind of innocent naïveté conditions a state of safety and "at-homeness." The risk entailed in the scientific technique of shadow modernism and the shadow modernist devices it generates is that, in the virtual world of the stories, they do indeed produce knowledge and repudiate ignorance with a horrible truth about the dangerously ephemeral nature of the ordinary. Erich Zann's bizarre music, Philip Hastane's demonic musical instrument, the mysterious heart of Yag-Kosha, and many other bizarre aesthetic objects: the shadow modernist *objets d'art* reveal the horrible truth that the ordinary is a temporary domestication of an eternal, hostile, strangeness. Therefore, properly speaking, these objects do not render the effect of the sublime in the traditional sense. For many, the sublime emphasizes ignorance and mystery. The strangeness and distinctiveness of "The Call of Cthulhu" and other pulp ekphrastic works of the *Weird Tales* Three is that the language of the sublime is utilized to describe not ignorance but knowledge, a violent process of epiphany.

The Shadow Modernist Sculpture of Henry Wilcox

Lovecraft's "The Call of Cthulhu" demonstrates the pulp ekphrastic narrative pattern, the translation of actual modernist art into fictional shadow modernist art that produces a terrible epiphany; moreover, like many of the pulp ekphrastic works of the *Weird Tales* Three, it frames the artistic enterprise as a collaborative, scientific endeavor. Textually speaking, "The Call of Cthulhu" consists not only of the papers and notes that Thurston draws from but also two stories contained within them: (1) that of George Angell's encounter with a shadow modernist artist named Henry Wilcox who was suffering from strange nightmares and creating art based on those dreams; and (2) that of Angell's encounter with a police inspector named John Legrasse who was seeking out an antiquarian/archaeologist who could help him on a case by identifying a sculpture he had recovered from a murderous cult in Louisiana. Let us consider Angell's encounter with Henry Wilcox, the shadow modernist artist.

Lovecraft's Henry Wilcox of "The Call of Cthulhu" is a fictional (shadow) modernist artist whose work, unattached to previously established artistic traditions, is framed as a dangerous transgression, an artistic undertaking that conveys occult knowledge. Wilcox is introduced as an intensely innovative artist, a radical figure who has been expelled from the Providence Art Club because it was "anxious to preserve its conservatism" (358). The narrative of "The Call of Cthulhu" begins to unfold when Wilcox brings a "singular clay bas-relief" sculpture adorned with strange hieroglyphics to an archaeological expert (24). It is in this fictional exchange between Professor Angell, the archaeologist, and Henry Wilcox, the shadow modernist, that we can see that Lovecraft has fully sharpened his technique for ekphrastically fictionalizing modernist art, the modernist artist, and the relationship of the artist-in-general to human society and the cosmos at large. Wilcox's strange art sculpture is useful for demonstrating this.

Wilcox's shadow modernist sculpture is an enduring form to the extent that it holds in tension both antiquity and novelty. It is equally ancient as well as modern, deriving from the "just now" of the night before (it is described as of plaster "exceedingly damp and fresh") and yet manifesting dreams "older than brooding Tyre" (356). Wilcox also shows Angell a sculpture of a monster from his dream. The monster is described by the narrator as similar in spirit to an "an octopus, a dragon, and a human caricature" and registers as a version of the sublime in the traditional sense: indefinite, obscure, beyond signification (23). His curiosity stoked, Angell attempts to help the artist and undertakes to interview Wilcox about his dreams. In describing the dream, there is another moment of the sublime:

8. Cthulhu Is Beautiful

> Hieroglyphics had covered the wall and pillars, and from some undetermined point below had come a voice that was not a voice; a chaotic sensation which only fancy could transmute into sound [...]. [His dreams] touched wildly on a gigantic thing "miles high" that walked or lumbered about. He at no time fully described this object, but occasional frantic words, as repeated by Dr. Tobey, convinced the professor that it must be identical with the nameless monstrosity he had sought to depict in his dream-sculpture [26–27].

"Cyclopean," "titan," "sky flung," "horror," "miles high," "chaotic": these adjectives suggest the sublime.

Now let us turn to Wilcox himself. He describes himself as "psychically hypersensitive," and, in response to certain geologic disturbances, has a "dream of Cyclopean cities of titan blocks and sky-flung monoliths, all dripping with green ooze and sinister with latent horror" (25, 26). Professor Angell, after analyzing Wilcox, studies other artists also influenced. He discovers during the length of the geologic disturbance that inspired Wilcox's strange work other sensitive people were inspired, particularly in Paris, France. It is related that in Paris "a fantastic painter named Ardois-Bonnot hangs a blasphemous 'Dream Landscape' in the Paris spring salon of 1926" (29). Paris, specifically the Left Bank area, was one of the epicenters of modernist artistic production in the early 1920s as well as an important headquarters of the continental European avant-garde.

It is telling that Lovecraft triangulates Wilcox in relation to what the author and other cultural elites would have understood as a hotbed of modernist artistic activity. Following the narrative logic of the story from beginning to end, Wilcox's fevered creation of sculptural art disconnected from previously established traditions results in the terrible revelation of Cthulhu, a monstrous entity sleeping in the ocean. Cthulhu, like Clark Ashton Smith's horrible Ubbo-Sathla, in its absolute formlessness and terror, allegorically transforms the ephemerality of the ordinary into a monster.

In the second story, the narrator relates the professor's notes regarding his encounter with a police inspector, John Legrasse. Inspector Legrasse explains how he had tracked down a mysterious cult in the swamps surrounding New Orleans. This cult had sacrificed a human before "a great granite monolith some eight feet in height" (36). After dispersing the cult and arresting them, Legrasse discovers, perched on top of the monolith, "a grotesque, repulsive, and apparently very ancient stone statuette" (30). Here is the narrator's description:

This thing [...] was of somewhat bloated corpulence, and squatted evilly on a rectangular block or pedestal covered with undecipherable characters [...]. Its vast, awesome, and incalculable age was unmistakable; yet not one link did it shew with any known type of art belonging to civilization's youth—or indeed to any other time [31–32].

"Vast," "awesome," "incalculable": once again, these adjectives seem to register the sublime. A kind of sublime, or something tending toward the sublime, pervades Lovecraft's "The Call of Cthulhu." And yet, none of the examples highlighted above register the sublime as it has been defined by traditional sources. This important distinction can be understood by examining the ideas regarding the sublime as it was initially formulated by Immanuel Kant and Edmund Burke.

Kant and Burke's Definitions of the Sublime

In his *A Philosophical Enquiry into the Origin of Our Ideas of the Sublime and Beautiful* (1757), Burke distinguishes the sublime from the beautiful by attempting to describe the emotions they evoke as well as the material qualities—shapes, textures, size—that are associated with them. Beauty, for Burke, is predominantly a function of our expectations and familiarity with aesthetic traditions; when an art object or nature conforms to our expectations of phenomena, then they are beautiful. Thus, the beautiful is a function of understanding, knowledge, recognition, and familiarity and is experienced by the subject when he or she understands fully their own and their society's expectations, i.e., the conditions of beauty. Conversely, Burke figures the sublime as emerging out of the subject's ignorance. A sublime phenomenon, then, is defined by its obscurity and its vagueness and the way it resists or fails to conform to our expectations. The subject experiences the sublime, according to Burke, as terrifying, vast, and beyond comprehension, and yet takes a kind of aesthetic delight in their cognitive incapacity in the face of sublimity. Though Burke understands the experience of the sublime as ultimately painful, he suggests that it can be married with beauty.

8. Cthulhu Is Beautiful

Immanuel Kant, in his *Critique of Judgment* (1790), modifies Burke's theory of the sublime and the beautiful. For Kant, the beautiful is not necessarily connected to phenomena, i.e., it is an idea primarily. His concept of beauty is somewhat paradoxical in that, to formulate it, Kant posits that subjective valuations of taste are necessarily imperative commands, i.e., they are subjective but tend toward universality. Thus, the beautiful becomes that which conforms to what we want it to conform to. Put another way, the beautiful is a quality that emerges when an arbitrary and prescriptive set of rules have been followed with precision in the instance of a specific work of art and it therefore is a kind of skillful conventionality. Furthermore, the beautiful emerges from a form of social consensus, from our collective striving to articulate an idealized form of beauty that does not in itself exist; therefore, it is an intellectual concept, a codified framework, ultimately connected to reason.

Kant understands the sublime, conversely, as an emotion unconnected to reason. But more importantly, the sublime is a feeling that signals the powerful capacity of the mind to reflect on things that transcend the conceptual frameworks that we have developed and utilize to aesthetically judge the world. It is not enough that a phenomenon be extremely large or vast to be considered sublime in Kant's framework. Sublimity is the emotional response one experiences that signals the powerful capacity of the mind to reflect on things that transcend the local scope of our conceptual frameworks.

The Sublime as Excess

Kant's and Burke's definitions of beauty conform much easier than their conceptions of the sublime. Both philosophers understand beauty as a function of conformity between human expectations of the world and the satisfaction of those expectations. When we gaze out at the world and, in a sense, see ourselves reflected back at us, that is beauty. However, the relationship between their concepts of the sublime is much more complicated. For Burke, the sublime signals an incapacity of the human mind; for Kant, however, the sublime signals a great capacity. For Burke, the sublime is a kind of profound symptom that there are phenomena beyond our comprehension and perceptive abilities and should, therefore delightfully, humble us. For Kant, sublimity signals the untapped potential of the human mind, its awesome ability to endure and take nourishment from an encounter with that which is beyond the range of its conceptual frameworks.

There is an obvious way these two thinkers' theories of the sublime correlate, and this is that for both Burke and Kant the sublime is registered as an excess; in Burke the sublime is in excess of our understanding, our comprehension; in Kant, though we can still conditionally comprehend the sublime in the sense that we can perceive it, it is only distinct from beauty to the extent that it transgresses its boundaries. Indeed, the Kantian sublime does not index a failure of cognition or perception, which is a distinctive feature of Burke's theory; however, the Kantian sublime is nevertheless in excess of any established conceptual frameworks we bring to it. In Kant, the sublime is boundless, yet conceivable; in Burke the sublime is indefinite and therefore beyond perception.

In both theories, however, the sublime is not stable or universalizing. It is excessive, partially absent, not fully present to our cognitive or merely conceptual frameworks.

Echoes of the Sublime in Lovecraft's Virtual Worlds

This is not the experience of Lovecraft's protagonists, specifically the protagonist of "The Call of Cthulhu." The crisis experienced by Lovecraft's protagonist is that of far too much knowledge, of mathematical correlation and geometrical proof, if not complete knowledge. In the opening passage the narrator calls "the inability of the human mind to correlate all of its content" "the most merciful thing in the world" (21). The narrator registers this point, articulates how it is knowledge (not ignorance) that has damned him: "I have looked upon all the universe has to hold of horror" (55). Of Cthulhu he states, "the thing cannot be described—there is no language for such abysms of shrieking and immemorial lunacy, such eldritch contradictions of all matter, force, and cosmic order"; however, the reader must remember that it was not Thurston who actually encountered Cthulhu, it was Johansen the sailor whose journal the narrator reads; thus, Johansen's language did, indeed, effectively signify the horror of seeing the mountain-sized monster. Of Johansen's writing, Thurston writes, "Poor Johansen's handwriting almost gave out when he wrote of this" (53). The key adjective here, it seems, is "almost" (53). His handwriting did not give out. The message was delivered. Thurston understood.

In these instances that tend toward the sublime, ignorance, lack of knowledge, i.e., the failure of signification, is valued, is a respite. Accordingly, absolute knowledge is figured as the cause of horror. These passages, then, do not conform with Burke's definition of the sublime, which depends on indefiniteness, obscurity, and vagueness. Consider some of the adjectives he uses to describe the sublime in his *Enquiry*: "rugged and negligent," "dark and gloomy," "obscure," these words seem to be defining the opposite of what the narrator is lamenting, is fearing at the story's beginning, things such as revelation, illumination, epiphany, correlation, and definition (548). This ill-matched relationship with Burke's notion of the sublime also holds with that of Kant's: "We call sublime what is absolutely large"; "[The sublime] is what is large beyond all comparison"; "unboundedness"; "ruleless disarray and definition" (520–521).

Here the sublime is once again framed as that which is beyond signification, conception within established epistemological frameworks. Though, in Kant, the sublime is still conceivable in its awesome vastness, it still transcends the framework of our human knowledge. In the passages cited above, the narrator's and Johansen's experience do not transcend human knowledge, they are absolutely facilitated by it, by the intellectual technologies of writing, correlation, and reading. Insofar as the citation of the material sciences, the theories that inform them, signify that measurement, indexing, categorization—methods so characteristic of sciences—are the source of horror, the opening of the story does not register the sublime in the sense of Burke or Kant. Something different is going on here. This is the story of a successful transmission of occult and cruel knowledge. Signification is not deferred.

The Negative Sublime

In Lovecraft's "The Call of Cthulhu," we have encountered a new variety of the sublime, a negative sublime to the extent that the emotion of grandeur evoked emerges not out of a failure of signification but out of a pervasive, absolute signification. In other words, here the sublime does not emerge out of ignorance, obscurity, transcendence of the symbolic; rather, it emerges as a response to absolute knowledge, and in this way is more akin to what Slavoj Žižek traces in his *The Sublime Object of Ideology* (1989). Taking Kant's and Burke's sublime as a starting point, he figures that sublime as an encounter with the Lacanian Real, that which is more than signification, the abject excess of the world that the subject of the sublime has experienced. This formulation, inasmuch as encountering the Real is akin to "learning the truth," is closer in spirit to the negative sublime than Kant's or Burke's formulations; however, it is nevertheless too strong as Lovecraft's protagonists generally succeed, to their horror, in understanding. They do not scream in horror because they have inadvertently stumbled outside of the symbolic to face the abject Real; rather, they follow the symbolic to its horrible conclusion, become wholly enclosed by a web of signification that has a horrible end. They translate the hieroglyphics, correlate the news stories, peer within the pages of ancient tomes, grasp the scientific theories, and, through these various signifiers, glimpse the Truth. Robert Weinberg, esteemed pulp magazine collector and historian, articulates this point quite clearly:

> Lovecraft's stories were as well constructed as any scientific paper. First, the statement by the narrator of a terrible horror to be revealed (the goal); next the facts are related through first hand evidence, newspaper clippings, or diaries (evidence); third, the confrontation between the narrator or another with the horror (the experiment); and finally, the realization of the horror as predicated and stated at the beginning (the conclusion) [30].

Here Weinberg highlights the degree to which moments that suggest the sublime in Lovecraft does not emerge out of uncertainty, vagueness, or the unknown. To the contrary, that which is known and has been proved through the convolutions of the plot is the source of the horror: "I must have forgetfulness or death," states the protagonist of "Dagon," the prototype story of Lovecraft's masterpiece, "The Call of Cthulhu" (52).

Cthulhu Is Beautiful

The negative sublime of "The Call of Cthulhu" is fictionalized by Lovecraft as the appropriate reaction to the apprehension of the ephemerality of the ordinary. This horrible awareness of the ephemerality of the ordinary emerges in the "The Call of Cthulhu" not directly because of the gelatinous, formless, eons-old monster sleeping in the Pacific. Following the twisting logic of narrative, it emerges, rather, out of viewing a piece of shadow modernist art, a plastic sculpture, still wet and new, that evokes antiquity. This strange sculpture, this enduring form, results in the transmission of occult knowledge about our ordinary realities: they are temporary domestications of strangeness, screens for dismissing a vast cosmic unfolding signified compactly in the story as Cthulhu wakes up: "After vigintillions of years great Cthulhu was loose again, and ravening for delight" (53). Here it is the word "vigintillion" that is key. Meaning ten to the 120th power, it evokes the temporal vastness that functions as a horrifying foil to human time.

The negative sublime is not indefiniteness, a threatening obscurity in the Burkean sense; nor is it an exhilarating boundlessness conceived that confirms the awesome power of the human mind in the Kantian sense. It is an inescapable truth founded on a conceptual framework informed by a science and is therefore more akin to Burkean and Kantian beauty than the sublime. Cthulhu, like Benjamin's angel of history with wings caught in the winds of history, is beautiful.

9. Lovecraft and the Threat of Modernism

Actual Modernism and Shadow Modernism

Let us consider the resemblance and lack of resemblance between actual modernism and the shadow modernism of the pulp ekphrastic works of the *Weird Tales* Three. The actual modernists pioneered aesthetic techniques for making enduring forms that held in tension the experience of novelty, and these aesthetic objects—"devices" that stabilized novelty— were believed to invigorate experience degraded by habit. The shadow modernists fictionalized by the *Weird Tales* Three, however, following them, did not set out to engineer new techniques. Their artistic enterprise, constrained by their fictional context, was always virtual; nevertheless, the artistic enterprise of the *Weird Tales* Three was an actual one. In their pulp ekphrastic works, the *Weird Tales* Three used an old technique—literary realism—and sutured it to a new, though virtual, one—modernism. Only in this grotesque way did they produce a new technique.

The *Weird Tales* Three are literary artistic innovators, but they are also ekphrasists, concerned with consolidating and celebrating previous techniques; their enterprise troubles the distinction between criticism and art. I imagine the pulp ekphrastic works of the *Weird Tales* Three as an attempt to understand the new "art devices" that were the fruit of earlier pioneering efforts. If the actual modernists thought of their task as a science for producing new techniques and new experiences, the *Weird Tales* Three thought of their task as descriptive, as tracing the implications of those techniques through fictionalization.

9. Lovecraft and the Threat of Modernism

But their project was not merely descriptive but also evaluative. For the *Weird Tales* Three, and Lovecraft in particular, the knowledge transmitted by the enduring forms of actual modernism was dangerous, an occult truth better left occult comparable to the catastrophe of history understood by Benjamin when gazing on Klee's painting. Using realism to stage confrontations with the non-representational forms of modernism was dramatized by these writers over and over as a violation, a transgression represented as the transmission of an occult truth about the ephemerality of the ordinary, about the brevity of our lives, about the fragility of the ordinary worlds we carve out for ourselves amid universal strangeness and unyielding, inhuman change.

Lovecraft's Scarecrow Modernism

Near the end of his life, after he had ceased writing fiction, Lovecraft sought to express this thesis in a critical register. For example, in a 1935 essay titled "Heritage or Modernism: Common Sense in Art Forms," published in a 1935 issue of Hyman Bradofsky's amateur journal, *The Californian*, H.P Lovecraft puts forth an argument in defense of traditional art styles and thereby censures those he characterizes by their intense levels of novelty. As a short-hand, he refers to these innovative styles and productions as "modernism," and, as concrete examples of the "art" he means to refer to by this term, he cites "Gertrude Stein," "Picasso," "James Joyce," "Frank Lloyd Wright," and others. He criticizes these artists for their belief that "all art ought to be divorced completely from tradition and from earlier art-forms" ("Heritage" 191). In response to the belief he attributes to these innovators of art, he scolds, "Remove all sources of familiarity—all the subtle landmarks supplied by what we know of the past—and no phase of art or life can have more than the slenderest vestige of appeal, beauty, or meaning" ("Heritage" 191). The risk here is nihilism. The subjective quality of familiarity and the social one of established formal convention, Lovecraft aligns with traditional art-forms, and in his enthusiasm elevates them to existential proportions: "There can be no such thing as value, purpose, direction, or meaning, or even interest, except in a strictly local and relative sense" ("Heritage" 191).

Lovecraft's scarecrow modernism in "Heritage or Modernism" is, of course, a caricature based less on an actual understanding of historical modernism—a largely academic concept—and more on an abstraction derived from experiencing modernist works out of their contexts, disassociated from the interpretive communities that understood their unique idiom. For example, one of the central premises in Lovecraft's essay, modernism's antagonistic relationship to tradition, is wrong. It does not take into consideration the extent to which many of the artists typically designated as modernists in classic and contemporary studies were concerned primarily not with severing their ties to artistic tradition but with the problem of reinvigorating that tradition, to salvaging it in an inauthentic world. But Lovecraft's inaccurate rendition of historical modernism is of less interest here when compared to his fictionalized distortion of modernism, a fiction that, when properly scrutinized, yields a complex theory of novelty and aesthetic production as a science that produces dangerous knowledge about the ephemerality of the ordinary. This final chapter focuses on Lovecraft's many fictional modernists and the modernist art they create and how their artistic enterprises are fictionalized as transgressive assaults on the ordinary.

Lovecraft's Shadow Modernism

Many of Lovecraft's short stories fictionalize artists as shadow modernists who produce knowledge-generating art clearly marked as severed from established aesthetic traditions, and can, in this way, be interpreted as allegories for actual modernists, particularly when the author's concrete historical situation is taken into consideration. Lovecraft was writing when modernism was being consolidated in the academy, historicized as not an insignificant experimental movement of elites but as the art of the early twentieth century. Furthermore, unlike Lovecraft's many expository polemics and parodies, where he censures historical and actual modernism directly, this literary discourse featuring fictional shadow modernists allows him to preserve the rich complexities of his reflections on modernist art as an occult science.

The adjective "shadow" is essential to capture the idea that Lovecraft's fictionalizations are not innocent representations but ideologically invested distortions, and the knowledge-producing modernist art they create at their (and our) peril is not actual modernism but modernism transformed into a monster. Below I trace an aesthetic theory outlined by Lovecraft's mode of fictionalizing modernist artists and art objects.

Shadow modernist artistic effort in these key instances is portrayed as a form of occult research, a struggle to bring into perception the cosmos-at-large, to bring its telescopic and microscopic scales into the local space of the ordinary that, consequently, is exposed as unstable. In other words, Lovecraft's shadow modernism is rendered as a transgressive totalizing gesture that juxtaposes incommensurate ontological planes of space and time. Home and hearth, coffee and madeleine, are thrown out of focus, made strange by the yawning vastness of outer space and cosmic time. Joyce's "mythic method," D.H. Lawrence's uncovering of primitive energies, Conrad's struggle to make us see, Woolf's attempt to formalize the intangible quality that distinguishes the post–Edwardian world, and what Schorer would call "techniques of discovery" thus emerge from Lovecraft's perspective as nothing less than the cruel violations of the enlightened philosopher in Plato's allegory: the modernist artist produces strange devices for extracting the unsuspecting dweller in the grotto wondering at the shadows. The shadow modernist art object reveals the ephemerality of the ordinary. Thus, the "shadow" in "shadow modernism" also refers to the phenomena the *Weird Tales* Three desire to preserve: the shadow is the protecting veil, the ordinary reality rippling on the wall of the cave. They do not wish to leave the grotto. They are afraid of the philosopher who, to them, the shadow modernist resembles. Whatever is outside of the grotto, beyond the horizon of the literary effect of reality, can mean nothing to them.

"From Beyond"

Not all of Lovecraft's stories treated here fictionalize artists as engaged in scientific research or feature art objects rendered as prosthetic devices for perceiving an otherwise hidden reality, what I have been calling the ephemerality of the ordinary. Some of Lovecraft's earlier, pre–*Weird Tales* stories invert this process and fictionalize scientists who behave like artists who produce technological devices that resemble art. Lovecraft's early tale, "From Beyond," is a good example of this type of inversion.

Published in 1920 in the privately printed magazine, *The Recluse*, H.P. Lovecraft's "From Beyond" offers an example of Lovecraft's early attempts to imagine the artistic enterprise as a form of occult and scientific research for producing a prosthetic device, an art object, that functions to reveal the ephemerality of the ordinary. This story of a mad scientist and his friend can be seen as having all the parts, at least at an embryonic stage, of that distorted vision of modernism as a science for producing knowledge outlined above and embedded in the pulp ekphrastic works of the *Weird Tales* Three. Adopting the outsider perspective of the artists who would congregate around that experimental magazine, we see that "From Beyond" is not only a story of weird science, a proto-version of what Hugo Gernsbeck in 1927 would come to call "scientifiction." It is also a story rendering shadow modernism as a grotesque and dangerous blending of scientific and artistic discourses, a suturing together of realism and modernism, empiricism and mathematics, poetry and prose. In this way, "From Beyond" is a story of a critic, a modernist artist, and a modernist art object, conceived here as a strange device that amplifies to cosmic levels the human sensorium.

Considered in this way, this story begins to establish an alternative vision to the mainstream "scientistic" frame of modernism as publicized in the critical writings of figures like Schorer, Pound, Eliot and Mencken, and many more. It will no doubt prove to be that less flattering alternative. "From Beyond" dramatizes and makes literal canonical articulations of key facets of modernist aesthetics, articulations that came well before modernism, such as Poe's "commencing with the consideration of an effect" in "The Philosophy of Composition," to some that followed on the heels of modernism, such as Viktor Shklovsky's concept of "estrangement," published in *Theory of Prose* in 1929. In his chapter "Art as Device," Shklovsky discusses an abstract, merely conceptual "device of art" that functions in this way: "by 'estranging' objects and complicating form, the device of art makes perception long and 'laborious'" (7). Accordingly, in Lovecraft's "From Beyond," we have an artistic device that makes the world strange in distinct but nevertheless approximate ways.

The story begins with the narrator lamenting the bodily changes

9. Lovecraft and the Threat of Modernism

undergone by his friend, the brilliant yet melancholy Crawford Tillinghast, because of his intense "physical and metaphysical researches" (192): "It is not pleasant to see a stout man suddenly grown thin, and it is even worse when the baggy skin becomes yellowed or grayed" (193). He attributes this wilting of Tillinghast's body to his excessive study of science, art, and philosophy and frames the mixing of scientific inquiry and aesthetic feeling as a dangerous transgression. What is the terrible nature of Tillinghast's grotesque blending of science and art? The demented Tillinghast outlines the concerns of his project in this way:

> What do we know [...] of the world and the universe about us? [...] With five feeble senses we pretend to comprehend the boundlessly complex cosmos, yet other beings with wider, stronger, or different range of senses might not only see very differently the things we see [193–94].

How does Tillinghast plan to amplify his sensorium? Drawing on his scientific and aesthetic knowledge, he has conceived and constructed a strange prosthetic device that will awake sleeping senses, and in this way literalizes a typical claim like Pound's that leverages the mythology of science to execute a thesis about the new art: "Any work of art which is not a beginning, an invention, a discovery is of little worth" (*Pavennes* 82). Growing agitated at his friend, the narrator's, confusion, Tillinghast describes his device thus: "The waves from that thing are waking a thousand sleeping senses in us" (196). He turns the device on without waiting for the narrator's consent, and it works. The narrator cannot speak because his sensory organs are amplified and a series of novel sensations perceived, through an expanded sensorium, begin to come. Notably, he describes his experience in aesthetic terms and frames it as listening to a new type of music: "It was infinitely faint, subtly vibrant, and unmistakably musical, but held a quality of surpassing wildness which made its impact feel like a delicate torture of my whole body" (197). The narrator's aesthetic pleasure in this strange music is short-lived, however, for, after struggling to describe its beauty to his demented friend, he is warned by Tillinghast that the device opens those affected by it to the threat of a hostile extra-dimensional being. Though the scientism of modernism may create awesome works of art, it is nevertheless a transgression and brings consequences. Hearing the warning, the narrator is, of course, horrified. Unable to speak, his eyes bulge as Tillinghast increases the vibrations of the device that expand the sensorium. Thousands of dormant sensory organs continue to be activated by Tillinghast's machine, and the tortured narrator is unable to stop the demented artist-scientist. In Tillinghast's pleasure in subjecting his friend to the effects of his aesthetic device, we have a vision of the modernist artist as torturer, a recurrent motif taken up on many later pulp ekphrastic works of the *Weird Tales* Three. A provocative passage from Clark Ashton Smith's "The Isle of the Torturers," published in *Weird Tales* in March of 1933, demonstrates this. This is the story of the inhabitants of the island of Uccastrog, and of their king, Ildrac, all of whom have grown weary with ennui. They have taken torture as their "art" and have become "artists" of it, producing artistic productions designed to cause pain through every sensory organ of the protagonist who is tortured: "They racked his ears with cacophonous sounds; with evil flutes that chilled the blood and curdled it upon his heart; with deep drums that seemed to ache in all his tissues; and thin tabors that wrenched his very bones" (70).

Like the torturers who have adapted cacophonous noise and various scents to torture their victim, Tillinghast continues to increase the horrible sensory-expanding vibrations of the machine, to the extent that the narrator, incapacitated by the quantity of impressions, experiences a moment of absolute novelty and formlessness. Form dissolves:

> Indescribable shapes both alive and otherwise were mixed in disgusting disarray, and close to every known thing were whole worlds of alien, unknown entities. It likewise seemed that all the known things entered into the composition of other unknown things and vice versa [199].

The narrator shudders convulsively at these perceptions of absolute novelty, and Tillinghast, perceiving his victim's horror, celebrates his triumph. On a thematic level, Tillinghast expresses the technical triumph the shadow modernists who set out first to establish the literary effect of reality and then to violate it. Almost driven insane by his former friend, the story ends tritely when the narrator brandishes a revolver and shoots—not at Tillinghast, but at his machine.

Lovecraft and the "Ideal of Axel"

From Lovecraft's perspective, Tillinghast is nothing less than a symbol for modernist artist; Tillinghast's machine is nothing less than a work of

9. Lovecraft and the Threat of Modernism

modernist art. The strange realms the device reveals are the ephemerality of the ordinary. Like a nervous child imagining a monster based upon a large, slanting shadow, Lovecraft has here read the shadow cast by scientistic modernism and fashioned a distorted vision of it: the artist and critic are madmen engaged together in cultivating inhuman sensations through blending science and art in order to create art devices that torturously expand the human sensorium to perverse, intolerable levels, to a state where form recedes and the fundamental ephemerality of ordinary phenomena is revealed. From Lovecraft's paranoid perspective, in their quest after novelty, the modernists are destroying the fragile conditions that make the establishment of the ordinary possible.

Less interesting here is the degree of Lovecraft's distortion of modernism, and more interesting, are the possible insights into historical modernism his distorted vision may point toward. What is the significance of the notable similarity between (1) Lovecraft's Crawford Tillinghast "harnessing shadows and striding from world to world to sow death and madness" and (2) Edmund Wilson's "Ideal of Axel," his archetype of the modernist artist in wide circulation when modernism was being consolidated academically? Wilson describes the archetypical modernist artist in this way: "Neurotic nobleman who arranges for himself an existence which will completely insulate him from the world and facilitate the cultivation of refined and bizarre sensations" (264). "Insulate him from the world." "Cultivation of bizarre sensations." For Lovecraft, these two ideas are incommensurate. The cultivation of bizarre sensations is equivalent to destroying ordinary reality.

The Music of Erich Zann and the Endurance of Form

The family resemblance between Lovecraft's fictional modernists and the "Ideal of Axel" theorized by Wilson as the prototypical modernist artist becomes clearer, in stories where Lovecraft portrays not scientists as artists (an indirect route) but rather artists as scientists engaged an enterprise that resembles less individual subjective expression and more collaborative research. Although many characters featured in earlier Lovecraft stories manifest the acute sensibilities of artists, or are directly portrayed as artists—e.g., Jervas Dudley of "The Tomb," Joe Slater of "Beyond the Wall of Sleep," Crawford Tillinghast of "From Beyond," and Randolph Carter of the Dream Cycle, Iranon of "The Quest of Iranon"—none of them are properly modernist artists until the strange violist of "The Music of Erich Zann." In this story, the narrator, lodging on the fifth story of a house on the strange "Rue d'Auseil," comes into contact with a decrepit hermit, Erich Zann, who, like Wilson's Axel, seems to be completely insulated from the world and lives alone as a hermit in an attic garret of the same house; however, at stake in his artistic enterprise is all of reality.

Zann is described as a violist who possesses "highly original genius" (282). Consider how Zann's music is described as disconnected from all previous traditions of music familiar to the narrator: "I was haunted by the weirdness of his music. Knowing little of art myself, I was yet certain that none of his harmonies had any relation to music I had heard before" (282). It is reported that Zann's beautiful music has attracted the attention of a hostile force, an incorporeal essence or spirit manifested as a kind of horrible dissonance, a note of music, a force that can only be kept at bay by Zann's playing. And when it arrives, it threatens to drown out Zann's music. Whereas Zann's music is complex, this opposing non-musical dissonance is cruelly simple, it is described as "a calm, deliberate, purposeful, mocking note from away in the west" (288). At the end of the story, Zann fails in warding off the entity, and, as a result, something horrible happens: the narrator perceives the ephemerality of the ordinary as a visual phenomenon beyond the attic window: "I saw [...] only the blackness of space illimitable; unimagined space alive with motion and music, and having no semblance with anything on earth" (289). Like Cthulhu and Ubbo-Sathla, this is the ephemerality of the ordinary translated into a literary image, a formless musical storm.

Strangely, unlike Tillinghast's device, Zann's art does not bring about the dissolution of form but rather attempts to make form endure. Zann's genius is in how it can hold the forms of ordinary reality in stasis. In this passage, we have displayed in literary discourse a moral idea Lovecraft proposed elsewhere in a critical register: "There can be no such thing as value, purpose, direction, or meaning, or even interest, except in a strictly local and relative sense" ("Heritage" 191). In the virtual world of this story,

Zann is both a modernist who transgresses and also a traditional artist who maintains the unknowledge of the ephemerality of the ordinary.

This story is an important instance of Lovecraft's struggling with ambivalence toward modernism, of his struggling to establish a coherent idiom to express what he thinks about modernism. Zann is the modernist artist who, striking out into new, original aesthetic realms nevertheless transgresses. And through the transgression of his artistic enterprise, Zann has brought upon himself and the narrator the stark reality of humanity's existence in a hostile universe, for which the terrible anti-musical entity stands as representative.

Erich Zann and the Mythic Method

In a thinly allegorical register, Lovecraft fictionalizes Zann, the modernist musician, as a steward of human meaning in a cosmos hostile to it. From this perspective, the literary character of Erich Zann facing his antagonist, a hostile chaos, formalizes a tension central to modernism, one apotheosized on the occasion of T.S. Eliot's analysis of James Joyce in his 1923 "Ulysses, Order, Myth": (1) the vision of the artist as acutely aware of the chaos of modernity, and (2) the vision of the artist as shaping and ordering that chaos. Compare the description of Zann as he plays in direct opposition to cosmic chaos with T.S. Eliot's famous analysis of Joyce's "mythical method" in *Ulysses*. Zann stands in agonizing opposition to the musical entity that heralds the ephemerality of the ordinary: "It would be useless to describe the playing of Erich Zann on that dreadful night. It was more horrible than I had ever overheard, because I could now see the expression on his face, and could realise that this time the motive was stark fear" (287).

Zann is maintaining the unknowge of the ephemerality of the ordinary through his playing. And now compare this to Eliot's description of Joyce's literary technique in *Ulysses*: "It is simply a way of controlling, of ordering, of giving a shape and a significance to the immense panorama of futility and anarchy which is contemporary history" ("Ulysses" 176). We can see a resemblance between the shadow modernist Zann and the actual modernist Joyce here. They are both artists facing the chaos of the cosmos as their enemy, attempting to preserve the ordinary against the erosions of accelerating change.

Lovecraft and the Ubiquity of Novelty

Many of Lovecraft's stories following "The Music of Erich Zann" feature shadow modernist artists whose artistic enterprises take them beyond established aesthetic traditions. Artists like the unnamed narrator of "Hypnos" (a sculptor) and his companion (who is transformed into a statue) instill intense subjective feeling into a kind of scientific project referred to as "impious exploration[s]" that are indescribable "for want of symbols or suggestions in any language" (327). The narrator of "The Hound" and his companion, St. John, construct grotesque art objects out of skeletons, play music on "nauseous musical instruments" that produce "dissonances of exquisite morbidity and cacaodamoniacal ghastliness," embark on "predatory excursions" to gather "tomb-loot," described as "artistically memorable events" (341). It is significant that these transgressive activities are undertaken in response to their boredom with previously established aesthetic movements. Of course, the figure of Randolph Carter can be brought up, and by slightly reframing his fictional theory of indescribability depicted in "The Unnameable," he can be seen as struggling with the same exigencies as those frequently cited as those of the modernists: the challenges associated with the task of aestheticizing or even describing novelty as such in a disenchanted modern world pervaded by ubiquitous novelty.

The Modern Studies of Richard Upton Pickman

Let us conclude this chapter by considering one more of Lovecraft's shadow modernists, Richard Upton Pickman. Pickman is transparently

9. Lovecraft and the Threat of Modernism

rendered as an experimental, modernist artist. The narrators, Thurber's, description of Pickman's work evokes a similar sensationalism to that that followed modernism's first appearance: "There's no use trying to tell you what they were like, because the awful, the blasphemous horror and the unbelievable loathsomeness and moral foetor came from simple touches quite beyond the power of words to classify" (63). Like Zann's music and many other examples of the fictional modernist art depicted by Lovecraft, Pickman's work is unfamiliar to such a pitch that it cannot be exhibited to the public, a situation referred to by Thurber: "As you know, the club wouldn't exhibit it, and the Museum of Fine Arts wouldn't accept it as a gift; and I can add that nobody would buy it" (59).

What comes into sharp focus in this story, a point vaguely outlined in "The Call of Cthulhu," is the nature of the relationship of the modernist artist to the ephemerality the ordinary. This story dramatizes an intriguing theory of the temporal nature of the ordinary, the way the strangeness of the past can intrude into the ordinary spaces of the present. This relationship can be seen clearly in the narrator's exploration of Pickman's private art collection at Copp's Hill. After a nighttime walk across Boston to Pickman's North End studio, the demented modernist shows Thurber his paintings depicting the witch and ghoul-haunted New England past. After being stirred to his core by these depictions of dog-faced ghoul changelings haunting Puritan homes and hearths, Pickman asks if Thurber would like to see his "modern studies" (386). Thurber is affected by the alteration of historical context and describes his reaction in this way: "The other chamber had shewn a pack of ghouls and witches overrunning the world of our forefathers, but this one brought the horror right into our own daily life!" (66). This suggests that shadow modernist art only appears to be a discrete "new" tradition. The bizarre, indescribable qualities of shadow modernist art, despite their appearance as a new "tradition," a new style, are in fact not new styles, but rather forms that transcend history, that stand out of the process of the establishment of tradition. Historical contexts do not apply to them just as historical contexts do not apply to mathematical concepts and abstractions. Hence, they tend to be described in terms of mathematical terms: as spheres, cones, cubes, and curves. They are enduring forms that transcend time which is why they can function as indexes to throw into focus the ephemerality of the ordinary.

In the context of viewing Lovecraft's fictional artists, the modernist who deviates from established traditions of aesthetic production does not create something new at all. The novelty of their work is an illusion as novelty is a function of time and perception. Rather than create novelty, these artists attempt to use aesthetics to turn away from the human context to face directly the totality of the cosmos. In bringing the ghoul-haunted New England past into the present day, Pickman (and perhaps even Lovecraft) reveal their structural resemblance, in terms of aesthetic strategies, to the very modernists they censure. They do so by manifesting acutely what T.S. Eliot famously termed "the historical sense" in his "Tradition and the Individual Talent"

> The historical sense involves a perception, not only of the pastness of the past, but of its presence; the historical sense compels a man to write not merely with his own generation in his bones, but with a feeling that the whole of the literature of Europe from Homer and within it the whole of the literature of his own country has a simultaneous existence and composes a simultaneous order [92].

The Dangerous Enterprise of Modernist Art

Lovecraft's shadow modernists offer a vision of modernist art as a dangerous enterprise, a grotesque, scientific discourse of knowledge that threatens to take away one's humanity and expose the ordinary as an ephemeral configuration that staves off absolute strangeness. And yet, despite the strangeness of its plot elements, on the level of allegory, Lovecraft's transformation of actual modernism into a monstrous enterprise is no more cynical than certain canonical accounts of modernist genius, for example, Malcolm Cowley's interpretation of James Joyce's life in *Exile's Return*:

> He looks at people as if they did not exist. At night, when he retires, he is left alone with three realities: thought, sleeplessness and migraine. He suffers from incurable headaches.—And why, we asked ourselves [...] does genius lead to this inhuman state in which suffering is the only reality? Why does it seem to exist in the atmosphere of a closed room, a sickroom, where the blinds are always drawn to exclude movement and sunlight of the streets and where there is nothing living, not even a red geranium in a pot? [131].

9. Lovecraft and the Threat of Modernism

What clearer image of the "inhuman state in which suffering is the only reality" than the human form carved of obsidian, a look of ecstatic horror frozen eternally on the face, an image that ends another shadow-modernist text, Clark Ashton Smith's "The Devotee of Evil"?

The stories of shadow modernists treated here can be seen as conservative polemics critiquing scientistic modernism framed as an inhuman form of art. These stories convey in a literary register what Ortega y Gasset argues in a philosophical one in *The Dehumanization of Art*, that the new art of his pre-fascist Spain reveals not a love but a hatred of art. The phenomenon of the new science of art, for Ortega y Gasset, does not signify, as we might be inclined to frame in other contexts as a worshipful gesture, a "purification" of art. Instead, from his perspective and the perspective of the pulp ekphrastic works of *Weird Tales* Three, to turn art into a science is to destroy it, to transform it from inherently human to something without human value at all, such as a drop of acid or a sliver of platinum: "What is behind this disgust at seeing art mixed up with life? Could it be disgust for the human sphere as such, for life, for reality? Or it is rather the opposite: respect for life and unwillingness to confuse it with art, so inferior a thing as art?" (29).

For the *Weird Tales* Three, the artistic techniques pioneered by modernists are indeed powerful and result in the creation of enduring, inhuman forms that reveal the ephemerality of the ordinary. But for these three writers, the ephemerality of the ordinary is a secret of history better left unknown.

10. Conclusion: Form and Formlessness

Some Reflections on Criticism and Methodology

Applying the elite genre of the academic literary criticism, a genre honed throughout the twentieth-century history of the literary academy for the scholarly use of a small and initiated intellectual aristocracy, to the populist literary work of triad of pulp writers whose fiction and poetry was originally published in cheap periodicals—writers whose enduring appeal extends far beyond the academy—has been a delicate operation in negotiating the tensions inherent in the modernist logic of high and low culture. This is because, in contrast to some readers and sometimes even the writers themselves, I view the *Weird Tales* Three as serious literary artists and historically significant masters of fiction, a perspective arguably at odds with their historically specific publishing context, a context that projects onto their work the status of ephemera, of literary kitsch unworthy of sustained hermeneutic treatment.

Moreover, working within the genre of academic literary criticism, using it to share appreciation and defend pulp fiction as art (and not merely as a symptom of historical causes), is itself considered by many a passé activity. Although academic literary criticism's social and academic function has been debatable since the rise of theory, aesthetics-based literary apologetics has been largely decried as politically suspect, methodologically shallow, and ideologically naive. It is only with the rise of new formalisms and recent critiques of literary critique, such as Rita Feltski's two wonderful books, *The Uses of Literature* (2008) and *The Limits of Critique*

(2015), that discursive conditions have gelled to allow the return of this more traditional, humanistic mode. But despite one's approach—apologetics, formalism, or critique—taking literary work seriously requires a bricolage mode of analysis, something humanely formless and wide-ranging, though also rigorously analytical, speculative, and even strategically hospitable to discursive heterogeneity.

The essay of literary criticism is better defined by what it is not. Although, when writing literary criticism, one might find oneself temporarily posing as a biographer, a historian, a sociologist, a philosopher, and/or an aesthete, as well as, occasionally, even a political vanguard, a literary critic—if one is really seeking to be a *literary* critic—one does not write historiography, sociology, philosophy, or technical description of artistic form and emphatically so. Instead, a literary critic writes literary criticism, which is none of the genres listed above but also a difficult genre to describe because it is so formless, so joyfully hospitable to a range of diverse discourses.

How to conclude?

The Key Note

The *Weird Tales* Three pioneered pulp ekphrasis as an aesthetic mode on the basis of rendering as horrible formlessness as such; accordingly, let us meditate briefly on the conditional value of acknowledging the aesthetic challenge posed by formlessness in general as well as explore the way that peering beyond domesticating form to formlessness can result in serendipitous artistic consequences.

In a way, the *Weird Tales* Three succeed artistically to the extent that they masterfully establish form and then dramatize its dissolution into formlessness. In their pulp ekphrastic work, epiphany emerges when decreation is dramatically staged. Of all their work's thematic preoccupations, it is their surprising focus on the challenge of formlessness—the decline of cultural/ethnic boundaries (Lovecraft), the decline of civilizations (Howard), the horrible deranging of the limited human sensorium (Smith)—

that most acutely distinguishes the *Weird Tales* Three from modernism, a movement that struggles to make triumphant form endure forever. For the *Weird Tales* Three, boundaries, orders, constraints, in a word, form, is impotent and ultimately doomed by an apocalyptic formlessness, and their pulp ekphrasist works succeed to the extent that they translate this ubiquitous process of disintegration into literary art. From the perspective of the *Weird Tales* Three, no form can endure time, and the horror of this realization is their key note.

The Deforming City

The recalcitrance of life, the tenacious untranscendability of formlessness, in the face of form, isn't the only way of articulating the problem; indeed, form ossifies as convention, as illusion, as boredom, as the ordinary, as the oppressive domestic, and the occult plenitude of the infinite, the contingent, and the extraordinary hides from artists who continuously seek it as hunters of the mythical White Stag. This strange elusiveness of formlessness—despite its undeniable ubiquity and universality—is pronounced clearly in the case of the compelling architectural photography project of Berenice Abbott. Recall that two years before H.P. Lovecraft's death in 1937, Abbott received federal aid from the depression-era economic program, the Federal Art Project, to photographically document New York in the process of change.

This is a compelling aesthetic enterprise: to capture the changing of a city's skyline in a static form like the photograph. Unlike the ebb and flow of formless waves mingling with sea shores and skies, cities, being artificial, change slowly and incrementally; the process of their formation and deformation is too incremental for the human sensorium to perceive. The most we can glimpse of a deforming and forming city are the local symptoms of transformation: the many sites of construction, the juxtaposition of old architecture with new architecture, the interactions of markedly distinct cultures, the establishment of newly arriving immigrant conclaves, and the diminishment of disappearing indigenous communities. These ele-

10. Conclusion

ments are what Abbott chose to emphasize in her photography project, and the effect of paging through her many compositions is to see 1935–1938 New York not as an enduring social and architectural form but a formless mass organizing, taking shape, and descending into a new shapelessness; we see the Manhattan skyline in her photography and it becomes strange; it crashes like surf, its forms coming, going, decaying, mutating between the two great wars.

Like Abbott, the *Weird Tales* Three were also fascinated with deforming cities. Such architectural and social forms were particularly useful for their aesthetic ends, for they express a strange paradox: they seem static even as they change, as they disintegrate, as they dissolve. Like Abbott, the *Weird Tales* Three fictionalized cities in their work that are not static forms but are instead changing, fluid forms, like dancing flames or storm clouds. Like Abbott, the *Weird Tales* Three thematized the changing city in their pulp ekphrasist works to further hone and strengthen their more fundamental theme about the ephemerality of the ordinary. In several stories, such as Lovecraft's "The Nameless City," Smith's "The City of the Singing Flame," and Robert E. Howard's, "Red Nails," the ancient city clearly deformed by time bears great symbolic weight. Such cities deformed by time give the reader access to a broad historical scope beyond the constrained range of the human sensorium and the temporally delimited experiences of three score and ten years. Indeed, such deforming cities, by virtue of their age and disintegration, reveal the contingent and fragile nature of the ordinary space they once supported.

The *Weird Tales* Three participated in a broader artistic fascination of the modernizing city. As a subject for ekphrastic reflection, it nourished many artists of the early twentieth century. Indeed, modernizing cities became a unique object for contemplating what seemed to be the powerful forces of human engineering and technological development, the invigorating but also terrifying increase in the human subject's power to shape formless nature, to force it to comply. Consider, for example, the eleventh proclamation of Marinetti's 1909 "Manifesto of Futurism":

> We will sing of the great crowds agitated by work, pleasure and revolt; the multi-colored and polyphonic surf of revolutions in modern capitals: the nocturnal vibration of the arsenals and the workshops beneath their violent electric moons: the gluttonous railway stations devouring smoking serpents; factories suspended from the clouds by the thread of their smoke; bridges with the leap of gymnasts flung across the diabolic cutlery of sunny rivers: adventurous

steamers sniffing the horizon; great-breasted locomotives, puffing on the rails like enormous steel horses with long tubes for bridle, and the gliding flight of aeroplanes whose propeller sounds like the flapping of a flag and the applause of enthusiastic crowds [251].

Here "modern capitals" are swiftly changed by "multi-colored and polyphonic surf of revolutions" as well as other technologies. The tone is ebullient and joyful, in contrast to the pessimistic account of the speaker of T.S. Eliot's "The Waste Land" of modern London in the midst of the Great War: "Unreal city / Under the brown fog of a winter dawn" (57). Here modernizing London animated for war by industrial production appears so artificial, so spiritual, so outside of nature, that it cannot even be said to be real. Indeed, for Marinetti, Eliot, and several other modernists, the city is an architectural form that endures, that swells the banks of time to stand outside of nature like an abstraction.

Not so for the *Weird Tales* Three. The city, like all forms, is doomed by formlessness.

In order to bring into focus the *Weird Tales* Three's sober acknowledgment of the untranscendable doom of formlessness and how formlessness as a theme is central to their pulp ekphrasist enterprise, consider a few deforming cities powerfully fictionalized by Lovecraft, Howard, and Smith: the sunken city of R'lyeh, the violence-haunted city of Xuchotl, the several crumbling citadels in the doomed continent of Zothique. Cities in the pulp ekphrastic works of the *Weird Tales* Three clearly manifest the wounds inflicted by history. Moreover, in the pulp ekphrasist works of the *Weird Tales* Three, the deforming city is sinister to the extent that, in its illusory formal endurance, it has the capacity to hide the forces of formlessness that, like the occult activity festering in the sewers beneath Red Hook, resides in its deepest and forgotten recesses and chambers. Consider, for example, Robert E. Howard's "The Valley of the Lost," a story unpublished in Howard's lifetime about a prehistoric race of humanoids who linger in an ancient city underground. Here is how the city is described:

> Its towers and battlements were those of an alien age. Its outline baffled his gaze with unnatural aspects; it was a city of lunacy to the normal human eye, with its hints of alien dimensions and abnormal principles of architecture. Through it moved strange figures, human, yet of a humanity definately different from his own [...]. He saw them in the twisting streets, and in their colossal buildings, and he shuddered at the inhumanness of their lives. Much they did was his ken;

10. Conclusion

> he could understand their actions no more than a Zulu savage might understand the events of modern London [...] [278–82].

Here Howard captures the fundamental uncanny quality of the deforming city, the way it strangely sutures the ordinary to the extraordinary. The protagonist recognizes the architectural forms and the humanoid denizens, and these shapes vaguely suggest humanity. But they also vaguely repudiate humanity. Such a city, bathed just so by an aesthetic and deforming gaze, oscillates from strange to ordinary, from ordinary to strange.

The deforming city reveals the *Weird Tales* Three's vision of the aesthetic gaze with all of its particularities shed: if form is an illusion, and the modern city, like modern art, possesses the secret of its illusory endurance, then the aesthetic gaze deforms. To profoundly contemplate aesthetic form is to discover its secret, its imbrication with formlessness. As a pulp ekphrasist, to look upon the city, the world, the self, the body, is to see the triumph of formlessness, to discover, like the protagonist of Lovecraft's "The Outsider," that the decaying corpse is us: "I stretched out my fingers to the abomination within that great gilded frame; stretched out my fingers and touched *a cold and unyielding surface of polished glass*" (272, emphasis original).

Form Matters

The *Weird Tales* Three pioneered pulp ekphrasis because a compelling development in European art (modernism) arrested their attention. From their outside and speculative perspective, this modernist art and literature, unframed by the robust defenses that often supplemented it in elite publications, exhibitions, and cosmopolitan conversations, appeared to them as a monster, as the hostile foil to art, the celebration of the inhuman, the aesthetic acceleration of formlessness. It is not surprising that for much of its existence the science fiction, fantasy, and supernatural horror traditions—the rich tradition of the literature of wonder of which the *Weird Tales* Three are central participants—suffered from a similar distortion through the misunderstanding gaze of academic literary criticism, a gaze trained, in large part, by modernism and flawed by discursive distance. The literary works of the unreal genres seemed the opposite of art, marked by an irresponsible indifference to form and degraded by the celebration of mere affect, mere entertainment, and the non-intellectual pleasures of repeated generic convention.

In a way, the *Weird Tales* Three's fictional modernism is absurd, and, to an extent, an aesthetically traditional interpretation of genre fiction is equally absurd, but what insights might such inaccurate renderings provide? Is modernism the token of an inevitable formlessness? Is pulp fiction unconcerned with form? Why this focus on form, this projection of value onto form, from both pulp and modernist perspectives?

Form matters. We have little purchase on the contingency, chaos, and formlessness of this ceaselessly unfolding drama that we call life, so we have devised the technology of form to fix the fluid, conditionally arrest the contingent, and spiritually console the vulnerable and finite bodies that we and our loved ones are. Like the "mighty tablets of star-quarried stone" that stood timeless in the "formless mass of Ubbo-Sathla […] headless, without organs," artistic form provides a compelling answer to the mystery of our finitude: we are finite but our various shaping's of the world seem to manifest a quality of endurance for a time. Both pulp ekphrasists and modernists are animated by this flickering and tenuous manifestation of hope (228). For the modernist, contra Ortega y Gasset, art is important; it bears the burden of making an alien world receptive to the production of fragile human meaning. For the pulp ekphrasist, art serves a similar function, and modernism, in the apparent violence it engages against previous traditions of art, appears unholy and evil, a herald not of form but of formlessness.

A Misunderstanding

Both views are undoubtedly wrong, yet we inherit several insights from such mistakes. What Andreas Huyssen termed "the great divide" between high and low art, between pulp fiction and modernist literature, might have as easily been termed "the great misunderstanding." If we squint, T.S. Eliot, James Joyce, H.P. Lovecraft, and Robert E. Howard begin to look similar; all become manifestations of a ubiquitous interwar cultural theme: artistically perceptive white males overwhelmed by the disintegration and defeat of European cultural hegemony and who use art to express sincere fear of change, fear of a new order of difference, the perceptible ascendency of the hitherto oppressed, subordinated, exploited, and violated: women, people of color, sexual minorities, religious minorities, indigenous people, the subaltern. But underpinning their tribalistic fear of difference, their horror at the defeat of European cultural hegemony, is a primal fear, an existential one, one that has been the engine of much art for thousands of years and certainly central to the pulp ekphrasist works of the *Weird Tales* Three: expressed beautifully by, according to Biblical tradition, an aging King Solomon, this is the fear of time: "I returned, and saw under the sun, that the race is not to the swift, nor the battle to the strong, neither yet bread to the wise, nor yet riches to men of understanding, nor yet favor to men of skill; but time and chance happeneth to them all" (Ecclesiastes 9.11 KJV). "Time and chance happeneth to them all." Irrespective of tribe, race, clique, or coterie, we are all ephemeral forms trembling in strange stasis destined for formlessness.

Formlessness and Popular Print Culture

One photograph from Berenice Abbott's photography project has always intrigued me. Titled "Newsstand, East 32nd Street and Third Avenue, Manhattan November 19, 1935," it depicts a bloated periodicals and tobacco station. A tired-looking man in a newsy cap stands nearby gazing listlessly at the racks bulging with magazines and newspapers, his hands at his hips. He does not seem particularly interested in the reading material and the diverse magazines seem to blur together, to lose their form; they appear less like entertainment commodities and more like a papery agglomeration or even evidence of urban flora, the ecological issue of concrete, steel, smoke and glass. This photograph that collapses distinctions of interwar print culture brings to mind an editorial about the newsstand and pulpwood magazine trade, published in *The New York Times* on August 28, 1935, a scant three months prior, titled, "Fiction by Volume": "The pulp magazines [...] go on pouring an endless stream into the newsstand trade" (16). "An endless stream." Echoing the deforming gaze inherent in Abbott's photograph, the pulp magazines' literary context wherein flourished the pulp ekphrastic works of the *Weird Tales* Three is also framed here as formless excess, a fecundity in sync with the great production powers of modern industry captured and documented by Abbott's photography. Formlessness, from this perspective, presents a methodological problem: by what principle do we navigate such a plenitude of literary artifacts?

Looking at this unflattering photograph of slick magazines, advertisements, popular daily newspapers, and pulps, and syncing it with *The New York Times* editorial published prior to it, one can understand and perhaps even briefly sympathize with the fear felt by critical theorists Theodor Adorno and Max Horkheimer and their statements about mass and popular culture in their essay, "The Culture Industry": "Marked differentiations such as those of A and B films, or of stories in different magazines in different price ranges depend not so much on subject matter as on classifying, organizing, and labeling consumers. Something is provided so that none may escape" (1112). In this essay, Adorno and Horkheimer frame mass culture as a kind of evil conspiracy hostile to human freedom; it is conceived as a technological, industrial, and political network, a "ruthless unity" that brings about mass hypnosis and consent and thereby participates in the same techno-utopian agenda of "the most powerful sectors" of the high capitalist economy: "steel, patroleum, electricity, and chemicals" (1112). And for the paranoid Adorno and Horkheimer, this industry does not serve consumers as much as imprison and then resource them, like cows in a dairy farm; but it is the lucre of the finite resource of our attention, they argue, that is captured, pooled, and organized to secure profit to reproduce and maintain "progress," an enterprise they understand, like Benjamin, not as the liberation of individuals but as a universal system of oppression, exploitation, and violence.

The pulp ekphrasist works of the *Weird Tales* Three should make us suspicious of this homogenization of mass culture, this deformation of popular culture into a homogeneous slime. The figure in Abbott's photograph stands subjected by a popular culture monopoly, and the papery growth he gazes on can be seen as ecologically and economically linked to the same techno-industrial system that was forming and deforming the world between the wars and producing unstable conditions that would, in a just few years after the photograph was snapped, bear the dark fruit of fascism, the atomic bomb, the holocaust, ethnic cleansing, and other countless atrocities and horrors; but the undiscerning figure is also unaware of the exceptional publications on that rack, such as *Weird Tales* that published the pulp ekphrasist works of the *Weird Tales* Three, works that, in their aesthetic and thematic focus on formlessness and modernity's acceleration of it, can be seen as quasi-prophetic warnings against that evil system that would render fascism, ethnic cleansing, the horror of mechanized warfare and atomic weapons, the tragedies of ecological degradation, and violence. Contra interwar intellectual culture's generalizing claims, "marked differentiations" between magazines do indeed matter.

The Aesthetic Fundamentals of the Weird Tales *Three*

In a 1919 essay titled, "The Case for Classicism," published in a privately printed magazine, *The United Co-operative*, H.P. Lovecraft lashes out at the modernist verse that disgusted him: "We moderns have overreached ourselves, and are blundering along with a dislocated sense of values amidst a bustle of heavy trivialities and false emotions which find reflection in the vague, hectic, hurried, impressionistic language of decadence" (213). Near the end of his life, in an age when modernism was being established as an academic category, his anti-modernism, still evident, had nevertheless become comparatively subdued. For example, writing in a 1934 anti-modernist polemic titled, "Heritage or Modernism: Common Sense in Art Forms," he adopts the stance of a sensible sage: "Every age has additions, subtractions, and modifications to make to its inherited art traditions. No one argues in behalf of a rigidly static art. [...] The point is that there is no need to destroy and replace accustomed aesthetic fundamentals when they can so much more advantageously be retained and developed as reason and conditions dictate. (197). "Destroying and replacing accustomed aesthetic fundamentals." This is a strange sin to affix to a movement in the arts that many of its key figures, like Eliot and Mencken, present as an effort to purify and make scientific aesthetic technique.

Lovecraft got it wrong. Yet, what he is ill-equipped to argue in a critical register, the *Weird Tales* Three skillfully execute in their pulp ekphrastic works. Gazing at modernism through the lens of the *Weird Tales* Three's distortions reveals fascinating and surprising elements of that aesthetic: the risk posed by modernism is not in destroying or replacing aesthetic fundamentals; it is instead a possibility that an artist might discover them; and in discovering aesthetic fundamentals—the horrible truth about form and formlessness—the ordinariness of novelty and the strangeness of ordinariness becomes clear: form becomes a matter of perspective, a powerful projection of the mind and culture, and matter and history becomes something we can artistically shape together forever.

Gothic Fiction and Staging Decreation

It is a commonplace idea that a new type of mimetic writing in Western Europe, the novel, emerged in the early eighteenth century with the quasi-experimental and fictional yet nevertheless journalistic narratives of Defoe, Fielding, and Richardson in the Anglophone context. The mysterious formation of this undeniable generic crystallization has most often been domesticated from a sociological, biographical, or antiquarian perspective: the novel is explained as a symbolic outgrowth and epiphenomenon of developments in printing technology, the dissemination of hypotheses and worldviews deriving from the emerging positivistic sciences and the individual innovating efforts of authors who found themselves socially functioning as journalist, cleric, poet, dramatist, philosopher, entertainer, propagandist, and theologian at the same time.

A less materialistic view of the novel and the reality effect it formalized—a multi-modal perspective that attempts to incorporate the materialistic, the discursive, and the hagiographic—is that the realism of the

10. Conclusion

novel emerged as a symbolic space for narrativizing and ultimately reifying a historically "novel" bourgeois social experience and reality. In other words, in order to write the novel, English writers needed first to experience the declamation or at least demotion of medieval mysticisms and the sacred and then collude in the widespread worship of a new secular idol occupying the sad hollow left by those now outmoded Medieval beliefs: an external, empirical material reality inhabited by individual blobs of quickened slime governed by consistent yet impersonal natural laws that had first a material rather than spiritual substance.

It would be difficult to argue against the idea that the early innovations of the novel were an outgrowth of what Max Weber refers to as the "disenchantment of the world," or that the nineteenth-century stylistic irruption known as "high realism" and "naturalism," an intensification and emphasis of the "disenchanted," "positivistic," and "impersonal" premises conditioning novelistic discourse, is likewise associated to a parallel intensification of positivism and secularization. Darwin begot Zola. Marx begot Eliot. Freud begot Conrad. From the corpse of god burst Scott, Balzac, and Dreiser.

But with the rise of the novel—that de facto narrative rhetoric of the secular, "disenchanted" world—came also, quick on its heels, the rise of the gothic novel, a culturally degraded category of sub-literary discourse expressing an undecided and downright skeptical relationship with the secular, "natural" world of science quite distinctive from that of the realistic novel. We can see, in the philosophical agnosticism of the *Weird Tales* Three, evidence of their participation in a tradition that connects their ideology to that of the early gothic novel. The various realisms associated with the novel were defined by innovative and powerful techniques used to render vividly concrete and empirically perceivable and measurable spaces and temporalities. They reified principles of history, biology, psychology and costume—in word, ordinary realities—rather than "abstract" spiritual realities such as the "good," "evil," and "spirit." The degraded gothic novel, conversely, distinguished itself not by its capacity to create new techniques but its capacity to use new techniques and to juxtapose them with other, older ones: it first engaged the new rhetoric of realism to produce the literary effect of reality pioneered by the early novelists and then, in the spirit of the ancient who first put human head and torso to horse body, grotesquely juxtaposed violations to that empirical reality by introducing old literary images derived from myth and medieval lore deliberately constructed to evoke the other world, the "outside" of reality suggested by the symbols and allegories of medieval religious experience: the piping satyr, the scythe-wielding skeleton, the fires of hell, the curving goat horns of Satan. In the pages of Walpole, Radcliffe, Lewis, Shelley, and Stoker, the corpse of god re-integrated itself and shambled around as zombie, vampire, and monster.

In this view, the formal rhetoric of the gothic novel and the effect it produces are literally "grotesque" in the primal sense of the term "grotesque" where it signifies impure hybridity through its reference of the ancient cave paintings depicting strange human-animal hybrids: the gothic combines the new technique with the old technique. Like Frankenstein in his laboratory and Lovecraft in *Weird Tales*, the gothic writer threads together disparate parts incommensurate in the light of day in the shadows.

The gothic novel and pulp ekphrastic works of the *Weird Tales* Three leverage the innovations of secular and "disenchanted" novelistic discourse and folds into its symbolic structure the literary images evoking spiritual/immaterial/unknown reality. The gothic and pulp ekphrasis are animated by a kind of historical spiral: a drag into the past and an acceleration into the future around a point of stability. In the gothic, the outward thrust of new technique is checked abruptly by a violent return of the old technique; in pulp ekphrasis, the old technique is propelled into the future by the new technique. It is Sisyphus with his rock and his hill: the labor up the hill represents the efforts to innovate technique, and the rock's sad fall represents the violence of the drag of the old style or the propulsion of the new. If the rhetoric of realism and modernism represents literature's sometime alliance with the enlightenment, the grotesque rhetoric of the gothic and pulp ekphrasis expresses literature's subsequent and even parallel alliance with the dark ages (those past and those to come).

The Gothic and Pulp Ekphrasis

The gothic resembles the pulp ekphrasis of the *Weird Tales* Three in its hybrid structure but deviates from it in its temporal dynamics.

10. Conclusion

Whereas the gothic sutures an old technique to a new technique, the pulp ekphrasist sutures a new technique (modernism) to an old technique (realism). The ephemerality of the ordinary is revealed in the gothic by expressing the persistence of the medieval past; the ephemerality of the ordinary is revealed in pulp ekphrasis by augury, by expressing the radical changes that are quickly approaching in the future. In both the gothic and pulp ekphrasis, we have the literary effect of reality dramatically violated.

To describe the rhetoric of gothic narratives as hybrid, as combing the innovation of realism with the traditional literary imagery of western mysticism and myth, echoes conventionalized formalistic accounts of novelistic discourse that, in their ahistorical and strictly formalist approach, would not be theoretically fit to distinguish the gothic novel from the realistic novel at all. For example, in the strictly formalist context of Bakhtin in "Epic and Novel," the distinctiveness of novelistic discourse has nothing whatsoever to do with the historically emergent empirical realities hypothesized by the positivistic sciences; rather, the novel is, par excellence, defined by its essential generic hybridity, its ability to absorb into its body, as in the concrete case of Daniel Defoe's *Robinson Crusoe*, the diverse genres of the philosophical dialog, the spiritual memoir, the journalistic account of colonial business proceedings, the captain's hearth-fire story, the monologue, the sermon. Like the technologies of the stone millwheel and the computer microprocessor, the technology of the novel always existed in theory; it only had to be "discovered."

From the narrowly synchronic and formalist perspective of Bakhtin, the apparent "realism" of novelistic discourse is not a necessary and sufficient condition for its categorical distinctiveness. The realism of the novel is incidental to its generic formlessness. For Bakhtin, *Robinson Crusoe* and *The Castle of Otranto* are equally novels; from the perspective of his theory, the only significant element that distinguishes the technique of Walpole from that of Defoe is that of historical emergence and differentiation, the incorporations of more genres into the insatiable genre of the novel. For Bakhtin, the novel will continue to develop steadily *ad infinitum*. It is effectively the horizon of literary innovation. It is a genre defined by its absolute generic promiscuity. The technology of the novel is like the absorbing chaos and the commensurate harmony of street art. The novel challenges the innovators to come up with something new, and then it swallows that innovation whole.

Bakhtin's theory of novelistic discourse reveals the horizon of synchronic theories of the novel. It would take an audacious and irresponsible reader to argue for the qualitative indistinguishability between literary renderings of, say, Marianne Dashwood getting caught in the rain, slipping, and hurting her ankle and the devil materializing and impaling Brother Ambrosio on a shelf of jagged rocks in retribution for his lasciviousness.

Both are scenes from novels, but these narrative events are functioning differently, and understanding their difference will require a nod to the referential elements of literary language, not to the actual world but to virtual worlds. Bakhtin's theory fails to help us understand the subtle and no-so-subtle distinctiveness in terms of rhetoric of fiction of historically separated novel's like *Robinson Crusoe* to *Finnegans Wake*, or even historically contemporary ones, like *Frankenstein* and *Sense and Sensibility*. This is because of Bakhtin's prejudiced "anti-representational" theory of literary language, a legacy of his modernism. To my mind, literary criticism needs to take seriously the idea of the special "referential nature" of literary language, the way it can and does create virtual and consistent worlds. To say something like a reality principle is operating in a scene depicting a tea party and to say a reality principle has been violated in a scene where dead organic matter is animated by a bolt of lightning is, from Bakhtin's analytic perspective, mere vagary. Both scenes are equally fictional, imaginary, unreal. This does not seem right. The virtual worlds rendered are distinct in important ways.

For Barthes, the novel cultivates "an effect of reality" through the cultivation of empirical concreteness and particularity, of space, of time, of character, and of idiomatic speech. Thus, the "incantatory" technique for summoning the magic of this effect of reality is, from Barthes's perspective, quite simplistic: we come to believe in—are conditioned to believe in—the virtual reality of characters and their stories in a realist novel by virtue of an approximate quantity of data and a sustained deployment of attention on the text at hand: sensory details about the phenomenal world of the novel, historical details about the characters, idiosyncrasies of these characters' speech, atmospheric touches of setting, depth of psychology, and so on.

As we deploy our attention, the virtual context swells and the actual context recedes.

10. Conclusion

The Magic of Rendering Reality through Narrative

But this cannot be the entire truth. There is something intangible, "occult," about the dark heart of a novel, hence the famous non-theoretical nature of "fiction" admitted by the master of the novel, Henry James, in his essay "The Art of Fiction." Of the novel, he writes, "It had no air of having a theory behind it—of being the expression of an artistic faith, the result of choice and comparison" (195). For James, the novelist experimentally weaves together details, details, and more details taken from his experience into a consistent narrative pattern: "The only reason for the existence of the novel is that it does attempt to represent life" (197). Thus, the novel either comes to life, as Frankenstein's monster, or lays dormant, like a torpid Count Dracula. Henry James writes: "It goes without saying that you will not write a good novel unless you possess the sense of reality; but it will be difficult to give you a recipe for calling that sense into being" (202). Despite his hesitation, James tries to offer that recipe:

> The power to guess the unseen from the seen, to trace the implication of things, to judge the whole piece by the pattern, the condition of feeling life in general so completely that you are well on your way to knowing any particular corner of it—this cluster of gifts may almost be said to constitute experience, and they occur in country and in town, and in the most differing stages of education [203].

"The power to guess the unseen from the seen." "Feeling life in general so completely." For James, the novelist emerges as a kind of initiate candidate into a mystery cult, a knower of occult secrets on par with the Magus initiate of Eliphas Levi's *Transcendental Magic* who possesses the first of the "seven least powers" of transcendental magus, "Samech": "To know at a glance the deep things in the souls of men." To my mind, James's statements engage the same rhetoric as that famous chronicler of the "Doctrine and Ritual" of magic. How do writers create tangible, substantive, virtual worlds with ink and paper? How do writers create personalities that we parasocially relate to and even grow to love and fear? Magic.

Pulp Ekphrasis as the Last Incantation

On August 26, 1928, Clark Ashton Smith wrote another *Weird Tales* writer, Donald Wandrei, about a story he was writing. Of his new story, "The Last Incantation," he writes that it "deals with an old sorcerer who tries to evoke the dead sweetheart of his youth with disastrous results" (*The End of the Story* 259). This story was published in *Weird Tales* in June of 1930, alongside H.P. Lovecraft's "The Rats in the Wall" and Robert E. Howard's "The Moon of Skulls." This story allegorizes the technique of fiction as an occult science engaged in by the sorcerer Malygris but ultimately fails to give the air of truth. The story begins and the sorcerer is beset with a terrible ennui. Malygris's flame for life has burned out. To reignite it, he decides to use his necromancy to summon the love of his youth, Nylissa, who died long ago:

> There stood the apparition of Nylissa, even as she had stood in the perished years, bending a little like a wind-blown flower, and smiling with the unmindful poignancy of youth. Fragile, pallid, and simply gowned, with anemone blossoms in her black hair, with eyes that held the new-born azure of vernal heavens, she was all that Malygris had remembered [...] [19].

Here is the writer as a sorcerer, a possessor of an occult knowledge of creating an effect of reality. But Malygris's art fails him. The youth and beauty of Nylissa does not satisfy, becomes horrible; rather than bringing the sorcerer pleasure, it serves as a mirror, an index of his own corruption and decay. When he talks with the summoned apparition of his lost love, her innocence and youth throws into stark focus the violence wrought by time on Malygris: "Somehow, as he gazed and listened, there grew a tiny doubt— a doubt no less absurd than intolerable" (20). Malygris can take no pleasure in his art: "He could believe no longer in love or youth or beauty; and even the memory of these things was a dubitable mirage, a thing of greyness and dust, nothing but the empty dark and cold, and a clutching weight of insufferable weariness, of immedicable anguish" (20). Malygris's art fails to rejuvenate experience. His art is ultimately no match for the march of time that produces the automated habits of perception, a process of decay captured in Viktor Shklovsky's famous "Art as Device" (1929), published the same year this story was being written: "Life fades into nothingness. Automization eats away at things, at clothes, at furniture, at our wives, and at our fear of war" (5).

Pulp ekphrasis, like the gothic, like Malygris's flawed art, collides with the limits of art and can be said to be acutely cognizant of the ephemerality of our experience, the way intensity of perception diminishes into habit, living bodies dissolve into dead earth, civilizations decay into ruins, and suns burn out. In triangulating the gothic, the pulp ekphrasis of the *Weird Tales* Three, and, by analogy, Malygris's impotent magic, we see a pervasive hopelessness that haunts literary history, that is foiled, perhaps, by hope treated elsewhere.

Pulp Ekphrasis and Awareness of Time

The pervasive melancholy of pulp ekphrastic works of *Weird Tales* Three that I have treated is linked to its acute sense of time, its apprehension of the secret of history, and the corollary sense that death, decay, and formlessness is approaching. Its insight is expressed in its preoccupation with crypts and tombs, corpses and decay, fallen civilizations, and ruins, and it reminds us that we are but base matter disintegrating, temporary configurations of the raw stuff of the cosmos. The other side of art—the modernism of Pound, the realism of James—tries to console by intoning that perhaps, through art, some forms might endure. In Lovecraft's "The Outsider," published in *Weird Tales* in April of 1926, at the height of the story the unnamed protagonist turns a corner and is confronted by a putrid, shambling, decaying corpse running toward him. He raises his hand to ward off the horrible avatar of death. He has run into a mirror. Compare this identification of living human being with death to Yeats, "Once out of nature I shall never take / My bodily form from any natural thing." In the end, the pulp ekphrasist focuses on formlessness; the modernist, form.

In the gothic's awareness of time is also an awareness that the reality we know is disintegrating. And in the pulp ekphrasis of the *Weird Tales* Three, awareness of time is also an awareness that the processes of modernity are speeding up that rate of change, and our ability to establish ordinary, quotidian realities that we can dwell in, take a deep breath in—a deep think in—is also flagging. Like the gothic, the pulp ekphrasists of *Weird Tales* are aware that we are disintegrating; they are aware that our cities are disintegrating, our ideologies, our visions of the cosmos and our place within it. Let Eliot's praise of Joyce's "mythic method" stand in here for the quasi-partisan commitment to form that I have been arguing characterizes modernism as seen by the *Weird Tales* Three: "It is simply a way of controlling, of ordering, of giving a shape and a significance to the immense panorama of futility and anarchy which is contemporary history" (12). It is as if a single day in Dublin is frozen in amber and thereby is inoculated against the disintegrating march of modernity.

"The Haunter of the Dark"

To Joyce's *Ulysses*, compare Lovecraft's final story before death, "The Haunter of the Dark," written in November of 1935. This story expresses powerfully the *Weird Tales* Three's embracing of the ephemerality of the ordinary through their pulp ekphrastic works of shadow modernism. Seven months after the publication of this story, Robert E. Howard would commit suicide. Just over a year later, Lovecraft would die of stomach cancer. Clark Ashton Smith would stop writing. And Farnsworth Wright would retire as *Weird Tales* editor, his Parkinson's disease killing him in 1940.

The protagonist, Blake, has discovered a "crazily angled stone," a geometric piece of sculptural art that defies mathematical description entombed in the bell tower of a Georgian steeple. It is called the "Shining Trapohezedron." Like many unfortunate protagonists before him, Blake gazes into the enduring form and perceives the ephemerality of the ordinary everywhere concealed and everywhere the same, and then Lovecraft's final story ends. A story hitherto written in a conventional realist style becomes a modernist montage that captures the disintegration of reality, the eclipse of the ordinary by universal weirdness:

10. Conclusion

> My name is Blake—Robert Harrison Blake of 620 East Knapp Street, Milwaukee, Wisconsin.... I am on this planet.... Azathoth have mercy!—the lightning no longer flashes—horrible—I can see everything with a monstrous sense that is not sight—light is dark and dark is light ... those people on the hill ... guard ... candles and charms ... their priests.... Sense of distance gone—far is near and near is far. [...] I am Robert Blake, but I see the tower in the dark. There is a monstrous odour ... senses transfigured ... boarding at that tower window cracking and giving way.... Iä ... ngai ... ygg...[477].

The "Shining Trapehozedron," a shadow modernist art object, has here revealed the ephemerality of the ordinary reality of Lovecraft's beloved hometown, the setting of the story, Providence, Rhode Island, in 1936. At the end of this story, Lovecraft stages the decreation of the literary effect of reality and dramatically renders the central thesis of the pulp ekphrastic works of the *Weird Tales* Three: everything is ephemeral; ordinary reality is but a finite stasis of an otherwise ceaseless fluidity and universal strangeness. Moreover, it is only through the perceptual apparatus of the enduring form of art—standing out from time and space—that this occult truth, everywhere the same and everywhere concealed, is revealed.

Works Cited

Baird, Edwin. "The Eyrie." *Weird Tales*, 1923, pp. 180–182.
Bakhtin, M.M. "The Epic and the Novel: Towards a Methodology for the Study in the Novel." *The Dialogic Imagination*. Ed. Michael Holquist. Austin: University of Texas Press, 1981.
Barthes, Roland. "The Reality Effect." *The Rustle of Language*. Trans. Richard Howard, Berkeley: University of California Press, 1989, pp. 141–148.
Bates, Henry. "Announcing Strange Tales." *Strange Tales of Mystery and Terror*, 1931, p. 7.
Beirce, Ambrose. "To the Editor of Town Talk." *The Shadow of the Unattained*. Ed. David E. Schultz and S.T. Joshi. New York: Hippocampus, 2005, pp. 288–289.
Benjamin, Walter. "Theses on the Philosophy of History." *Illuminations*. Trans. Harry Zohn. New York: Schocken, 1969, pp. 253–264.
"Boy Publishes More Poems." *San Francisco Examiner*. 17 December 1922, pp. 20.
Burke, Edmund. "A Philosophical Enquiry into the Origin of Our Ideas of the Sublime and Beautiful." *The Norton Anthology of Theory and Criticism*. Eds. Vincent B. Leitch, et al. New York: Norton, 2001, pp. 539–51.
Carey, John. *The Intellectuals and the Masses*. Chicago: Academy Press, 1992.
Clune, Michael. *Writing Against Time*. Palo Alto: Stanford University Press, 2013.
Connors, Scott, ed. *The Freedom of Fantastic Things: Selected Criticism on Clark Ashton Smith*. New York: Hippocampus Press, 2006.
Cowley, Malcolm. *Exile's Return: Literary Odyssey of the 1920s*. 1934. Ed. Donald Faulkner. New York: Penguin, 1994.
Eliot, T.S. "The Metaphysical Poets." *Selected Prose of T.S. Eliot*. Ed. Frank Kermode. New York: Harcourt, 1975, pp. 59–67.
_____. "Tradition and the Individual Talent." *Selected Prose of T.S. Eliot*. Ed. Frank Kermode. New York: Harcourt, 1975. 37–45.
_____. "*Ulysses*, Order, Myth." *Selected Prose of T.S. Eliot*. Ed. Frank Kermode. New York: Harcourt, 1975, pp. 175–178.
_____. "The Waste Land." *The Waste Land and Other Poems*. Ed. Frank Kermode. New York: Penguin, 1998, pp. 53–69.
Everett, Justin and Jeffrey Shanks, eds. *The Unique Legacy of Weird Tales: The Evolution of Modern Fantasy and Horror*. Lanham, MD: Rowman and Littlefield, 2015.
Feltski, Rita. *Limits of Critique*. Chicago: University of Chicago Press, 2015.
_____. *Uses of Literature*. New York: Wiley-Blackwell, 2008.
"Fiction by Volume." *The New York Times*, 28 August 1935, p16.
Finn, Mark. *Blood and Thunder: The Life and Art of Robert E. Howard*. Austin: Monkeybrain, 2006.
Galpin, Alfred. "Some Tendencies in Modern Poetry." *H.P. Lovecraft: Letters to Alfred Galpin*. Eds. S.T. Joshi and David E. Schultz. New York: Hippocampus, 2003, pp. 240–43.

Works Cited

Hays, H.R. "Superman on a Psychotic Bender." *The New York Times*, 29 September 1946, p. 167.
Herron, Don, ed. *The Dark Barbarian: The Writings of Robert E. Howard, a Critical Anthology*. Santa Barbara: Greenwood, 1984.
Hersey, Harold. *Pulpwood Editor: The Fabulous World of Thriller Magazines Revealed by a Veteran Editor and Publisher*. 1937. Silver Spring, MD: Adventure House, 2002.
Horkheimer, Max, and Theodor W. Adorno. "*From* The Culture Industry: Enlightenment as Mass Deception." *The Norton Anthology of Theory and Criticism*. 2nd ed., Eds. Vincent B. Leitch, et al. New York: Norton, 2010, pp. 1110–1127.
Howard, Robert E. "Beyond the Black River." *The Conquering Sword of Conan*. New York: Del Rey, 2005, pp. 43–100.
———. "The Mirrors of Tuzun Thune." *Kull: Exile of Atlantis*. New York: Del Rey, 2006, pp. 53–64.
———. "The People of the Black Circle." *The Bloody Crown of Conan*. New York: Del Rey, 2003, pp. 1–79.
———. *Post Oaks and Sand Roughs*. Hampton Falls, NH: Donald M. Grant, 1990.
———. "The Screaming Skull of Silence." *Kull: Exile of Atlantis*. New York: Del Rey, 2006, pp. 117–26.
———. "The Striking of the Gong." *Kull: Exile of Atlantis*. New York: Del Rey, 2006, pp. 127–32.
———. "The Tower of the Elephant." *The Coming of Conan the Barbarian*. New York: Del Ray, 2003, pp. 59–82.
———. "The Valley of the Lost." *The Horror Stories of Robert E. Howard*. New York: Del Rey, 2008, pp. 269–288.
Huxtable, Ada Louis. "How We See, or Think We See the City." *The New York Times*, 25 November 1973, p. 182.
James, Henry. "The Art of Fiction." *American Realism*. Ed. Jane Berardete. New York: Putnam, 1972, pp. 195–215.
Jones, H. Bedford. "The Changing Market." *Pulp Fictioneers: Adventures in the Storytelling Business*. Ed. John Locke. Silver Spring, MD: Adventure House, 2004, pp. 36–39.
Joshi, S.T. *I Am Providence: The Life and Times of H.P. Lovecraft*. New York: Hippocampus, 2010.
Joshi, S.T., and David E. Schultz. *An H.P. Lovecraft Encyclopedia*. New York: Hippocampus, 2001.
Joshi, S.T., David Schultz, and Rusty Burke. Introduction. *A Means to Freedom: The Letters of H.P. Lovecraft and Robert E. Howard*. 2 vols. New York: Hippocampus, 2009, pp. 7–14.
Kandinsky, Wassily. *Concerning the Spiritual in Art*. Trans. M.T.H. Sadler. New York: Dover, 1977.
Kant, Immanuel. "Critique of Judgment." *The Norton Anthology of Theory and Criticism*. Eds. Vincent B. Leitch, et al. New York: Norton, 2001, pp. 504–535.
Leiber, Fritz. "On What We Should Call the Kind of Story This Magazine Is." *Amra* 2.16, 1961, p. 21.
Lichtbau, Joseph. "The Psycho-Mystic, Horror, and Weird Story Field." *Windy City Pulp Stories* 13, 2013, pp. 63–69.
Lovecraft, H.P. "At the Mountains of Madness." *H.P. Lovecraft: A Variorum Edition*. Ed. S.T. Joshi, vol. 3. New York: Hippocampus, 2015, pp. 11–157.
———. "Background." *The Ancient Track: Complete Poetical Works of H.P. Lovecraft*. New York: Hippocampus, 2013, pp. 92.
———. "The Call of Cthulhu." *H.P. Lovecraft: A Variorum Edition*. Ed. S.T. Joshi, vol. 2. New York: Hippocampus, 2015, pp. 21–55.
———. "A Case for Classicism." *Miscellaneous Writings*. Ed. S.T. Joshi, Sauk City, WI: Arkham House, 1995, pp. 210–213.

Works Cited

———. "A Confession of Unfaith." *Miscellaneous Writings*. Ed. S.T. Joshi, Sauk City, WI: Arkham House, 1995, pp. 533–537.
———. "Dagon." *H.P. Lovecraft: A Variorum Edition*. Ed. S.T. Joshi, vol. 1. New York: Hippocampus, 2015, pp. 52–58.
———. "From Beyond." *H.P. Lovecraft: A Variorum Edition*. Ed. S.T. Joshi, vol. 1. New York: Hippocampus, 2015, pp. 192–201.
———. "The Haunter of the Dark." *H.P. Lovecraft: A Variorum Edition*. Ed. S.T. Joshi, vol. 3. New York: Hippocampus, 2015, pp. 451–478.
———. "Heritage or Modernism: Common Sense in Art Forms." *Miscellaneous Writings*. Ed. S.T. Joshi. Sauk City, WI: Arkham House, 1995, pp. 190–98.
———. "The Hound." *H.P. Lovecraft: A Variorum Edition*. Ed. S.T. Joshi, vol. 1. New York: Hippocampus, 2015, pp. 339–348.
———. "Hypnos." *H.P. Lovecraft: A Variorum Edition*. Ed. S.T. Joshi, vol. 1. New York: Hippocampus, 2015, pp. 325–333.
———. "In Defense of Dagon." *Miscellaneous Writings*. Ed. S.T. Joshi. Sauk City, WI: Arkham House, 1995, pp. 147–171.
———. "The Music of Erich Zann." *H.P. Lovecraft: A Variorum Edition*. Ed. S.T Joshi, vol. 1. New York: Hippocampus, 2015, pp. 280–290.
———. "Nyarlathotep." *H.P. Lovecraft: A Variorum Edition*. Ed. S.T. Joshi, vol. 1. New York: Hippocampus, 2015, pp. 202–205.
———. "The Outsider." *H.P. Lovecraft: A Variorum Edition*. Ed. S.T. Joshi, vol. 1. New York: Hippocampus, 2015, pp. 265–272.
———. "Pickman's Model." *H.P. Lovecraft: A Variorum Edition*. Ed. S.T. Joshi, vol. 2. New York: Hippocampus, 2015, pp. 56–72.
———. "The Rats in the Walls." *H.P. Lovecraft: A Variorum Edition*. Ed. S.T. Joshi, vol. 1. New York: Hippocampus, 2015, pp. 374–396.
———. "The Shadow Over Innsmouth." *H.P. Lovecraft: A Variorum Edition*. Ed. S.T. Joshi, vol. 3. New York: Hippocampus, 2015, pp. 158–230.
———. "Supernatural Horror in Literature." *H.P. Lovecraft: The Complete Fiction*. Ed. S.T. Joshi. New York: Barnes and Noble, 2008, pp. 1041–1098.
———. "To Reinhardt Kleiner—November 16, 1916." *Selected Letters of H.P. Lovecraft* Eds. August Derleth and Donald Wandrei, vol. 1, Sauk City, WI: Arkham House, 1965, pp. 29–42.
———. "The Tomb." *H.P. Lovecraft: A Variorum Edition*. Ed. S.T. Joshi, vol. 1. New York: Hippocampus, 2015, pp. 38–51.
———, and Clark Ashton Smith. *Dawnward Spire, Lonely Hill: The Letters of H.P. Lovecraft and Clark Ashton Smith*. Eds. David E. Scultz and S.T. Joshi. New York: Hippocampus, 2017.
Lovecraft, H.P., and Robert E. Howard. *A Means to Freedom: The Letters of H.P. Lovecraft and Clark Ashton Smith*. 2 vols. Eds. S.T. Joshi, David Schultz, and Rusty Burke. New York: Hippocampus, 2009.
Lukács, Georg. *The Historical Novel*. 1937. London: Merlin, 1962.
Macdonald, Robert R. Foreword. *Berenice Abbot: Changing New York*. New York: New Press, 1997, pp. 8.
Madison, Nathan Vernon. *Anti-Foreign Imagery in American Pulps and Comic Books, 1920–1960*. Jefferson, NC: McFarland, 2013.
Marinetti, Filippo Tommaso. "The Founding and Manifesto of Futurism." *Modernism: An Anthology of Sources and Documents*. Eds. Vassiliki Kolootroni, Jane Goldman, and Olga Taxidou. Chicago: Chicago University Press, 1998, pp. 249–256.
Marx, Karl, and Frederick Engels. *The Communist Manifesto*. New York: International Publishers, 1948.
McCann, Sean. *Gumshoe America: Hard-boiled Crime Fiction and the Rise and Fall of New Deal Liberalism*. Durham, NC: Duke University Press, 2000.

Works Cited

McCracken, Scott. *Pulp: Reading Popular Literature*. Manchester: Manchester University Press, 1998.
Mencken, H.L. "The Criticism of Criticism of Criticism." *Prejudices: First, Second, and Third Series*. New York: Library of America, pp. 48–56, 3–10.
———. "The New Poetry Movement." *Prejudices: First, Second, and Third Series*. New York: Library of America, pp. 48–56.
Monroe, Harriet. "The Poetry of George Sterling." *Poetry* 7.4, 1916, pp. 307–313.
Mott, Frank Luther. *A History of American Magazines*. Cambridge: Harvard University Press, 1968.
Ortega y Gasset, Jose. "The Dehumanization of Art." *The Dehumanization of Art and Other Writings on Art and Culture*. New York: Doubleday Anchor, 1956, pp. 1–50.
Poe, Edgar Allan. "The Philosophy of Composition." *The Norton Anthology of Theory and Criticism*. Eds. Vincent B. Leitch, et al. New York: Norton, 2001, pp. 742–750.
Pound, Ezra. *Pavannes and Divagations*. London: Owen, 1960.
———. Appendix. "Studies in Contemporary Mentality." *Modernism in the Magazines*. Robert Scholes and Clifford Wulfman. New Haven, CT: Yale University Press, 2010, pp. 223–326.
Prida, Jonas. Introduction. *Conan Meets the Academy: Multidisciplinary Essays on the Enduring Barbarian*. Jefferson, NC: McFarland, 2013, pp. 5–12.
"Pulp Magazines Called a Menace." *The New York Times*, 29 November 1936, p. 27.
Rudd, Anthony. "A Square of Canvas." *Weird Tales: 32 Unearthed Horrors*. Eds. Stefan R. Dziemianowicz, Robert Weinberg, and Martin H. Greenberg. New York: Bonanza Books, 1988, pp. 1–12.
Saler, Michael. *As If: Modern Enchantment and the Literary Prehistory of Virtual Reality*. New York: Oxford University Press, 2012.
Scholes, Robert, and Clifford Wulfmann. *Modernism in the Magazines: An Introduction*. New Haven, CT: Yale University Press, 2010.
Schorer, Mark. "Technique as Discovery." *The Hudson Review* 1.1, 1948, pp. 67–87.
Shklovsky, Viktor. "Art as Device." *Theory of Prose*. Normal, IL: Dalkey Archive P, 1991, pp. 1–14.
Smith, Clark Ashton. *The Black Book of Clark Ashton Smith*. Sauk City, WI: Arkham House, 1979.
———. "The City of Singing Flame." *The Door of Saturn: The Collected Fantasies of Clark Ashton Smith*. Eds. Scott Connors and Ron Hilger, vol. 2. New York: Night Shade, 2007, pp. 157–170.
———. "The Devotee of Evil [The Manichaean]." *Strange Shadows: The Uncollected Fiction and Essays of Clark Ashton Smith*. Ed. Steve Behrends. New York: Greenwood, 1989, p. 157.
———. "The Devotee of Evil." *The End of the Story: The Collected Fantasies of Clark Ashton Smith*. Eds. Scott Connors and Ron Hilger, vol. 1. New York: Night Shade, 2006, pp. 153–162.
———. "The Empire of the Necromancers." *A Vintage from Atlantis: The Collected Fantasies of Clark Ashton Smith*. Eds. Scott Connors and Ron Hilger, vol. 3. New York: Night Shade, 2007, pp. 193–200.
———. "The End of the Story." *The End of the Story: The Collected Fantasies of Clark Ashton Smith*. Eds. Scott Connors and Ron Hilger, vol. 1. New York: Night Shade, 2006, pp. 21–34.
———. "The Hashish-Eater; Or, the Apocalypse of Evil." *The Last Oblivion: Best Fantastic Poems of Clark Ashton Smith*. Eds. S.T. Joshi and David E. Schultz. New York: Hippocampus, 2002, pp. 15–29.
———. "The Isle of the Torturers." *The Maze of the Enchanter: The Collected Fantasies of Clark Ashton Smith*. Eds. Scott Connors and Ron Hilger, vol. 4. New York: Night Shade, 2009, pp. 63–74.

Works Cited

———. "The Last Incantation." *The End of the Story: The Collected Fantasies of Clark Ashton Smith.* Eds. Scott Connors and Ron Hilger, vol. 1. New York: Night Shade, 2006, pp. 17–20.

———. "Nero." *The Last Oblivion: Best Fantastic Poems of Clark Ashton Smith.* Eds. S.T. Joshi and David E. Schultz. New York: Hippocampus, 2002, pp. 49–51.

———. "The Ninth Skeleton." *The End of the Story: The Collected Fantasies of Clark Ashton Smith.* Eds. Scott Connors and Ron Hilger, vol. 1. New York: Night Shade, 2006, pp. 13–16.

———. *Selected Letters of Clark Ashton Smith.* Eds. David E. Schultz and Scott Connors, Sauk City, WI: Arkham House, 2003.

———. "The Star-Treader." *The Last Oblivion: Best Fantastic Poems of Clark Ashton Smith.* Eds. S.T. Joshi and David E. Schultz. New York: Hippocampus, 2002, pp. 30–33.

———. "Ubbo-Sathla." *A Vintage from Atlantis: The Collected Fantasies of Clark Ashton Smith.* Eds. Scott Connors and Ron Hilger, vol. 3. New York: Night Shade, 2007, pp. 223–228.

Smith, Erin. *Hard-Boiled: Working Class Readers and Pulp Magazines.* Philadelphia: Temple University Press, 2000.

Suvin, Darko. *Metamorphoses of Science Fiction: On the Poetics and History of a Literary Genre.* New Haven, CT: Yale University Press, 1979.

Weber, Max. *The Protestant Ethic and the Spirit of Capitalism.* New York: Routledge, 1992.

Weinberg, Robert. *The Weird Tales Story.* Berkeley Heights, CA: Wildside Press, 1999.

"Why Weird Tales?" *Weird Tales* 4.2, 1924, pp. 1–2.

Wilson, Edmund. *Axel's Castle: A Study in the Imaginative Literature of 1870–1930.* 1931. New York: Norton, 1959.

Wright, Farnsworth. "The Eyrie." *Weird Tales* 7.4 ,1926, pp. 566–568.

———. "Letter to the Editor of *Writers Digest,* July 1929." *Pulp Fictioneers: Adventures in the Storytelling Business.* Ed. John Locke, Silver Spring, Adventure House, 2004, pp. 27.

Wyn, A.A. "Pulp Magazines A Publisher Cites Figures of Their Number Printing Patronage." *The New York Times,* 4 September 1935, pp. 18.

Yeats, W.B. "Sailing to Byzantium." *The Collected Poems of W.B. Yeats.* Ed. Richard J. Finneran. New York: Scribner's, 1996. 193.

Yochelson, Bonnie. Introduction. *Berenice Abbott: Changing New York.* New York: New Press, 1997, pp. 9–34.

Žižek, Slavoj. *The Sublime Object of Ideology.* London: Verso, 2009.

Index

Abbott, Berenice 22, 36–40, 168–169, 173–174
Adorno, Theodor 9, 37, 174
advertisements 51–54, 59
aesthetic form 8, 10, 37, 44, 78, 80, 91, 137
affect 31, 140, 172
alienation 10, 66, 73, 100–113, 117, 125–126
alterity 14, 76, 112
amateur press association 66, 141
Amra (periodical) 141
Anderson, Margaret 50–51
Anderson, Sherwood 117–118
Angell, George (fictional character) 142–145
Angel of History 10, 30, 43, 151
Anglo-American 20, 28, 50, 71–72, 137
antitechnologism 61
The Arcades Project (Benjamin) 129
The Argosy (periodical) 45, 54–56
Arkham House 116
"Art as Device" (Shklovsky) 156, 182
"The Art of Fiction" (James) 181
artistic ambition 16, 62–63, 69, 89, 105, 140
Astounding Stories (periodical) 15, 58
At the Mountains of Madness (Lovecraft) 94
Atlantic (periodical) 53, 64, 86, 88
Author and Journalist (periodical) 102
Averoigne 18, 93
Axel's Castle (Wilson) 71, 158–160

Baird, Edwin 57–58
Bakhtin, Mikhail 179–180
Barlow, Robert H. 64
Barnes, Djuna 36
Barthes, Roland 7, 180
Bates, Harry 58
Baudelaire, Charles 90
Beach, Sylvia 36
beauty (aesthetic category) 89, 91–96, 146–148, 151

Beckett, Samuel 49
Benjamin, Walter 10, 22–23, 29–35, 38, 40, 140, 151, 153, 174
"Beyond the Black River" (Howard) 98
"Beyond the Wall of Sleep" (Lovecraft) 160
bibliophilia 47
Bierce, Ambrose 83, 85, 89
Black Mask (periodical) 57
Blackwood, Algernon 122
Blast! (periodical) 49,
Blue Book (periodical) 56
Bohemian Club of San Francisco 18, 83
bourgeoisie 11, 23, 30–31, 86, 141, 177
Brooklyn Bridge 37–38
Browning, Robert 77, 109
Burke, Edmund 36, 142–143, 146–151
"By This Axe I Rule!" (Howard) 131

The Call (periodical) 86
"The Call of Cthulhu" (Lovecraft) 41, 142–146, 148–151, 163
Carey, John 11–13, 117
Carter, Randolph 160, 162
Carver, Raymond 125
"Case for Classicism" (Lovecraft) 175
The Castle of Otranto 179
catalysis 137–139
Celts 108
censorship 82
Chandler, Raymond 57
Chicago, Illinois 71, 73, 111–112
"The City of Singing Flame" (Smith) 94
Clayton, William 58
The Clayton Group 101, 102–103
Cleveland, Ohio 66–69, 72
Clune, Michael 19
Cocteau, Jean 36
collaborative authorship 66, 137–141, 144, 160
"The Colour Out of Space" (Lovecraft) 122
comic books 47, 110, 114
commodity fetishization 48

193

Index

"The Communist Manifesto" 2, 31
Conan 18, 98, 101, 109, 116, 119–120, 129–131
Conan Meets the Academy: Multidisciplinary Essays on the Enduring Barbarian 109
"Concerning the Spiritual in Art" (Kandinsky) 77
"A Confession of Unfaith" (Lovecraft) 70, 89
Conrad, Joseph 9, 15, 155, 177
correspondence, literary 69, 71, 74, 82, 85–88, 90, 104, 108, 111, 122
cosmic horror 58–59
cosmicism 69
Cosmopolitan (periodical) 51, 52, 53
Costigan, Steve 123–128
Cowley, Malcolm 22, 27–29, 36, 38, 40, 71, 137, 164
Crane, Hart 27, 68–69, 90
The Criterion (periodical) 74
criticism 8–9, 17–20, 21–23, 44, 49, 50, 52, 59, 67, 71, 73, 130–133, 137, 152, 166–167, 171, 180,
"Criticism of Criticism of Criticism" (Mencken) 137
Critique of Judgment (Kant) 147
Cross Plains, Texas 111–112, 125, 129
Cthulhu 18, 41, 133, 136–151
Cubism 19
culture industry 44, 174

Dada 29
"Dagon" (Lovecraft) 150
The Dark Barbarian: The Writings of Robert E. Howard, a Critical Anthology 17
Darwin 177
Debussy, Claude 24
deep ones 47
defamiliarization 75, 121
Defoe, Daniel 176, 179
deformation 2, 7, 11, 21, 23, 25–28, 32–33, 38–41, 168, 174
"Degenerate Art Exhibition" ("Entartete Kunst") 81
"The Dehumanization of Art" 22–26, 165
Derleth, August 128
The Destructive Element (Spender) 71
Detective Story Magazine (periodical) 55
"The Devotee of Evil" (Smith) 96–97, 165
The Dial (periodical) 49, 90
Dialectical Materialism 31–32, 46
dime novel 11, 15, 46, 54
disenchantment 177
Dreiser, Theodore 117, 118, 177
Duchamp, Marcel 36

Ebony and Crystal (Smith) 74, 86
editorial 54, 56–58, 73, 102, 174
Edwardian era 155
The Egoist (periodical) 49
Eliot, T.S. 15, 74–80, 111, 137–140, 156, 161, 164, 170, 173, 176–177, 184
"Empire of the Necromancers" (Smith) 25
"The End of the Story" (Smith) 93–97, 133
entertainment 14–15, 44, 53, 60–63, 172–173
"Epic and Novel" (Bakhtin) 179
eugenics 18
Exile's Return 22, 27, 36, 164
experimental literature and art 27, 29, 39, 42, 48–49, 50, 58, 81, 117, 122–123, 130–132, 136–137, 154, 156, 163, 176, 181
"The Eyrie" (letter column) 60–62

fantasy (genre) 5, 39, 70, 72, 109, 114–115, 123, 131, 171
The Fantasy Fan (periodical) 16, 17
fanzines 16–17, 115
fascism 165, 175
Faulkner, William 27
Federal Art Project 36–37, 168
Feltski, Rita 166
Fielding, Henry 176
Finnegans Wake 180
Fitzgerald, Edmund 27
Fitzgerald, F. Scott 117
formalism 12, 119, 167
France 34, 36, 93, 145
Frankenstein (novel) 178, 180–181
Frankfurt School 29, 44
The Freedom of Fantastic Things: Selected Criticism on Clark Ashton Smith 17
Freud, Sigmund 177
"From Beyond" (Lovecraft) 16, 155–156, 160
Futurism 19, 169

Gaelic 107, 108
Gaiman, Neil 84
Galpin, Alfred 66–70, 108
Garland, Hamlin 56
genre fiction 55, 70, 84–85, 114, 172
Gernsbeck, Hugo 156
The Golden Argosy (periodical) 54
gothic 106–107, 176–179, 183–184
the great divide 117, 172
Grey, Zane 118, 121
Guggenheim, Peggy 36

hackwork 64
Hammett, Dashiell 57
hard-boiled detective (genre) 13

Index

"The Hashish Eater" (Smith) 76
"The Haunter of the Dark" (Lovecraft) 184–185
Hays, H.R. 116
Hecht, Ben 56, 117–118
Hemingway, Ernest 9, 27, 111, 125, 136
Henneberger, J.C. 56–57, 89
"Heritage or Modernism: Common Sense in Art Forms" (Lovecraft) 3, 153–154, 160, 175
Hersey, Harold 62–63, 100
historical fiction 130
The Historical Novel 33
historicism 12
A History of American Magazines (Mott) 71
Hitler, Adolf 29
Holmes, Sherlock (fictional character) 13
Horkheimer, Max 9, 38, 174
horror 1, 4–5, 31–32, 39, 44, 47–48, 70, 72, 89, 91–93, 95–97, 114–115, 121, 123, 140, 142–143, 145, 149–150, 163, 171
Hough, Emerson 56
"The Hound" (Lovecraft) 162
Huyssen, Andreas 117, 172
"Hypnos" (Lovecraft) 162

ideology 47, 49, 75, 139
imaginative literature 60, 62
"In Defense of Dagon" (Lovecraft) 64, 141
Irish heritage 107
"The Isle of the Torturers" (Smith) 41, 158

James, Henry 181
Jones, H. Bedford 102
Joshi, S.T. 57
Joyce, James 9, 36, 136, 153, 161, 164, 173

Kandinsky, Wassily 77–78
Kant, Immanuel 142–143, 146–151
Keats, John 4, 23, 86, 93, 96, 109
"Kings of the Night" (Howard) 131
Klee, Paul 22–23, 32–33, 35, 153
Kleiner, Reinhardt 45
Kull 116, 130–135

"The Last Incantation" (Smith) 182
Lawrence, D.H. 90, 155
Legrasse, John 144–145
Leiber, Fritz 115
Levi, Eliphas 181
Lewis, Sinclair 117–118, 178
Lichtblau, Joseph 102–103
The Limits of Critique (Feltski) 166–167
literary art 9, 11, 42, 45–47, 51, 57, 168
little magazine 49–53, 59, 66, 71, 137
The Little Review (periodical) 51, 90

Locke, John 100
London, Jack 83, 85
Long, Frank Belknap 107
Lord Dunsany 122
Love Story Magazine (periodical) 55
Lovecraft Studies (periodical) 17
Loveman, Samuel 66–68, 70
Lowell, Amy 66
Lukács, György 33–35
Lumley, William 140

Machen, Arthur 121, 122
Madison, Nathan Vernon 18–19
madness 159
magazines 5, 11–15, 18, 38, 43–46, 48–57, 59–62, 64, 71–73, 82, 86, 89–90, 101–104, 110–111, 140, 173–175
Malygris (fictional character) 182–183
"Manifesto of Futurism" 169
Marinetti, F.T. 169–170
Martin, George R.R. 84
mass culture 10–11, 16, 117, 174
Masters, Edgar Lee 66
McCann, Sean 13
McCracken, Scott 10, 46
Mencken, H.L. 9, 47, 51, 72, 74, 86, 118, 137–139, 156, 176
"The Metaphysical Poets" (Eliot) 77
"The Mirrors of Tuzun Thume" (Howard) 131
modern art 2, 4, 16–17, 19, 26, 40, 49, 52, 120, 140, 171
Modernism 1–3, 8, 12, 16, 19–24, 26–29, 36, 38–39, 48–53, 62, 66, 69–74, 78–82, 84, 88, 104–105, 109–110, 112–113, 117–118, 120, 122, 136–140, 142–143, 152–157, 159, 161, 163–165, 168, 171–172, 175–176, 178–180, 183–184
modernist ekphrasis 22
Monroe, Harriet 51, 71, 73–74, 83–84, 88
"The Moon of Skulls" (Howard) 182
Mott, Frank Luther 71–72
Munsey, Frank Andrew 54–55
"The Music of Erich Zann" (Lovecraft) 143, 159–163
mythic method 155, 161, 184

Nathan, George Jean 117
Nazism 28, 81
"Nero" (Smith) 89
Neruda, Pablo 116
The New Age (periodical) 9
New York City 22, 37–38
The New York Times 42–44, 86, 116, 174
"The Ninth Skeleton" (Smith) 91
North Atlantic Review 86, 88
"Nyarlathotep" (Lovecraft) 28–29

Index

O'Brien, Fitz 64
"Ode on a Grecian Urn" (Keats) 23, 93, 96
Odes and Sonnets (Smith) 86
Ortega y Gasset, José 22–29, 38, 40, 77, 81, 165, 172
"The Outsider" (Lovecraft) 171, 183

"Pastorale" (Crane) 68
Pater, Walter 17
pathos 24, 31, 35
Pavannes and Divagations (Pound) 67
"The People of the Black Circle" (Howard) 41
phenomenology 34,
The Philosopher (periodical) 66
A Philosophical Enquiry into the Origin of Our Ideas of the Sublime and the Beautiful 146
Pickman, Richard Upton 21, 32, 35, 41, 162–164
"Pickman's Model" (Lovecraft) 32, 41
"Plaster-All" (Lovecraft) 68
Plato 48, 155
poetics 67–68
poetry 4, 8, 23, 48–49, 51,-52, 54, 66–74, 77, 80, 83–86, 88, 90, 109–110, 116, 156, 166,
Poetry (periodical) 49, 51, 71–73, 83–84, 86, 90
popular culture 10–11, 15, 17, 109, 114, 174
Popular Photography (periodical) 38,
populism 87, 115, 117, 166
Post Oaks and Sand Roughs (Howard) 122–127
Pound, Ezra 9, 47, 67–69, 71–73, 85, 90, 156–157, 183
Prida, Joseph 109
print and periodical culture 14, 50, 173–174
The Providence Journal (periodical) 68
psychological realism 118
publishing 43–45, 49, 56–57, 60, 82–83, 89, 101–103, 111, 166
pulp ekphrasis 15–16, 21, 23, 32, 39, 41, 42, 47, 65–66, 69, 76, 78, 80, 82–83, 84, 97, 105, 113, 114–115, 119, 130, 132, 139, 142, 167–175, 178–179, 183–184
pulp magazine collecting 47
Pulpwood Editor (Hersey) 100
pulpwood magazine 12–14, 16, 38, 42–46, 52–56, 59, 62–63, 100, 174

quantity writer 63
"The Quest of Iranon" (Lovecraft) 160

Radcliffe, Anne 178
The Railroad Man's Magazine (periodical) 55, 57

"The Rats in the Walls" (Lovecraft) 106–108, 182
readers 5, 8, 13, 16, 43, 45, 52, 53, 55, 57–60, 62, 63, 64, 101, 104, 106, 121–122, 131, 137, 166
realism 8, 11–12, 19–20, 60, 105, 118–125, 129–130, 152–153, 156, 176–179, 183
The Recluse (periodical) 156
"Retrospect" (Pound) 67
"The Return of the Sorcerer" (Smith) 102
rhetoric 7–8, 23, 28, 30–31, 34, 37, 46–48, 54, 67, 73, 81–82, 94, 109, 119, 136, 139, 142
Richardson, Samuel 176
Robertson, A.M. 69, 85
Robinson Crusoe 179, 180
Rudd, Anthony 39–41

"Sailing to Byzantium" (poem) 183
Saler, Michael 8
San Francisco 18, 69, 74, 83, 86, 111
The San Francisco Examiner (periodical) 74
Sandalwood (Smith) 86
Sandburg, Carl 66
The Saturday Evening Post (periodical) 52
Scholes, Robert 49, 52–53, 59
Schorer, Mark 136–140, 155–156
science fiction 5, 12, 15, 39, 46–47, 58, 70, 72, 75, 123, 131, 171
scientism 139, 157
"The Screaming Skull of Silence" (Howard) 132–133
Scribner's (periodical) 51
semiotics 50
Sense and Sensibility 180
sensorium 16, 30, 33, 35, 38, 65, 73, 76, 123–124, 126, 128, 138, 156–159, 167–169
serialized fiction 54
"The Shadow Kingdom" (Howard) 131
shadow modernism 16, 19–21, 26, 29, 32, 38–41, 79, 82–83, 96, 117, 130, 139, 143, 152–156, 184
"The Shadow Over Innsmouth" (Lovecraft) 47
Shakespeare, William 62, 109
Shelley, Mary 178
shining trapehozedron 184–185
Shklovksy, Viktor 138, 156, 182
signification 7, 40, 45, 121, 144, 149–150
Skull-face and Other Stories 116
slick magazine 51–54, 71, 174
The Smart Set (periodical) 51, 53, 86
Smith, Erin 13
socioeconomic class 11, 44
Solomon Kane 116, 173

Index

"Some Tendencies in Modern Poetry" (Galpin) 66
The Spanish Civil War 29
"Spear and Fang" (Howard) 105
Spender, Stephen 71
"A Square of Canvas" (Rudd) 22, 39–40
The Star-Treader and Other Poems (Smith) 69, 70, 85, 89
Sterling, George 73, 83–90
Stoker, Bram 178
Strange Tales of Mystery and Terror (periodical) 15, 58, 101–104
"The Striking of the Gong" (Howard) 132–134
sublime 142–151
The Sublime Object of Ideology (Žižek) 150
Sully, Genevieve K. 91
Supernatural Horror in Literature (Lovecraft) 1, 106
supernatural literature 118
surrealism 19
Suvin, Darko 75
sword and sorcery 115–117, 123, 127

"Technique as Discovery" (Schorer) 136, 138
"Theses on the Philosophy of History" 22, 29
The Thing's Incredible: The Secret Origins of Weird Tales (Locke) 100
"Through the Gates of the Silver Key" (Lovecraft) 63
"The Tomb" (Lovecraft) 20, 160
"The Tower of the Elephant" (Howard) 129
Tillinghast, Crawford 157–160
Town Talk (periodical) 85
"Tradition and the Individual Talent" (Eliot) 77, 138, 164

"Ubbo-Sathla" (Smith) 78–80, 145, 160, 172

Ulysses (novel) 161, 184
"Ulysses, Order, Myth" (Eliot) 161
The Unique Legacy of Weird Tales: The Evolution of Modern Fantasy and Horror 17
United Amateur (periodical) 28
"The United Co-operative" (periodical) 175
"The Unnameable" (Lovecraft) 162
The Uses of Literature (Feltski) 166

"The Valley of the Lost" (Howard) 170
violence 115, 127–131, 170, 172, 174–175, 178, 182

Walpole, Horace 178
Wandrei, Donald 182
The Waste Land (Eliot) 74–80, 170
Weber, Max 177
Weinberg, Robert 150
Weird Tales, history of 56–64
Wells, H.G. 81, 136
Western Story Magazine (periodical) 55, 58
"Why Weird Tales" (editorial) 60
Wilcox, Henry 23, 41, 143–145
Wilde, Oscar 23
Wilson, Edmund 47, 71, 139–140, 159–160
Wonder Stories (periodical) 64, 94
Woolf, Virginia 9, 15, 111, 136, 155
World War I 72, 81, 170
Wright, Farnsworth 60–64, 97, 101, 104, 106, 108, 112, 130–131, 153, 184
Writer's Digest (periodical) 101–104
Wulfman, Clifford 49, 52–53, 59
Wyn, A.A. 61–62

Yeats, William Butler 72, 85, 90, 183

Zann, Erich 143, 159–163
Žižek, Slavoj 150

www.ingramcontent.com/pod-product-compliance
Lightning Source LLC
Chambersburg PA
CBHW032101300426
44116CB00007B/834